DATE DUE

JY 30 '98			
DE 16 '98			
DE 8 '99			
MY 1 '00			
S 02 8 '02			
DE 5 '01			
OC 30 '03			
		'06	
	4 '06		
E 2 3 '08			

THE LIPSTICK PROVISO

THE
LIPSTICK
PROVISO

WOMEN, SEX &
POWER IN THE
REAL WORLD

KAREN LEHRMAN

An Anchor Book

DOUBLEDAY
New York   London   Toronto   Sydney   Auckland

AN ANCHOR BOOK
PUBLISHED BY DOUBLEDAY
a division of Bantam Doubleday Dell Publishing Group, Inc.
1540 Broadway, New York, New York 10036

ANCHOR BOOKS, DOUBLEDAY, and the portrayal of an anchor are trademarks of
Doubleday, a division of Bantam Doubleday Dell Publishing Group, Inc.

Book design by Richard Oriolo

Library of Congress Cataloging-in-Publication Data

Lehrman, Karen.
The lipstick proviso : women, sex, and power in the real
world / Karen Lehrman. — 1st Anchor Books ed.
p.   cm.
Includes bibliographical references.
1. Feminist theory.   2. Feminism.   I. Title.
HQ1190.L44   1997
305.42—dc21   96-49392
CIP

ISBN 0-385-47481-4

For my parents,
with much love and
gratitude

Contents

◆

THE LIPSTICK PROVISO

◆

THE LIPSTICK PROVISO

IN THE SUMMER of 1996, a new breed of rock star was sweeping the country. The artists were tough, angry, iconoclastic—and female. Singing brazenly about sex and power, these women rockers—Alanis Morissette, Liz Phair, PJ Harvey, Tori Amos—had not only attitude but an audience: they were winning Grammys and selling millions of albums a year.

Their provocative demeanor, however, and onstage attire (evening gowns, slip dresses, skin-tight jeans) were not going over very well in some quarters. "You can't fight the patriarchy in a tube top," one critic told Amos, who is famous for straddling the piano bench while playing. Another critic wrote in a British magazine that Louise Post, lead singer of the band Veruca Salt, had "set feminism back ten years" because she had applied lipstick onstage. To which band member Nina Gordon responded: "Who is this woman who thinks it's important to point that out?"[1]

Most likely, she is a woman well-versed in current feminist theory on the subjects of makeup and fashion. For centuries, lipstick and all the other tools of feminine allurement were condemned by religious puritans as decadent and shameful, the cause of sin and suffering. In recent years such popular feminist writers as Naomi Wolf (*The Beauty Myth*), Susan Faludi (*Backlash*), and Susan Brownmiller (*Femininity*) and a host of academic types have argued that makeup, revealing clothing, and coquettish manners are degrading and exploitative, weapons in society's war to keep women in the role of sex objects. A "backlash" against feminism, these theorists argue, is forcing women to spend excessive amounts of time and money on their appearance, and to use feminine adornment as camouflage—so that they will appear less threatening to men.

It's true, of course, that the behavior of many women today does seem rather self-contradictory. Many women order their male colleagues around, while waiting for those same men to open their doors and help them on with their coats. Some women will prepare for a big meeting by reading a stack of folders and getting a manicure. Many women have higher-status jobs than the men they date, yet they never call men or ask them out. Some women work ferociously throughout their twenties to build their careers and then, at the crack of thirty, suddenly decide that they want to get married and stay home to raise a family.

While many women, in other words, have rather easily acquired some traditionally masculine traits—ambition, competitiveness, assertiveness—they have also happily retained much of traditional femininity. Yet the explanation for this apparent inconsistency would seem to be a little more complicated than the backlash analysis suggests. In fact, such analysis mostly shows how far feminist theory has lagged behind feminist reality. This is as true for political issues as it is for matters of personal relations. Most feminist theorists support unnecessarily broad definitions of sexual harassment and date rape, some version of quotas, and some level of censorship of pornography and sexual imagery. They tend to see women as a homogenous sisterhood with the same political opinions and values, men as misogynistic predators, sexuality as a weakness, and real freedom as problematic.

This is not very helpful to women today. Actually, as these theories make their way into laws and corporate policies, it is potentially quite harmful.

The easy answer would be to write off feminist theory, pronounce feminism dead, and say that we are living happily ever after in a post-feminist world. But we are not living in a post-feminist world, happily or otherwise. We have just begun to achieve a society that can even remotely be called feminist in the original meaning of the term: a society in which women enjoy equal rights, equal opportunities, and equal responsibilities.

There's still considerable work to be done in the political realm, especially regarding such issues as sexual assault, domestic violence, and abortion. Equally important, there's still much in the way of personal work to accomplish. Women can't rightly be called autonomous if we stay with abusive or even emotionally challenged lovers; say yes to sex when we mean no; overeat or undereat to hide a sexuality or avoid assuming responsibility; or allow any man—or woman—to tell us what to wear, how to behave, or whom to vote for.

Although real feminism cannot prescribe our choices, it can offer us a guide to making rational ones. To do that, of course, feminist theory needs to be not only rational itself but realistic and accessible to women outside the academy. I don't think many would use these words to describe reigning feminist theory. Indeed, contemporary feminist theory is in desperate need of being updated for the real world. And what seems to be happening in the real world is that women have entered a new stage of relations with society, with men, and with themselves.

During the sixties and seventies, the emphasis of feminist activism was on promoting the inherent equality of women: women could do anything men could do (and quite often they could do it better). By the eighties, the emphasis in some quarters began to shift to the fact that men and women are not identical: men, for instance, don't get pregnant. We are now moving into a stage of feminism—probably the last stage—in which each woman can finally be seen as fundamentally unique. Not coincidentally, it is a woman's inherent individuality that most inspired feminism's founding foremothers more than a century ago.

But what does it mean, exactly, for a woman to be an individual? Well, to begin with, she certainly doesn't have to conform to any "feminist" rules of behavior. For the sake of clarity, I suggest adding an amendment onto feminism's proverbial contract with society, what I have come to call the lipstick proviso: women don't have to sacrifice their individuality, or even their femininity—whatever that means to each of them—in order to be equal. The larger point is that we no longer have to deny or fear differences between the sexes—even if those differences turn out to be firmly rooted in biology. Indeed, as the legal and social restrictions on women have nearly all been lifted, we're now beginning to see which of the traditionally feminine behaviors were more solidly grounded in cultural norms, and which in biological imperatives. A strong desire to mother, for instance, appears to have outlasted a need to submissively obey one's husband. If more behaviors than not turn out to have a strong biological basis, this is no cause for feminist embarrassment. Nor does it mean that these behaviors can't, to some degree, be modified.

Nevertheless, a feminism predicated on women's individuality is not without its complexities (which is at least partially why it has been resisted for so long). The corporate world, for instance, must judge women on their merits, not on their similarities to other women or their differences from men. Yet women do share a reproductive system that has been known to exert a substantial influence on their lives. Can the corporate world ever become sophisticated enough to treat women as both equal and potentially different? Do we ourselves understand what that means?

Consider a woman's sexuality. How does it figure into an office environment? Should a liberated woman well in touch with her sensuality and desires hide her sexuality, exploit it, or simply ignore it? Finally, does women's inherent individuality mean that sisterhood—the idea that women are uniquely bonded spiritually and politically—is dead? Should we mourn its loss?

In the world of personal relations, the individuality of women would seem to be a little more clearcut: women are free to make their own choices about their lives. We don't have to jettison all of traditional femininity, romance, and the nuclear family just because they existed before the sixties. Rather, the line can now be drawn at self-destructiveness: which feminine traits, beauty procedures, romantic practices, and so on undermine women's health and autonomy? Wearing lipstick or a tube top clearly doesn't. But what about cosmetic surgery, courtship, full-time motherhood, and chivalry? The answer, no doubt, can differ with the woman. And each woman is obliged to figure it out. Under real feminism, women have ultimate responsibility for their problems, happiness, and lives. The personal, in other words, is no longer political.

Because women and men are still behaving in significantly different ways, I have resorted in this book to something that I generally distrust: generalization. I say that women tend to be more nurturing and men more aggressive; that women appear more compassionate and men more emotionally controlled.

I do so to help make a point. Indeed, it's hard to write a book about women and men without doing so. Still, my generalizations—based on studies, surveys, and my own observations—are only pictures of the average case: *all* women are surely not nurturing and *all* men are not aggressive. Moreover, these observations do not imply "normalcy" and may very well change in another fifty years. No matter what happens, though, women and men will always fall somewhere on a spectrum, a continuum: some men will be more nurturing than some women, just as some women will be taller than some men. As a result, an assumption, a prejudgment, about a *particular* woman's (or man's) behavior, values, or goals can never be legitimately drawn.

I am not a feminist scholar, an evolutionary theorist, or a social scientist. I am a writer, a feminist, a liberal. In addition to the latest research on these subjects, my arguments and thoughts are based on conversations with women. Yes, most of those I come in contact with are white, middle-class women. But I believe that most of the larger issues involving identity and relations between the sexes apply to nearly all women at some point in their lives. Yes, I focus primarily on heterosexual women. But the fact is, the vast majority of women are heterosexual.

And yes, my focus is largely on women. This hardly means that men don't have a lot of work to do. But women have their share—a fact that feminists typically ignore. Indeed, many of the changes men and society in general need to make at this point will not come about unless women—as individuals—first become strong enough to demand them.

The first chapter of this book deals with some of the broader theoretical questions that need to be confronted before we can move on to the more basic problems in women's personal lives, problems involving beauty, sex, power, and female friendship. We first have to understand what feminism is—and is not—before we can apply it to our lives.

I wrote this book as much for myself as for anyone. And if there is one thing that has been reinforced in the process, it is a sense of optimism. We have come a tremendous distance in the past three decades, a greater distance than was traveled in the previous three centuries. In the end, feminism may be impossible to realize completely. But we have no reason to believe that, because of a "backlash," our genes, or even naysaying feminist theorists, we aren't capable of coming quite close.

One

◆

LIBERATION

I

BY THE TIME I was gaining my feminist bearings in high school during the late seventies, the phrase "liberated woman" had already become a disparaging epithet. Stripped of its original promise of strength, independence, and adventure, the phrase had been media-sentenced to represent the worst stereotype of the women's movement: a saggy-breasted, hairy-legged, man-hating militant who spends her days denouncing capitalism and Western culture and her nights doing God knows what with other women.

Nevertheless, as a young woman eager to escape the confines of a traditional household, I continued to put much stock in the original meaning of the phrase. Feminism, I believed, was going to turn all women into liberated women, into women who would unfailingly exhibit serene confidence, steely resolve, and steadfast courage. Unburdened by the behavioral and sartorial restrictions of traditional femininity, we would all want to trek alone through the wilds of Indonesia, head IBM, run for president. Our ambitions would be boundless, our achievements awesome. Men, marriage, children—each would have to wait. The world needed to be conquered first.

Well, as it turns out, I do have one female friend who has hiked unaccompanied through the forests of Indonesia (and returned unscathed), and many women in their early thirties have already risen to the top of their fields. Yet it doesn't seem as though the first generation of women to come of age with feminism—born in the freedom-drenched sixties, reared in the androgynous seventies, educated in the power-tie eighties—has metamorphosed en masse into briefcase-toting, world-wandering Mistresses of the Universe.

Many women would prefer not to work outside the home at all. Others want a job that allows them the flexibility to be at home with their kids for at least part of the day. Some scale back their career ambitions as soon as thoughts turn to children. And while many women walk around flaunting a confident "I am woman; hear me roar" attitude, at least as many are far less sure of themselves. Even women who have been quite successful professionally often seem lost emotionally. They have trouble asking their bosses for a raise, their landlords for heat, their boyfriends for support. They can't live without a man, lose their identities once they are in a relationship, overeat or undereat to relieve their anxiety and loneliness. They hardly seem happy, let alone strong and independent.

In recent years many women have also returned to practices that were once thought to subsidize male oppression. They're wearing provocative clothes and heels again, painting their faces and nails, treating their skin and hair to the latest styles and fads. They dream of romance and big weddings, wish to be courted with flowers and chocolates, and expect doors to be—literally—opened for them. Many women, it seems, like to celebrate their femaleness, their femininity, and want to be treated like, well, ladies.

What's going on here? Has feminism failed women? Have women failed feminism? Or has society failed them both?

Such questions lie at the center of the current debate over the "true" meaning of feminism, a debate between what are being called "establishment" or "gender" feminists (Gloria Steinem, Susan Faludi, Patricia Ireland, Gloria Allred, Catharine MacKinnon, and much of the women's studies community) and their critics (Camille Paglia, Christina Hoff Sommers, Elizabeth Fox-Genovese, Daphne Patai, Katie Roiphe). These issues, though, are not merely academic: they touch directly on women's daily struggles with their identities, their relations with men, and their relations with each other.

Feminist theory has never been monolithic. But for the past quarter century a number of closely related feminist beliefs have dominated both academic and popular writing on the subject of women. According to this set of beliefs, the reason all women haven't yet turned into liberated women is that the "patriarchy," typically defined as a pervasive and self-sustaining system of male domination and privilege, stands resolutely in the way. Every time women make progress, the patriarchy responds with "backlash"— discrimination, harassment, abuse, and misogynistic social messages (career women are miserable, fat women are ugly, and so on). Women who internalize these messages not only revert to traditional roles and behaviors but also suffer from low self-esteem, depression, and eating disorders.

To counter this "war against women," some feminist activists argue, government must be called in to mandate that women represent 51 percent (in proportion to the population) of Congress, corporate boardrooms, and powerful media outlets. Others think employers should simply be subjected to constant criticism until they hire equal numbers of women. Some theorists believe that government must also step in to ban pornography and "sexist" speech and to "sensitize" men through mandatory workshops. Oth-

to see the media continually denounced for using
~~dels and actresses or showing happy housewives.[1]

The critique of reigning feminism has also been far from
monolithic. Underlying much of the criticism, though, are four
basic points. One, gender feminists have undermined the original
conception of feminism—the emancipation of women from all laws
and social regulations confining them to one type of life—by hard-
ening the theory into an inflexible set of political opinions, professional goals, and androgynous behaviors and attire. Two, many
"feminist" expectations are not only unrealistic but contrary to the
desires and values of women today. Three, even the more realistic
objectives—eliminating street harassment or sexist speech, for instance—either cannot or should not be achieved by government
intervention.

And four, much of what is being called a backlash against
feminism is actually legitimate resistance by both women and men
to the *extremes* of establishment feminism—the rhetoric or policy
proposals that can be construed as anti-men, anti-sex, anti-family,
anti-beauty, anti-religion, or anti-nature; the assumption that all
women have the same (leftist) political opinions; and the calls for
special privileges for women (quotas or the lowering of job standards) and mandatory behavior modification for men.

This critique, for the most part, has been quite useful. It has
helped to remind us that for most of its history feminism has not
embodied a specific ideology or political agenda. Indeed, feminism
stems from a variety of commitments—the abolitionist cause, anar-
chism, socialism, and the "social purity" movements. Nor was feminism ever meant to prescribe a set of professional goals or personal
behaviors. Rather, for most of the past century and a half, feminism
has represented an ideal of liberation—of equal rights, opportunities, and responsibilities for women. That's it.

No one (including myself) should have expected that, when
the legal and social barriers were lifted, all women would want
high-powered careers and would shun every aspect of traditional
femininity. A liberated woman is, by definition, a woman who has

been liberated. She is not a woman who has to fit any preconceived design: there is no *one* liberated woman. And if women choose not to go into every profession, be it auto repair or brain surgery, in the same numbers as men, this represents no affront to feminism. Feminism, like (classical) liberalism, requires equality of opportunity, not equality of result.

At the same time, no one can knowledgeably say that women will *never* be as ambitious as men and will forever be more inclined to work part time and raise their kids than to run a corporation or run for president. We can generalize only about what is happening today, not about the future. We have no idea if the next generation of women—those raised predominantly by mothers working outside the home—will make the same choices women today are making. All we can say is that if those choices are made freely, then feminism is being served.

While the critique of reigning feminism has been quite useful in breaking apart the ideological orthodoxy that feminism had become, it still is only a critique: it doesn't do very much to solve the problems that remain for women. Moreover, some of the critics, in their efforts to reinforce their arguments (not to mention gain media exposure), have tended to minimize these very real problems. For instance, in *The Morning After* Katie Roiphe aptly describes the sensationalism surrounding date rape. But she barely addresses a serious underlying problem: many women are still saying yes to sex when they would prefer to say no. Just because government or university fiat shouldn't attempt to solve a problem doesn't mean the problem isn't a real one.

Indeed, feminism—liberation—involves more than removing the political obstacles to women's autonomy. Feminism requires a society that is capable of accepting the widest array of women's choices—and women who are strong and independent enough to make rational ones.

And the fact is, feminism hasn't yet succeeded as completely as many of us would have liked. Sexism, discrimination, and men who believe that women possess a gene for toilet cleaning continue to influence the choices of many women as well as obstruct their career paths. Many women have parents who discourage their independence, husbands who encourage their subservience, and bosses who exploit them both professionally and sexually. No doubt years of this treatment can wear down even an Amazon's self-esteem. In addition, the corporate world is still far from ready to accommodate our predominantly two-working-parent society. Social conservatives who put such a high priority on "family values" have been notably silent about the need for more family-friendly workplaces.

Yet while stalled socialization and unevolved men have no doubt contributed to women's lagging emotional progress, they can't take all of the blame. Many women have lived basically charmed lives and still consistently make self-destructive or irrational choices. Financial independence may help generate emotional independence, but it clearly is no guarantee.

At least part of the explanation may be that while establishment feminists have been focusing intensely on such "issues" as beautiful models, flirting, and sexy imagery, they have barely dealt with women's very real personal problems. Enormous attention has been paid to how the "patriarchy" mistreats women, but little has been written (with the notable exception of Gloria Steinem's *Revolution from Within*) about how women mistreat themselves. Even focusing on how women should take responsibility for their problems—encouraging overweight women, for example, to exercise and eat balanced meals—is often dismissed as "blaming the victim."

But we don't excuse men for hurting others, even when the fault lies in failed socialization; why should we be excusing women for hurting themselves, for not taking control of their lives? Now that society has finally begun to treat women like adults, they have to learn how to act like adults.

What's important to keep in mind, however, is that in the personal realm, feminism can represent only an ideal, a set of challenges for women and society. Unfortunately, given the foibles of both human nature and society, we will probably never meet these challenges: some men will always indulge in sexist behavior and most women (just like most men) will always have bouts of emotional weakness. But that should in no way distract us or deter us.

To continue the considerable progress that has been made, I think we need to make two major modifications in the way we look at feminist issues. First, we need to understand that, as a result of this progress, the feminist debate has largely shifted from the realm of the political to the realm of the personal.

This is not to say that the political work of feminism is done. In fact, it may never be done. Even when all of the necessary laws are passed or reformed and enforcement procedures are as good as can be expected, there will always be a need for vigilance. Complacency regarding women's rights would be foolish, especially given the irrepressibility of social conservatives in this country and most especially concerning the issue of abortion. But many of the problems that plague most women (in the West) on a daily basis now fall in the personal realm: government can do little to solve them.

The second shift needs to be made in our emphasis on gender, on women as a group, a class, a self-consciously unified sisterhood. Many feminist theorists—through their near-obsessive focus on numerical equality, their calls for changing schools and corporations to better "accommodate" women, their support of laws and policies that would protect women's supposedly frail nature, and their promotion of a distinct "women's" way of thinking and voting—have wound up emphasizing gender in women's professional and political lives. But the primary goal of feminism was to make the public world as gender-neutral and gender-blind as possible: no special privileges for either men or women—so that women can participate on an equal basis with men, so that women can be judged on their competence and not their gender.

Meanwhile, in their often complete dismissal of even the possibility of biological differences between women and men, many feminist theorists still seem glued to the notion that feminism necessitates androgyny. But women don't have to be sexless to be equal. Indeed, even courtship and chivalry can coexist quite peacefully with feminism. If feminist theorists can't learn to respect

13

women's choices—from wearing sensuous Galliano gowns to stay-ing at home to raise their children—how will society?

Women are individuals. They differ from one another just as men differ from one another. Despite both biology and shared experiences, to expect women to think and act as a class is no better than expecting Asians or Jews or Native Americans to think and act as a class. Not coincidentally, the original ideal of feminism is rooted in the individuality of women. We're finally ready to return to it.

I I

Feminism represents the ideal of liberty for women. Commitment to this ideal doesn't mean you must love Toni Morrison, hate rough sex, worship a goddess, or believe that fashion is silly. It doesn't mean you must think that the West, capitalism, and men in general are the source of all misery and that multiculturalism, the state, and women are the source of all good. It doesn't mean you must accept that morality is relative, truth is unknowable, and the self doesn't exist.

All feminism means is that the female half of the human race should enjoy the same rights, and have the same opportunities to fulfill those rights, as the male half. How women exercise their rights and what they decide to do with their opportunities—these are matters of personal choice. Feminism asks only that women make those choices responsibly, as clear-headed, rational adults.

The feminist idea descends from the writings of such classical liberal thinkers as Mary Wollstonecraft, John Stuart Mill, Margaret Fuller, and Elizabeth Cady Stanton. In her monumental treatise *A Vindication of the Rights of Woman*, published in 1792 and considered the first modern writing on the subject, Wollstonecraft sought to apply to women the principles of Enlightenment rationalism—indi-vidual liberty, equality, fairness, and personal responsibility—principles that also formed the foundation for the political doctrine of liberalism.

The Enlightenment *philosophes* believed that what makes humans human is their ability to control their instincts through rationality and conscience, their innate desire to seek pleasure and avoid pain. Although humans don't always live up to their universal nature, that nature offers a moral guide ("natural law") for their behavior and endows them with certain inalienable rights ("natural rights"), namely, the rights to life, liberty, and the pursuit of happiness.

If rationality is the capacity that distinguishes humans from animals, Wollstonecraft reasoned, then women must have this capacity as well. And that means that women must also hold those coveted inalienable rights. Which would then mean that no government or institution could discriminate against women merely because they are women.

It took, however, more than a century and what's considered the "First Wave" of feminist activism for enlightened governments to grant women most of the legal rights held by men—the rights to seek an education, to work outside the home, to own property; and it took another quarter century before women were allowed to vote.

Despite such political progress, throughout the nineteenth and much of the twentieth centuries society continued to think it best that the world of governing, industry, and adventure be reserved exclusively for men (the so-called public sphere), while that of the home and hearth be the province of women (the private sphere). Designated social roles didn't really begin to collapse until the sixties, when the contemporary women's movement (the "Second Wave") succeeded in opening up to women nearly every opportunity in the public sphere, and the seventies, when the burgeoning need for two incomes allowed women an excuse to exit the home.

Thus, as Wollstonecraft and the other intellectual forebears of feminism predicted, social roles were reworked in this country without a massive overhaul of our basic institutions. Family, church, corporation, the political and economic systems—all have needed (and in some cases still need) to be reformed to accommodate feminism. But they haven't needed to be abolished. Wollstonecraft and the others also believed that feminism didn't require androgyny: equality and sexual difference seemed to them perfectly compatible. Even if "a large proportion of women would give themselves to the same employments as now," wrote Margaret Fuller in *Woman in the Nineteenth Century* (1845), this would represent no affront to equality. "The difference would be that *all* need not be constrained to employments for which *some* are unfit."[2]

In academia, this original conception of feminism—removal of the political, social, and personal barriers to women's freedom without a major upheaval in society—now goes by the name of "liberal feminism." This is to distinguish it from Marxist feminism, psychoanalytic feminism, radical feminism, existentialist feminism, socialist feminism, ecofeminism, and postmodern feminism. (Yes, people who write about feminism like to give it names. In the more popular literature, we now have—in addition to gender feminism, establishment feminism, and orthodox feminism—power feminism, equity feminism, difference feminism, individualistic feminism, victim feminism, protectionist feminism, neo-Victorian feminism, therapeutic feminism, and confessional feminism.)

Yet despite the historical roots of liberal feminism, few feminist academics today call themselves liberal feminists. They tend to believe that feminism has outgrown liberalism, that reform of society has liberated only a small percentage of women in male-created structures under male-defined criteria. Gender oppression, they argue, is as pernicious and pervasive as ever.

Actually, the term "liberal feminism" is redundant. Feminism, in its original conception, is merely a subset of classical liberalism, an application of liberal principles to women. The other feminisms aren't necessarily "wrong." Indeed, each has added some important ideas to the feminist debate. But, as I hope to show throughout this book, liberal feminism—rooted as it is in the inherent autonomy, individuality, and rationality of women—accords women not only the greatest freedom of choice, but the greatest respect as human beings.

Since many of the feminist theories and policies regarding such issues as sexual harassment, date rape, and discrimination emanate from the academy, the fact that few academics take liberal feminism seriously is a problem. But perhaps an even bigger problem is that outside the academy the term "feminism" is viewed—by feminists and nonfeminists alike—as a compendium of the most radical feminist theories and leftist political proposals. Worse, establishment feminists assume not only that all self-described feminists accept these positions, but that all *women* accept them. In 1992, the National Organization for Women tried to start a "women's party," which offered a distinctly leftist "women's agenda." Gloria Steinem has labeled a Republican woman politician a "female impersonator." And during the 1996 presidential campaign, Representative Pat Schroeder, Bella Abzug, and other feminist activists promoted a "Contract with the Women of the U.S.A.," which was pledged to, among other things, support comparable-worth policies and preferential treatment for women.[3]

This is feminism as partisan ideology, and it isn't confined to feminist issues. When you go to a rally for abortion rights, for instance, much of the program is often devoted to issues that have no direct connection to feminism—the Persian Gulf War, NAFTA, saving baby seals.

But feminism has nothing to say about baby seals. Nor does it have anything definitive to say about subsidized child care, parental leave, single-sex schools—all of which are political questions, open to debate. Liberal feminism is not a totalizing ideology; there is much room for disagreement.

At the base of what I'm going to have to call "ideological feminism" is an astonishingly unfeminist assumption: that all women think alike, that all women hold the same political opinions, values, and goals. And if they don't hold these views, then they're living under a false consciousness—they've internalized the "backlash." But women do not comprise a political class, a homogeneous sisterhood. Indeed, the fundamental feminist idea was to get society to see women as individuals who happen to be female, not the other way around. Under liberal feminism, the fact that a woman is female may not be the most interesting or important thing about her.

What seems to have been lost over the years is what Yale historian Nancy Cott in *The Grounding of Modern Feminism* calls one of the central paradoxes of feminism: it requires that "women recognize their unity while it stands for diversity among women." In other words, the fact that women are individuals doesn't mean that they can't band together to fight for various feminist causes. Indeed, they have certainly had to do so in the past, and may have to do so again. But at the same time, the political, professional, and personal identity of a woman can never be subsumed under the classification "Woman." That in fact was precisely the problem feminism was supposed to fix.[4]

The fact that women are individuals also doesn't undermine their ability to form social groups. No woman is an island, and women may need the support of their friends—especially (but not necessarily) their female friends—now more than ever. But friends are not political statements: women don't have to like, support, or nurture other women just because they are female. The notion that all women should love one another is not much of an improvement over the traditional stereotype that all women hate one another. I am a sister only to my brother.

Because of the influence of multiculturalism, establishment feminists in the past decade or so have been forced to recognize the class, racial, and ethnic diversity of women. But they have yet to make the same leap regarding political views: Republicans can be feminists, too.

Indeed, establishment feminists still seem to be in denial, blaming the media for turning feminism into a radical orthodoxy. To be sure, the media have certainly not been above mocking the extremes of the women's movement. But the media are only doing their job when they report that NOW president Patricia Ireland says women should vote for only "authentic" female candidates. Or that Heidi Hartmann, director of the Institute for Women's Policy Research, believes that "a states-rights, free-market agenda will never be a women's agenda." Or that Naomi Wolf and Susan Faludi have written that there are intricately designed conspiracies arrayed against women. Or that Catharine MacKinnon and Andrea Dworkin have argued that the line between sex and rape in a patriarchal society is nearly nonexistent.[5]

What the media can be blamed for is continuing to turn to these feminist "leaders" when they need *the* feminist interpretation of an event. There is no one feminist interpretation of anything (much less a "woman's point of view"). And there should be no feminist leaders, no feminist spokeswomen, no singular feminist agenda. There are only feminists—those who believe in the essential equality of women—feminist theories, and, thanks to the beneficial work of feminist activists, a near-feminist society.

I I I

So, now what? Well, liberal feminism doesn't offer us any more of a detailed blueprint for the future than it did for the past—there is still much room for debate. Nevertheless, the few general principles it does hold need to reassert themselves.

One of these concerns the line between the political and the personal aspects of a woman's life, between the parts that government should stick its nose into and those that it should keep its nose out of. A primary task of feminists during the First Wave and the beginning of the Second Wave was to show that the line between the personal and the political was often drawn unjustly.

First Wave feminists argued that government had no business prohibiting women from obtaining a public school education, from working outside the home, from keeping their money and property. In turn, Second Wave feminists argued that many of women's problems that society deemed "personal" were actually in dire need of government attention. The most blatant example was domestic violence, which the police and even the courts treated (and sometimes still treat) as a "family problem" to be worked out between the husband and wife.

This "personal is political" analysis was able not only to sensitize the legal system to such issues as sexual harassment and marital rape, but also to help women understand that they are not alone in suffering from many of their problems. Unfortunately, sometime during the seventies the interpretation of this phrase went haywire. First, the word "political" was broadened from its humble definition of "relating to government" to encompass anything bearing upon "power relations," that is, male domination over women.

Then, since many feminist theorists believe that *all* of society is shaped by such domination, every aspect of a woman's life—from her choice of underwear to her choice of sexual partner to her choice of career—was soon considered a problem in need of "political" dissection. In *Backlash,* Susan Faludi blames the resurgence of sexy lingerie on a corporate culture that wishes to keep women in the role of Playboy bunnies. In her essay "Compulsory Heterosexuality," Adrienne Rich asserts that women are basically forced by patriarchal imperatives to fall in love with and marry men. In congressional testimony, Heidi Hartmann argues that women are still overwhelmingly ending up in jobs in the traditionally female "pink ghetto"—nursing, teaching, child care—primarily because of sexist socialization and discrimination.[6]

Since many of these issues are also considered political in the old sense of the word, government is often called upon to do the fixing. One of the more ironic and disturbing results has been the proposals by many feminist activists to put consensual sexual encounters back under the scrutiny of, if not the state, then university administrators and corporate personnel officers. So far, these activists have succeeded in getting the academic and corporate worlds to formulate policies forbidding women from dating their colleagues, professors, or students and to pass anti-rape ordinances requiring explicit verbal consent at each stage of sexual relations.[7]

These sorts of measures interfere with women's autonomy and right to privacy, assume women are incapable of making rational choices, and unnecessarily attempt to cleanse offices and class-rooms of sexual undertones. They also absolve women of responsi-bility for their actions—or inaction. Courts in several states have begun to take seriously MacKinnon's theory that in a patriarchal world, consent for women is a dubious construct. Thus, a woman can have what would appear to be consensual sex and then say she was raped the next morning (or the next day or week or month or year) when she feels regret for her behavior.[8]

To get feminism back on the liberal track, we need to first return the word "political" to its conventional definition: state ac-tion. A problem deemed political should require more government intervention, less government intervention, or different government intervention. That's it. Thus, rape, domestic violence, blatant sexual harassment, and discrimination are clearly political problems.

What, though, about pornography, "insensitive" speech, "of-fensive" humor, wolf whistles? Various feminists have found each of these to be in need of government attention. Yet politicizing these issues not only assumes that these are actual "problems," but is a tacit admission that women—and not men—are incapable of deal-ing with them, that women are in need of more protection from government than men. Underlying the feminist contract, however, is the notion that women are just as capable as men of, say, ignor-ing, rebutting, or laughing at speech they find distasteful. More-over, many women read or watch pornography, like to tell dirty jokes, and even engage in conversations that some might call sexist.

Perhaps one of the more curious issues to have become politicized in recent years partly because of feminist activism is surrogate motherhood. Some theorists oppose surrogate mother-hood because, they claim, a mother can't make a truly voluntary, informed decision about whether to keep a baby before its birth.

Others apply a Marxist analysis to the issue: surrogate motherhood is a form of exploitation in which middle- and upper-middle-class couples turn the bodies of poor women into mere commodities.

Of course, no one should underestimate the bonds that can develop between a pregnant woman and the fetus growing in her womb. But no one—most especially the law—should also underestimate the rationality of a woman, of her ability to make a clear-headed decision about her life. Indeed, the same argument that feminists have used to make abortion legal applies to surrogacy. If a woman has a right—stemming from the right to privacy, self-ownership, or equality—to abort a fetus or give a baby up for adoption, she should certainly have a right to give a baby to its biological father in exchange for money. (How, by the way, could any woman have an abortion if prebirth maternal bonds are always so strong?)

The Marxist slam on upper-middle-class mothers is even more curious. I wonder if these theorists would feel any differently if they desperately wanted a child yet weren't able to conceive or carry a fetus to term. Interestingly, according to an article in the journal *Dissent,* surrogate mothers typically describe their motivations for entering into pregnancy contracts with childless couples as, at least in part, altruistic ones. They want to perform a good deed for others and give something of themselves; the monetary gain is secondary. Of course, the motivations of surrogate mothers are really moot. They have just as much a right to sell their babies as they do to sell their bodies.[9]

Not coincidentally, prostitution is another issue on which many feminist theorists and activists have tried to constrict women's rights for the ostensible good of Women. The argument is similar: prostitution is a fundamental exploitation of women who have, thanks to capitalism, no economic alternative.

No doubt many prostitutes end up selling their bodies because of dire economic circumstances. No doubt many do so because of child abuse, rape, sexual harassment, or discrimination. These are all significant problems that government, as well as femi-

nist activists, can do much to alleviate. But not all women, especially those at the high end of the profession (consider, for example, the "Mayflower Madam"), choose prostitution as a last resort.
Moreover, even if they did, it wouldn't matter. Again, under liberal
feminism, laws have to be made on the assumption that women are
clearheaded and rational—whether they always are or not.

The orthodox feminist tendency to overpoliticize women's
lives has had another deleterious effect. Writers have taken to arguing that women have no personal problems (to bolster her theory
that misogynistic conspirators were intentionally spreading myths
about the failure of feminism, Susan Faludi nearly asserts in *Backlash*
that working women do not suffer from any stress-related ailments,
depression, or low self-esteem) or that all of women's personal
problems are caused by society (Naomi Wolf compares anorexia to
the Holocaust in *The Beauty Myth*). Some writers have even gone so
far as to state that women may be imagining some of their problems (in *The Mismeasure of Woman*, Carol Tavris writes that PMS is
basically a male fabrication).[10]

Clearly, women do have many personal problems, some of
which may have been exacerbated by feminism. While many
women feel obvious stress from tending to both a job and a family,
others feel depressed and lonely from focusing solely on their careers. While some women overeat to obscure their sexuality, others
starve themselves to avoid the responsibility of becoming adults.
Just because feminism may have contributed to these problems, of
course, doesn't make it wrong. Yet women hardly benefit from a
minimization of these problems or a masking of their sources.

[Meanwhile, unnecessarily blaming society for all of these
problems both undermines women's autonomy and promotes the
fatalistic view that their lives won't change until society changes.
Yet while societal changes will no doubt mitigate some of these
problems, most have to be dealt with by women themselves.][In-
deed, women can do just as much damage to themselves, through
their actions or inaction, as "the patriarchy" could ever do to them.
To a certain degree, many women allow themselves to be verbally

or physically abused, exploited or harassed, obese or anorexic. Even if there were no "thinness culture" or pornography industry, even if women ruled Congress and every Fortune 500 company, women with little emotional fortitude would (like men) still subject themselves to abuse or make irrational choices.]

Building emotional strength and independence—self-development—was a prominent part of feminist theorizing and activism in the early days of the Second Wave. But throughout the seventies, the emphasis shifted to dissecting and dismantling the societal, "structural" barriers to women's progress. In recent years, focusing on women's personal development and responsibility has typically been dismissed as naive or even sexist. Worse, much of the rhetoric and policy proposals concerning sexual harassment, date rape, and feminine traditions seem almost geared to the promotion of weakness and dependence. [Women are said to be victimized by diets, exercise, beautiful models, fashion designers, high heels, makeup, compliments, movies featuring fulfilled housewives, not to mention every male co-worker and date. The fact that women have a great deal of control over their lives—both to help themselves and to hurt themselves—rarely makes it into feminist discourse.]

Women need emotional strength not only for their own well-being but also to push the men in their lives and the companies they work for to better accept and accommodate equality. Just because government can do only so much to hasten the pace of social and cultural change doesn't mean individual women can't achieve a great deal on their own. In fact, they have to.

Women's personal lives and choices need to be free of not just intrusion by government, but intrusion by society as well—and that includes feminist theorists. [Women cannot be burdened by anyone asserting that certain behaviors are "immoral" or "unfeminist." Of course, just because women are now free to do something—casual sex, single motherhood, adultery—doesn't mean it's the most rational thing to do. But only each woman can decide if her actions are self-destructive and thus unfeminist: what is self-destructive for one woman—entering a wet T-shirt contest, for instance, or being a full-time housewife—may be liberating for another. You may not like my choices (and I may not like yours). But aside from warning me about the possible pitfalls, my choices are really none of your business.]

IV

Another principle of liberal feminism holds that the public sphere—the world of laws, jobs, and education—must be as gender-neutral as possible. This means there can be no special privileges for men—or for women. Protectionist legislation, such as limiting the hours or types of jobs women can work, has been off the books for a good twenty years. But recently, some feminist activists have supported both lowering standards (not just changing sexist standards) for jobs like firefighting and "gender-norming" standardized tests. "Institutions have to adjust," explains Bella Abzug. But "adjusting" institutions for the sake of women is not only potentially dangerous—a female firefighter not capable of lifting a body out of a burning building does not promote the cause of equality—but sexist, reinforcing the stereotype that women can't compete as well as men.[11]

The most pervasive special privilege is rarely seen as such: quotas, both those that are implicit and those that are explicit. Feminists who support quotas or preferential hiring tend to believe that justice—feminism—requires that positions at every level of power be split 50/50 (or 51/49, to match the female proportion of the population at large). The only reason this has not happened, they argue, is because of gross discrimination and residual sexist stereotypes.

But liberal feminism—like liberalism—requires only equality of opportunity, not equality of result. "Feminism is not concerned with a group of people it wants to benefit," writes Janet Radcliffe Richards in The Sceptical Feminist, "but with a type of injustice it wants to eliminate." Equality of opportunity means that the playing field has to be made as level as possible and that none of the participants is too disadvantaged to compete. Thus, you could argue that, for instance, subsidized child care is critical to feminism. But given the complexity of human life—the fact that some women will always have more education, more talent, more intelligence, and, yes, more charm and beauty—feminism cannot possibly mean that everyone comes out a "winner." Nor should it.[12]

Indeed, there is no female consensus on what exactly constitutes a "winner." Just as all women don't have the same political opinions and taste in clothes, they also all don't have the same goals. Some women aspire to be full-time mothers. Others prefer jobs with flexible hours and low levels of responsibility. Still others desire to stabilize at middle management. Are all of these women living under a false consciousness, so overpowered by antifeminist messages that they can't think for themselves?

Well, it is no doubt true that society's less than wholehearted embrace of feminism is still influencing the choices of many women, from the parents who don't encourage daughters to the husbands who don't do dishes. And in another fifty years the picture could look completely different. But at the moment that seems unlikely. Most young women in their twenties—well-educated women who grew up with nearly every option open to them—are still choosing jobs that allow them to give their families greater priority than their careers. Surveys show that only 14 percent of women in middle management (compared with 45 percent of men) aspire to be CEOs and that employed mothers are far more likely than employed fathers to want to work part time or fewer hours and to value flexibility over advancement.[13]

This is no cause for feminist embarrassment. Even if a hundred years from now fewer women than men still want jobs with high levels of prestige and responsibility, even if men continue to be far better represented in the top echelons of society, even if patriarchy—narrowly defined as men holding disproportionately more of the positions of influence in the public sphere—persists, this would not undermine feminism. Liberty and justice can exist in a world in which a woman does not become president, Speaker of the House, or secretary of state; in which women do not constitute more than a third of Congress, corporate boards, or CEOs; in which women remain a small percentage of newspaper editors.

This is not to say that it wouldn't be far *better* if enough qualified women did aspire to such heights. It's no doubt true that female legislators, lawyers, doctors, editors, and manufacturers are more likely to understand women's experiences and needs better than their male counterparts do. And it will no doubt be harder to reach the feminist ideal—in terms of both a nonsexist society and strong, self-directed, independent-minded women—without women better represented at the top: the value of inspiring role models should never be underestimated. But as long as women have as much of an opportunity for advancement as men, we will all have to learn to respect the choices of women. Indeed, unless you want to enslave both women and men to self-appointed social engineers, there is nothing that can be done about it.

An additional problem with obsessing about numerical equality is that it implies that the power of prestigious positions is the only type of power worth having. This doesn't say very much about the importance of teachers, nurses, day care workers, and, most especially, mothers. Conservatives are right when they argue that power can take many forms and that women have never been exactly powerless. Again, the key issue is freedom of choice, which women in the past clearly did not have.

Meanwhile, some feminist theorists have been trying to undermine the gender neutrality of the public sphere in more subtle ways. One is through promotion of a supposedly distinct "women's" way of working. These feminists consider it the mission of feminism to transform the public sphere from a world of competition and hierarchy into a world of compassion and cooperation. If women ruled the government, large corporations, and the media, they claim, there would be a lot less violence, greed, and exploitation.

This is, of course, just an updated version of the argument

some First Wave feminists used to try to get the vote: women would apply their morally superior thoughts and behaviors—so supposedly obvious in the domestic sphere—to the political world as well. And the argument is still just as specious and even sexist. Women are no doubt different from men. But at the moment it appears that those differences have little to do with competition, hierarchy, or even ethics. Historically, women's competitive drive and dishonesty were allowed only subtle, indirect expression; today, they are being vented far more explicitly. Moreover, whatever the differences between the sexes turn out to be, they will be far from pervasive: there will always be women who will lie, cheat, and sell junk bonds as well as any man.

Most important, the ideal of liberal feminism has nothing to say about whether women *should* be more competitive or less, whether the public sphere *should* be more hierarchical or less. Some women, it seems, are going to continue to choose fields—nursing, teaching, child care—that allow them to be more empathetic and less aggressive; others are going to want to play hardball on Wall Street, in journalism, politics, or law. If some women eventually make some fields or offices more compassionate, that will be an interesting development. But feminism hardly requires this.

The same gratuitous gender promotion is apparent in feminist attempts to advance a "women's literature" or a "women's science" or to hold all-female art and photo exhibits. Again, many women, either because of nature or nurture, may very well incline toward a certain manner of writing or painting. But asserting that there is a particular women's style is insulting both to those women who adhere to it and to those who don't.

The whole purpose of making the public sphere gender-blind was to allow women to be judged by objective criteria, not by their secondary sex characteristics. "I want my work considered as mine, not as some tour de force or bit of presumptuous rivalry on the part of an eccentric member of an excluded group," the writer Miriam Allen de Ford declared in the late twenties. "I want to stand before the world and say: 'I am myself. I have defects, weaknesses, and faults. I want them judged as mine—not as a woman's.'"[14]

V

Creating a gender-neutral public sphere, however, doesn't require the neutering of women. Indeed, there's no reason women can't thoroughly enjoy sexual differences in their private interactions both in and out of the office.

Reigning feminist theory has often disagreed. Implicit in much feminist writing is the belief that until women shun all aspects of traditional femininity, they will continue to be exploited by men. Therefore, women shouldn't accentuate sexual differences through clothes, makeup, and mannerisms. They shouldn't allow men to court them or be chivalrous. And by no means should they do more than half of the "mothering" and housekeeping.

During the late seventies, a strain of feminist theorists began to turn away from support of this rather androgynous vision. Variously called "difference," "cultural," or "relational" feminists, these theorists have argued that such traditionally feminine traits as compassion, intuitiveness, and sensitivity need to be not only "valorized" (that is, valued) but celebrated. And such traditionally masculine traits as rationality, emotional control, and "abstract" thinking need to be seen as, at best, problematic.

While any efforts to better appreciate mothering and nurturing are certainly worthwhile, this type of analysis can undermine women's individuality as much as the more androgynous notions. Theorists like Carol Gilligan, Sara Ruddick, and Nel Noddings write not only as though *all* women are more relational than men, but as though this fact is immutable. Fortunately, this is far from the case. Indeed, in many situations, an abundance of these traits may not be all that useful to women. (And the fact that some feminists have taken to disparaging rationality—the linchpin to

Wollstonecraft's argument for equality—is more than a little ironic.)

(Feminists have certainly needed to puncture the notion that to be accepted as a "woman," a member of the female sex had to look, act, talk, and live in a societally prescribed way.) But a historically rigid feminine identity didn't need to be replaced by an equally rigid feminist one. A woman today is capable of *choosing* to engage in many traditionally feminine behaviors and mannerisms. She can wear slinky dresses and heels or baggy overalls and combat boots; move with studied grace or lumber casually; pursue men or wait to be pursued; take her husband's name in marriage or keep her own; stay home to raise her children or go to work while her husband raises the children.

Obviously, not all women are making these choices completely unencumbered by social influences. (Indeed, culture affects all decisions, even subversive ones.) Yet most women today, I would imagine, are making personal choices fully aware of their options. And if more of these women than not continue to take more traditional routes, I don't think it should come as much of a surprise. Nor should their doing so be self-righteously dismissed as a product of "backlash."

If anything, it could be called progress. It is proof that many women now feel liberated enough to act in any way they please: they no longer have to renounce certain pleasures—fashion, courtship, chivalry—merely to make a symbolic point. In fact, it may turn out that the more equality women gain in the political realm, the more they may want to celebrate their differences from men in the personal realm.

It also may turn out that the closer some behaviors are to the imperatives of reproduction, to the passage of our genes to the next generation, the more this may differ between the sexes. For instance, studies continue to show that men and women, on average, still have very different views about love and sex: women tend to believe that love should come first; men the opposite. Women who enter (or reenter) the dating game and try to ignore these differences are apt to spend many nights, at the very least, feeling completely confused.

[The larger point is that women have made enough progress to be able to discuss the fact that some emotional and behaviorial differences between the sexes may have biological roots: traditional femininity and masculinity do not appear to be fully constructed by society.]

Feminist resistance in the past to the mere mention of the possibility of psychological differences between the sexes was understandable. Scientists studying the brain at the end of the nineteenth century argued that because women's brains are (on average) smaller than men's, their intelligence must be inferior. Moreover, when Charles Darwin first proposed his theory of natural selection—the process by which traits that promoted reproduction are preserved—it was immediately misappropriated by what came to be called "social Darwinists" to justify social inequality. Social Darwinists claimed, for instance, that since women are apparently naturally better at childrearing, they should remain permanently ensconced in the domestic sphere: biology is destiny.

The rift between feminism and the sciences that explores the biological basis of behavior—variously called sociobiology, or its more refined offspring, evolutionary psychology—was further widened by a prevailing bias among the (mostly male) evolutionary theorists, who tended to look primarily at male behavior and often made merely stereotypical assumptions about females.

But we've come a long way intellectually in the past couple of decades. There are now evolutionary theorists who are looking closely at female behavior as well—and they're making some rather surprising discoveries. For example, anthropologist Sarah Blaffer Hrdy has found that other female primates—chimpanzees, gorillas, baboons—are actually far more ambitious, competitive, and assertive than female humans have historically been. And although the world of primates can in no way be called androgynous—the females are the primary caretakers of the young—much of it is far more egalitarian than our society has been: the females do not exist to serve the males. Hrdy speculates that our human ancestors inhabited a more egalitarian world as well.[15]

Even more fascinating, scientists are finally able to study the brains of women and men more closely, and they are finding subtle but significant differences that hardly slight women. Yes, women do have smaller brains—but they have 11 percent more neurons packed into those efficient units. And scans of those brains have found that women and men use different parts of their limbic systems, which regulate emotions. Men, on average, have higher brain activity in the more ancient and primitive regions, the parts more involved with action, while women, on average, have more activity in the newer and more complex parts, which are involved with symbols. This may at least partially explain women's age-old complaint that men never express their feelings, and men's age-old response that they did precisely that by washing the car.[16]

Unfortunately, many ideological feminists remain unmoved. Research into biological differences is "really the remnant of anti-American, crazy thinking," declared Gloria Steinem on a television show devoted to the latest studies. "It's what's keeping us down, not what's helping us." Ideological feminists may be the only group besides creationists who refuse to believe in evolution.[17]

Clearly, biology is no longer specific destiny for women—some women today choose to live with neither husband nor children. But biology does play a role in the destinies of many women, and ignoring this reality doesn't help women better plan their lives—or force society to better accommodate two-career families. Biology (for the moment) circumscribes when a woman can have children, and it may very well influence whether she wants to stay home with her children when they are young and even which field she chooses to work in. What if it turns out that the bond between mothers and infants really is more pronounced than the bond between fathers and infants? What good would it do women—let alone children—to try to wish this morality away?

While the pivotal role biology plays in many women's lives does shape the boundaries of their autonomy, it doesn't make women slaves to the womb. Our choices are also strongly influenced by culture, family, friends, and our own unique desires. The goal of feminism is not only to allow women an endless array of options but to help them understand what may or may not be motivating their decisions. To do this, of course, you can't live in fear of either the potential motivations or the ultimate choices.

Moreover, acknowledging that some traits may be rooted in biology—may be "natural"—doesn't mean that they're necessarily beneficial or that we're necessarily stuck with them. Consider the trait of sensitivity. According to many evolutionary theorists, women are naturally more sensitive than men: our female ancestors needed large doses of empathy and compassion to communicate with and care for their children. An overly sensitive nature, meanwhile, would have inhibited our male ancestors from successfully protecting and feeding their families.

Outside of childrearing, however, being highly sensitive is not always useful for women today—it can cause them to take offense at the slightest affront, to take everything personally, or to give too much nurturing and demand too little. Fortunately, as a million pop psych books will tell you, oversensitivity is negotiable: women can learn to control their relational tendencies just as (most) men have learned to control their aggressive ones.

At the same time, contrary to ideological feminism's blanket condemnation of traditional masculinity, men have typically held title to quite a few traits that women can now put to good use. In addition to ambition, assertiveness, and independence, there's also decisiveness, the ability to compartmentalize various areas of one's life, the ability not to be self-destructive when depressed or anxious, and so on. Moreover, there's nothing inconsistent about emphasizing more traditionally masculine traits in the public sphere and more traditionally feminine ones in the private.

It should also not cause alarm if women decide to retain the more culturally inspired aspects of classic femininity—from wearing bras to carrying themselves with poise. Many customs developed as ways of enhancing the natural grace, elegance, and beauty of the female body, not as means of restricting women mentally and physically. More important, most women appear to derive enormous pleasure from enveloping themselves in all of the rites and rituals of traditional womanhood, and there's nothing wrong with that.

Unfortunately, much of the new feminist commentary that is trying to jettison the puritanical aspects of reigning feminist theory has not exactly encouraged a thoughtful analysis of traditional femininity. Victim feminism is being replaced with in-your-face feminism, and its message is crude: women are not just tough and assertive; we're all just as vulgar as Roseanne and Courtney Love and we'll use lots of dirty words to prove it. Women don't just like sex; we're all fully in thrall to hard-core pornography and spanking, and we will divulge the most intimate aspects of our sex lives to prove it. Women are not only capable of anger, we're all really bitches. Women are not only capable of abusing and cheating on our spouses, but we really do so *more* than men.

How pleasant. Actually, I think women are now beyond having to prove that they can be just as disgusting as men: being the "bad girl" all the time can be just as conformist as being the perennial "good girl." Perhaps it's even time to retrieve the dignity and self-possession inherent in the term "lady" and give it a hip, feminist spin.

More important, perhaps it's time to retrieve the term "gentleman" and have it now include real respect for women. In fact, it's on the general loss of "civility" in society that conservatives actually have a point. Women could use something in between the personal (individual responsibility) and the political (government responsibility) to help teach men to behave like humans. Liberation never meant that pregnant women should have to stand on crowded buses, that men should stop offering to carry groceries for an overburdened mother, that the check should always have to be split— even if the woman earns less. Chivalry, in other words, needs to be revived and updated. Gallant behavior and feminism are not incompatible. The problem wasn't that women were put on a pedestal, but that they were chained to it.

V I

In her book on female primates, anthropologist Sarah Blaffer Hrdy speculates that the more egalitarian world of our ancestors was destroyed when human society began to erect a set of controls over women, especially controls on women's sexuality. At that point, what you might call a devolution of woman began, leading to the far more dependent, passive, and sexually inhibited stereotype that reigned rather consistently until the sixties.

But Hrdy sees room for optimism. A society that was smart enough to erect those kinds of controls should be smart enough to dismantle them. She goes so far as to dedicate her book to "the liberated woman who never evolved but who with imagination, intelligence, an open mind, and perseverance many of us may yet become."[18]

We have every reason to continue to be optimistic. After all, an entire revolution in social roles has occurred in just thirty years. More work needs to be done, especially regarding rape and domestic violence, and vigilance needs to be constant, especially regarding the right to abortion. Yet those who wish to reestablish legal and social controls on women are far from popular.

At this point, completing the feminist revolution is largely up to women themselves: it primarily involves completing their own personal evolutions. For this reason, most of this book is devoted to the personal sides of feminist issues, those involving beauty, sex, love, power, and female friendship. There are now, I believe, two fundamental questions underlying women's personal lives: What exactly does it mean to be equal yet different, both in the private and public spheres? And what exactly does it mean to be autonomous?

I hardly answer either of these sufficiently. But I think it's time that we begin to better address them. If the First Wave of feminism concerned itself mostly with political issues (gaining women's rights) and the Second Wave dealt mostly with economic issues (expanding women's freedoms), this next wave needs to be primarily devoted to developing our emotional independence.

It has become part of feminist dogma to say that all barriers to self-realization are political barriers. Unfortunately, many are painfully personal. Despite the influences of both biology and culture, we are continually making choices, choices, as the Enlightenment *philosophes* put it, to seek pleasure and avoid pain—or the opposite. Liberation offers women the possibility of happy, fulfilled lives. But just the possibility.

◆

FEMININITY

I

A TRULY FEMININE woman, it was said not long ago, always knew her place. Meek and subservient, she would gratefully sacrifice her own needs in order to nurture round the clock, cooing over every passing stroller, baking pies for the neighbors, brushing dandruff from her husband's shoulders. At the same time, she could be rather emotional—moody, easily frightened or brought to tears—and dependent, not good with money or mechanical things. In fact, a model of femininity was believed to have little in the way of ambition and was certainly not competitive (though she did tend to boast about her husband's salary and worked awfully hard at being considered an icon of style). A real woman, it was believed, didn't care much for sex, despised lewd behavior, and liked a clean house.

Today, women sit on the Supreme Court, conduct Senate hearings, run multimillion-dollar firms, and orbit the earth. Many put off marriage until they're established in their careers, show minimal aptitude for housework, and don't cook. Quite a few wear combat boots, sit with their legs spread apart, call their bosses "asshole," and say "Fuck you" to street harassers. Some have little interest in children—their own or anyone else's—and are not nice.

On talk shows and in pop psych books, experts exhort women to find their inner bitches, develop their darker sides, run with the wolves. Courtney Love exposes her breasts during concerts and teenage girls go wild. Sharon Stone, Linda Fiorentino, and Heather Locklear play mean and unethical femmes fatales and women adore them. Roseanne grabs her crotch while singing the national anthem, spews out vulgarity on her weekly sitcom, and is invited to advise the *New Yorker* on its issue dedicated to women.

Femininity, it would appear, has vanished.

In fact, the word is rarely used anymore, turning up mostly in advertisements for products serving women's "special" needs. Given its prominent place in American society just thirty years ago, its disappearance is rather remarkable. Of course, "feminine" never actually had a precise or fixed meaning—"of or belonging to the female sex" is how *Webster's* defines it. And few women in the real world ever conformed to every aspect of the feminine ideal. Nevertheless, prior to the sixties, a certain set of behaviors, mannerisms, and values was widely believed to characterize womanhood, or at least "proper" womanhood. Women who didn't conform were considered unattractive, immoral, abnormal, or lesbian.

Dismantling the notion of a socially approved womanhood has been one of the main tasks of feminists during the past century. Most feminist theorists have argued that not only is all of "femininity" an invention, like Santa Claus, but that it was devised explicitly to oppress women. Women have been forced to wear restrictive clothing and to abide by constraining rules of behavior in order to reinforce their supposedly natural passivity and dependency; women are pressured to obsess about their appearance so that they don't have the time or energy to do anything else. Some feminists have even argued that women's desires to marry and mother are also products of social conditioning. Until women are free of femininity, runs the argument, they will never be free at all.

Clearly, the vast changes that have taken place in women's goals, behaviors, and demeanors during the past thirty years confirm much of the feminist argument: the traditional notion of femininity has been strongly shaped by cultural norms.

What's equally apparent, however, is that much of traditional femininity has not disappeared. Women still get married and want to have children. They are still far more likely than men to exhibit compassion and empathy, and to get up when the baby cries. Although most women now work outside the home, they still do two-thirds of the childrearing and housework. They continue to be more dependent than men, both financially and emotionally, more apt to make relationships the center of their lives, and more likely to act coy in romantic situations. Women today also overwhelmingly wear dresses, makeup, and longish hair, speak in a slightly modulated voice, shave their underarms, cross their legs at the knee if not the ankle, and move and gesture with an element of grace.

There are, of course, a variety of possible reasons why each of these practices continues to thrive. Most obviously, customs, attitudes, and behaviors can be rather resilient. It has been, after all, only thirty years, and much of society continues to reward women for acting "properly" and to punish women who breach gender lines.

Yet the standard feminist explanation—that continued interest in feminine behaviors is due wholly to a backlash against feminism—seems far too pat, not to mention condescending to women. Given the enormous progress that has been made, I think it's safe to say that most women are not being subconsciously programmed by a patriarchal conspiracy. At the very least, they are aware of alternative lifestyles. If a misogynist backlash were as powerful as Susan Faludi, Marilyn French, Naomi Wolf, and other theorists have made it out to be, how could women also be able to exhibit such previously taboo traits as ambition and assertiveness?

Perhaps what we're beginning to see is that some aspects of traditional femininity, especially those dealing with nurturing and relations with men, are far more deeply rooted in biology than in culture and thus more resistant to change.

Most feminist theorists have been loath to acknowledge any psychological differences between the sexes, believing that even discussing the possibility will send women back to waxing floors and baking soufflés. Some feminists have even argued that premenstrual syndrome and the pain of childbirth are socially constructed and would not exist in a feminist society. Even so-called difference feminists, who believe that women are not only different from men but morally superior to them, are careful not to attribute those differences to any sort of genetic predisposition. Most disconcerting, more than a few "feminist" social scientists, anthropologists, and psychiatrists apparently view any research that attempts to explore these differences as a betrayal of feminism; some have even made efforts to quash such research or stigmatize those doing it as "anti-woman."[1]

But to recognize the possibility that some aspects of traditional femininity may have a biological basis is neither to betray feminism nor to pose an insurmountable problem for women. To the contrary, acknowledging biology can be enormously helpful. Knowing that some of our behaviors are rooted in our natures can be as liberating as knowing that many have been influenced by culture. At the very least, it leads to a better understanding of who we are.

Nor is it a problem for feminism if women choose to retain the more superficial aspects of traditional femininity, from wearing nail polish to walking with a come-hither swish, or if they allow themselves such traditionally masculine traits as competitiveness, rationality, and objectivity—despite the fact that various feminists have denounced all of these as tools of the patriarchy.

[What *is* a problem for both feminism and women is self-destructiveness. And unfortunately, more than a few habits associated with traditional femininity are quite self-punishing. Unhealthy dieting, wearing five-inch heels, undergoing endless plastic surgery—each has been well discussed by now (and I discuss them even more in the next chapter). But there are also more subtle and indirect forms of self-destructiveness: excessive dependence on men; gratuitous self-sacrifice; acting helpless, indecisive, or irrational. Men too, of course, can be quite self-destructive. But there is far less in the traditional concept of masculinity that is inherently self-destructive; indeed, the real problem is that it fosters aggression.]

Why would women still be more vulnerable to self-destructive behaviors? [Again, the explanation is no doubt partly social and cultural. Many women are still being (inadvertently) socialized to respond poorly to life's daily challenges, and the challenges faced by many women are colossal, especially given the corporate world's failure to keep up with the two-career family. While Hollywood and the media in general have been doing a better job of making room for strong female characters and public figures, there still aren't many role models, both real and imagined, that truly inspire. Finally, a helpless woman—especially if she's beautiful—is still quite appealing to many men (and women).]

But it also seems that biology may be partly responsible for making many women more susceptible to self-destructive thoughts and acts. Scientists now confidently attribute premenstrual, postpartum, and postmenopausal sensitivity and depression to hormonal changes, and some researchers believe that women may have a genetic predisposition to depression. Could it also be that women's stronger nurturing drive has predisposed some women to extreme dependence and indiscriminate self-sacrifice? We don't yet know. But ignoring the possibility of biological differences doesn't expedite the process of finding out.

Just because certain traits may be more firmly grounded in biology doesn't mean that they too can't be changed. Women are no more puppets of their genes than they are of the patriarchy. Indeed, women can't afford to use explanations of any sort as excuses. Even after society becomes more egalitarian, women will continue to be faced with a medley of struggles. Being able to deal with them is as important to feminism as being allowed to deal with them. Freedom is not exactly useful if we can't take full advantage of them.

Fifty years ago, Simone de Beauvoir wrote that a woman was not born into society, but made by it. To a considerable extent, we've seen that de Beauvoir was right. Now that the cages of restrictive femininity have finally been opened, women in many ways have to be remade—but this task can be accomplished only by each woman herself. No one promised that this would be painless. Indeed, in some ways life may have been far easier when a woman was just someone's daughter, girlfriend, wife, or mother, when she had a feminine ideal looming over her head telling her how to sit, stand, speak, and order her life. Now each of us has to get up every day and figure out who we want to be.

To help in this matter, I've broken traditional femininity down into three layers. These layers are in no way scientifically drawn and are hardly comprehensive. Nonetheless, I offer them as an introductory guide to what has changed in the past thirty years, what hasn't changed, and what should have changed.

The first layer consists of those aspects of traditional femininity that appear to have altered the least. For this and other reasons, they are probably the most deeply rooted in biology. I have put into this category the nurturing or "relational" qualities: compassion, caring, gentleness, empathy, patience, and selflessness.

The second layer consists of those traits that are far less visible among women today—helplessness, passivity, uncompetitiveness, submissiveness, obedience, and the like. While some of these traits may have a more subtle evolutionary basis—such as the attraction of men—their rather quick disappearance seems to indicate that culture had far more to do with their persistence than survival of the species.

The final layer consists of the most superficial aspects of traditional femininity—dainty gestures, figure-enhancing clothing, mascara, and so on. [Although much of this layer no doubt also stems from an evolutionary need to attract men, it is now clearly far more an artifact of culture than of DNA.] Despite its relative superficiality, though, this layer has not changed as much as the second, probably because the other behaviors were less useful to women and these are more fun. Assertiveness is more useful than passivity; acting "feminine" is (apparently) more fun than not.

What's crucial to emphasize in any discussion of biological difference is a fact that typically gets overlooked by those on all ideological sides: women's individuality. No matter how much the average woman turns out to be different from the average man, women are also quite different from one another. Each woman is a product of her unique genetic code, experiences, choices, and luck. Knowledge of biological differences can't predict how any particular woman will think, act, or vote. It doesn't undermine a woman's distinctive identity; it simply complicates the discussion. And for the sake of women and feminism (not to mention truth), this discussion is ready to be complicated.

I I

Women's relational traits have received a lot of attention in recent years, especially since the 1982 publication of Carol Gilligan's now famous *In a Different Voice*. According to Gilligan, women's capacity for relating to others is not only the focus of their lives but also the basis of their moral reasoning. Women use a subjective sense of compassion in making decisions; men, abstract principles of justice. The world would be a saner place, Gilligan argues, if it better valued relational traits and if men acted more like women.[2]

Although *In a Different Voice* spawned a virtual "difference" in-

dustry of books and articles purporting to show that women's problems—from depression to the glass ceiling—stem from society's
inability to appreciate women's relational qualities, the book's reception was chilly in many feminist circles. Gilligan and other difference feminists have been roundly attacked for asserting not only
that women are more nurturing than men, but that *all* women are
that way, and that women's motherliness makes them superior to
men.[3]

Indeed, in the past couple of years a feminist backlash against
Gilligan and her cohorts has erupted. A slew of psychologists and
journalists/pundits (most notably, Carol Tavris, Katherine Dunn,
and Kate Fillion) have been arguing that women are not only no
more nurturing than men but just as aggressive, violent, and unethical. Some have argued that women's relationships with one another
are based more often on malice than on kindness and that women's
true promiscuous and adulterous natures are still being inhibited by
social restrictions.[4]

Well, leaving aside for a moment virtue, promiscuity, and aggression, it certainly *appears* that women are still, on average, more
nurturing than men. Women—even young women who have
grown up with feminism largely in place—are still far more likely
to provide care and comfort, to express a strong desire to have
children, to fret over a child's needs and moods. No doubt socialization continues to have much to do with this. Researchers still
find that the same baby will elicit very different responses from
adults depending on whether it is dressed in pink or blue. And little
girls are still given dolls to cuddle while little boys get to thrash
around with trucks.

But studies also show (and even the most egalitarian-minded
parents will confess) that a few hours after birth girls are more
sensitive to touch, sound, and pain. Baby girls are more easily com-
forted by soothing words and are much more interested in people
and faces. Girl toddlers learn to speak earlier, are far more talkative,
and are more apt to talk about their feelings. Baby boys, on the
other hand, are far more exploratory; boy toddlers are far more

hyperactive, inclined to rough games, and are likely to use dolls for sword fighting than for playing house. These differences have even survived experiments at kibbutzim in Israel specifically geared toward discouraging sex-role identifications.[5]

Clearly, something else is going on here, something that feminist theorists are still loath to admit. The absolutely-no-difference feminists dismiss the possibility of innate psychological differences between the sexes flat out; Gilligan and most of the other difference feminists either argue that the differences stem from culture or are purposefully vague on the question. No doubt part of the reason for this skittishness is the even greater hostility they would have received from the larger no-difference feminist community if they had given any credence to biological factors.

For most feminist theorists, it seems, biological differences between the sexes involve only chromosomes, hormones, and reproductive organs. Everything else, including psychology, falls under the category of "gender," meaning that any perceived differences are solely a product of social conditioning. (The only exception is aggression, which is often implicitly or explicitly attributed to male biology.) As feminist psychologist Sandra Lipsitz Bem puts it in *The Lenses of Gender*, a person's biological sex should in no way "be at the core of individual identity and sexuality."[6]

Even some feminist scientists who *believe* in biologically grounded differences between the sexes get nervous when talk turns to subjects like nurturing. "You can get us into a lot of trouble if you write about this," one feminist anthropologist warned me. "You can send women back forty years."

No doubt some social conservatives will try to use any theory about women's "natural" nurturing capabilities as proof that God intended women to spend their days changing diapers and choosing wallpaper. But it seems that enough progress has now been made that such talk will get nowhere politically. Feminism has succeeded precisely because it is a cause for sexual justice that says nothing about sexual difference. Indeed, proof that a woman's biology doesn't undermine her ability to work in the public sphere can be found in the scientists doing the highly specialized, highly *analytical* work of researching sexual differences: more than half are women.[7]

What feminist-minded biologists, psychologists, and anthropologists not concerned with the "political" ramifications of their remarks will tell you is that women are biologically predisposed to be more nurturing than men. Females have been found to be more nurturing than males across cultures, throughout the mammalian world, and, perhaps most important, in the traditional hunter-gatherer societies, the earliest form of human society, where most of evolution is thought to have taken place. Ovarian hormones, specifically estrogen, are believed to be responsible for women's greater ability to communicate and form intimate bonds and for their often intense yearning to have children. Testosterone, by contrast, has been found to undermine maternal behavior. This has been most strikingly demonstrated in two genetic aberrations— adrenogenital syndrome, which causes the secretion of abnormally large quantities of a testosterone-like substance in utero, and Turner's syndrome, which creates ovaries so underdeveloped that no testosterone at all reaches the developing brain. Girls with adrenogenital syndrome are far more tomboyish and express less of a desire to marry and have children when they grow up, while girls with Turner's syndrome show exaggerated "feminine" behavior.[8]

More to the point, researchers have found that during labor, breastfeeding, and physical contact with her child, a mother releases the peptide hormone oxytocin, which is believed to facilitate bonding. Contrary to Susan Faludi and other no-difference feminists, in other words, movies featuring happy mothers and miserable single women cannot take the blame for the fact that many childless women in their thirties find it painful to even look at little kids and get deeply jealous if their friends have children first.[9]

It has been widely believed that hormones not only have a direct effect on behavior, but also affect it indirectly by determining the organization of the brain as it develops in the womb. Through anatomical studies and electronic imaging technologies,

scientists have now been able to confirm this, finding both structural and functional differences in the brains of men and women.
Exactly how these differences translate into behavior is still the
source of much controversy. Nevertheless, neuroscientists have discovered that, for example, the corpus callosum is thicker in women
than in men, allowing for a larger number of connections between
the left side of the brain, which controls language, and the right
side of the brain, which controls emotion and visual-spatial perception. These connections are believed to promote a greater capacity
to cross-relate verbal and visual information while at the same time
integrating emotions, perhaps enabling women to better recognize
emotional nuances in voice, gesture, and facial expression—skills
our female ancestors would have found essential to understand the
needs of children even before they were able to speak.[10]

Brain scans of men and women carrying out language tasks
have reinforced this theory—men use only the left side of their
brains while women use both. Meanwhile, psychological studies
have consistently found that women, on average, are better at verbal tasks, reading emotions on people's faces, and picking up nuances of meaning from tones of voice or intensity of expression.[11]

Evolutionary psychologists attribute women's greater nurturing proclivities to the fact that the mother's investment in her offspring is far greater (nine months of pregnancy, up to two years of
nursing) than a man's. Moreover, until relatively recently in human
history, infants had to be breast-fed or they would die. Our female
ancestors were often left to rear children on their own. Since females just as much as males need to pass on their genes, our most
reproductively successful female ancestors not only would have selected the best mates but would have cared most conscientiously
for their offspring. (Our most reproductively successful male ancestors, by contrast, were equipped with the most aggressive and self-
reliant qualities, which enabled them to compete for females, hunt
for food, and protect their families.)[12]

However. Saying that a particular set of traits may be firmly
rooted in female biology doesn't mean that *all* women are well

endowed with those traits and that if they're not, then they're abnormal. It means that more women than men have a genetic *predisposition* for those traits; whether or not a woman actually exhibits them and how strongly she does so has much to do with culture, individual circumstances, conscious decisions, and, in the case of nurturing, the level of estrogen in her body. "Every behavior pattern," writes anthropologist Donald Symons in *The Evolution of Human Sexuality*, "is the product of both genes and the environment."[13]

Indeed, culture starts shaping the way people think from the moment they leave the womb. Moreover, an event or act of learning can directly affect the brain's biochemistry and physiology, deeply modifying inherited characteristics.

Culture's potentially profound effect on biology can be seen in how easily many women today are able to put their biological clocks on pause during their twenties so that they can concentrate on their careers. My mother gave birth to my older brother when she was twenty-two. Like many women in my generation, I didn't even begin to take note of a desire to have children until I turned thirty. The problem for many of us now is that we find having a career and having children equally attractive, a conflict that will no doubt persist no matter how much society rearranges itself.

Actually, from an evolutionary perspective a tension of this sort may be quite "natural." As science writer Robert Wright has pointed out, women weren't designed to be suburban housewives, with little to do except clean, cook, and rear children. Although women were the primary caregivers in hunter-gatherer societies, they also had a career: gathering. This got them out of the house and mingling with other gatherers. Fifties suburbia, Wright points out, forced "mothers into artificial isolation—removed from their kin, often lacking close friends and devoid of purpose beyond child-rearing." Indeed, the "breadwinner era," from post–Civil War industrialization to the 1960s, when few women worked outside the home, is now considered an aberration. Narrowly prescribed gender roles, in other words, have been mandated by culture, not evolution.[14]

Being a member of the more nurturing sex doesn't even mean you have to be a child's primary caretaker. Biological predisposition is not necessarily biological destiny: saying that since women are more naturally inclined to be maternal, they should all be mothers, is the same as saying that since men are more naturally inclined toward aggression, they should all play football. Some women, as I discuss later, are simply inept at mothering, while some men seem to be born for the task. Psychological differences, like all differences, fall on bell curves; there will always be much overlap between men and women. Indeed, researchers now believe that the more testosterone coursing through the brain of a female fetus and the less estrogen emitted at puberty, the less desire a woman may have to nurture. And the less testosterone a male fetus is exposed to, the more the adult male may be "feminine" in behavior. More important, mothering is—to some degree—a learnable task. When circumstances demand it, even an uber-alpha male can suddenly figure out how to coo, cuddle, and change diapers.[15]

Nevertheless, the evidence still suggests that women—on average—are more nurturing than men. Perhaps this will change in fifty years, but I wouldn't bet on it. Clearly, this is far from an inherently bad thing: nurturing is crucial to raising children, and there are many benefits to being able to express one's feelings, show affection, and form intensely intimate bonds is rather beneficial. Yet—contrary to the beliefs of Gilligan and her followers— having your sense of self defined primarily through feelings and relationships is not without its problems. Again, just because a behavior or psychological trait is more "natural" doesn't mean it's always useful (or even morally "good").

As we all know from TV talk shows and self-help books, women can connect too much. Both have offered endless stories of women who desperately need to mother their friends, their lovers, their neighbors. And the flip side of needing to love too much is needing too much love. Many women, it seems, go to great, often self-destructive lengths to receive even the mere semblance of love, comfort, or security. They'll stay in abusive relationships, have sex with men they don't find attractive (let alone like), eat too much, shop too much, drink too much—all to fill what often feels like an emotional black hole.

A relational capacity gone awry can also make women overly sensitive and selfless. Again, sensitivity and selflessness are crucial for rearing children. But outside the world of child-rearing oversensitivity can make a woman take offense at the slightest affront, and selflessness can be, well, selfless.

No doubt centuries of women's confinement to subservient roles have greatly contributed to making the essential qualities of nurturing self-destructive for many women: women were and still are socialized to put the feelings and needs of others above their own. And no doubt some women internalize their purported inferiority. Yet clearly these tendencies have not been so easy to shake off, suggesting that a biological influence, however irrational, may be at work.

That same biological influence may also lie at the root of women's greater proclivity toward depression. Studies on mood disorders consistently show that, from early adolescence on, women's rates of depression are twice as high as those of men: one in four women suffer from a major depression at some point in their lives.[16]

This depression gap was supposed to close after women were finally allowed out of the house and into the public arena. And studies do show that the least depressed women are those who work outside the home (though only if they also have a husband and family). At the same time, there hasn't been a significant drop in the rate of depression for women since the sixties. In fact, although long-term comparisons are not completely reliable (because, for example, women today may be more apt to delve into their personal problems), the evidence does suggest that in the past fifty years, clinical depression has either increased for women or stabilized.[17]

Many feminists now blame the depression gap on society's continued inability to fully accept feminism, forcing women to work double shifts, to be overly concerned with physical appearance, and to be subjected to sexual abuse, discrimination, and harassment.

It's no doubt true, of course, that these factors can affect a woman's ability to feel in control of her life. But this analysis doesn't appear to tell the whole story. The fact that women's higher rate of depression begins after puberty and declines after menopause has led many researchers to speculate that it may be related in some way to the activity of ovarian hormones during menstruation. (Before puberty, girls and boys have the same kinds of hormones circulating at the same levels.) Ovarian hormones have already been implicated in premenstrual syndrome (PMS), the mood and/or bodily changes that many women experience before their periods. Researchers speculate that our bodies have not fully adjusted to the fact that, thanks to birth control, a relatively short period of nursing, and a longer reproductive life span, women now cycle nearly continuously for more than forty years; ovulation and menstruation averaged only two years among hunter-gatherer women. Women's brains may not be geared to handle the monthly influx of hormones, making them more vulnerable to depression.[18]

Another theory holds that many women may respond differently than men to the neurotransmitter serotonin, which regulates moods. Prozac and other serotonin-enhancing antidepressants have been found to be effective for treating not only depression but severe PMS, obsessive-compulsive disorders, and bulimia. Yet another theory has arisen from use of the new imaging technologies. Brain scans have found that when women and men are asked to recall sad memories, the active area in a woman's limbic system is eight times as large as in a man's. Researchers speculate that all of this activity during normal bouts of sadness may leave the limbic systems of many women unresponsive when faced with actual depression.[19]

Biological factors may turn out to explain little in the end, or they may be able to explain only the more severe cases of depression. But research into these questions shouldn't be suppressed out of fear that it will somehow be used against women, as some "feminist" scientists have apparently sought to do.

Nor should a different set of social factors be dismissed out of hand. Evolutionary psychologists tend to believe that the high incidence of depression among women in their childbearing years could be related to the absence of a steady, loving relationship or a lack of close contact with relatives and friends. Again, studies do show that the happiest women are both married and working outside the home. It's hard to live in the real world and not notice that women who are not in a relationship are far more apt to be depressed than men not in a relationship. I often hear from single women in their late twenties and early thirties some version of: "I'm at the top of my career, I've never felt stronger, and I've never looked better. Yet I'm still miserable." It's hard to believe that society's reputed emphasis on happy homemakers is fully responsible for making these women feel this way.

Perhaps the most convincing theory is that certain cognitive and psychological traits may predispose women to mood disorders, especially when dealing with stress and setbacks. When things go wrong, according to psychological studies, women tend to blame themselves and men tend to blame others. Women tend to feel "out of control," helpless, and incapable of improving the situation; men tend to attribute a setback to either external factors or something they can change. Women also tend to ruminate more over their problems, while men take direct action to solve them or at least to distract themselves.[20]

Why more women than men have this "pessimistic explanatory style" is an interesting question. According to work done at the University of North Carolina Population Center and the Kinsey Institute, women with high testosterone levels, either naturally or artificially induced, tend to be more self-sufficient, self-assured, and independent than women with more average levels. Researchers have also found that men with lower levels of testosterone are less likely to be competitive, ambitious, and assertive. But, as University of Pennsylvania psychologist Martin Seligman has shown through numerous studies throughout his career, optimism and a sense of agency can also be learned.[21]

In other words, no matter how great the influence of biology and how strong the power of social conditioning, women can better adapt themselves to the stresses of life through better control of their thoughts and emotions. Unfortunately, many feminists—both of the difference and no-difference varieties—still disparage self-sufficiency, rationality, and emotional control as hopelessly "male." And difference feminists continue to unreservedly tout the relational qualities as gloriously female. In *Silencing the Self: Women and Depression*, Dana Crowley Jack argues that the depression gap is a result not of women being overdependent and selfless but of society's undervaluing of connectedness and intimacy as healthy human needs.[22]

Of course, intimacy should be valued, and there is much in women's nurturing tendencies to celebrate. Women should take pleasure (if they want) in their greater abilities to be soft, tender, and empathetic. But women need to also understand how these same qualities can turn against them. And feminists need to understand that women are smart enough to distinguish the two faces of intimacy.

Changing negative patterns of thought can be quite difficult—especially if they are rooted in biology. Many women today appear to fear autonomy, responsibility, and independence as much as they desire them, the so-called Cinderella Complex. But, again, explanations can't be turned into excuses. Every generation of women has had its own set of problems to contend with. This is ours. Relatively, it's not so bad.

Moreover, knowing that our ambivalence regarding autonomy and responsibility may be rooted in biochemistry can be oddly reassuring: if we're fighting biological tendencies, not just internalizing a cultural backlash, then obviously it's going to be difficult. A biological explanation, ironically, can allow women to be a little more patient with themselves.

What all of this individual work amounts to is the continual separation of womanhood from motherhood. Birth control and abortion permanently separated femininity from maternity in terms of reproduction; women now need to continue the process emotionally, to separate their fates from the first impulse of their emotions. Indeed, this first layer of traits—compassion, patience, gentleness—far better describes mothers than women. They are wonderful traits for any nonmother to have—male or female. But not only are they not "superior" to such traits as autonomy and rationality, they can actually—in immoderate dosages—be quite inferior. A liberated femininity, it seems, would need to continually analyze them with a healthy degree of skepticism.

I I I

My second layer of traditional femininity consists of those traits that have shown a significant change in the past quarter century, and for that reason are probably far more rooted in culture than biology. In this category I would put such traits as helplessness, indecisiveness, naiveté; unambitiousness, uncompetitiveness, unassertiveness; meekness, submissiveness, obedience.

These are not what you would call an attractive set of traits. Indeed, while some of the relational qualities may lead to self-destructiveness, many of these—meekness, passivity, submissiveness—are *inherently* self-destructive (the dictionary defines *meekness* as "enduring injury with patience and without resentment"). What's also striking is how most of them actually characterize little girls, not women. Indeed, if the first layer of traditional femininity could better be called "maternal," the second layer could better be called "girlish." Perhaps what's most curious about these traits is how they would seem to undermine the benefits of the first layer. It's hard to see how helplessness and indecisiveness, for example, would be all that useful in childrearing.

Nevertheless, evolutionary psychologists offer a couple of theories that may explain their biological origins. Since youth signals to men reproductive potential, men have historically been most attracted to youthful women. Men have also been big on purity—it apparently signals a greater likelihood of future fidelity. To both attract and keep men, Donald Symons and others speculate, females many a millennium ago may have used naiveté and passivity to advertise youth and virtue. Another theory holds that males were designed not only to be aggressive, but also to protect. Thus, as wild boars became less of a threat throughout the years, females had to increasingly show males that they were needed—voilà, the faint, the swoon, the wobbling high heels.

There would seem to be some truth to all of this. Just as some animals developed characteristics—elaborate plumage, large antlers—that are potentially a hindrance to survival yet benefit them in their respective mate markets, so too may women have developed characteristics that are not very useful for anything but attracting men.

Yet the fact that many women have so easily cast off these traits in such a short period of time seems to suggest the strong influence of culture. Although some of them—innocence, naiveté, meekness—were considered Christian virtues for boys as well as girls, they were far more expected of women than of men. Of course, throughout history, a lot of women—kept out of public schools, universities, good jobs—actually *were* helpless and naive. But many more dumbed themselves down so as not to threaten pseudo-masculine men—or other traditionally feminine women.

Unfortunately, this still goes on. Indeed, the traits in this group that have probably changed the least are those that directly suggest vulnerability—helplessness, indecisiveness, innocence, and the like.

It might seem that women today who coat their personalities with these traits would receive a less than favorable response from, say, their co-workers. But many women, consciously or not, still resort to vulnerability tricks when convenient—when, for instance, they don't want to appear too strong, too much in control, too competent. Women will claim that they can't figure out the tip at a business lunch, can't turn on the VCR without a husband's assistance, can't be alone during a thunderstorm. They will forget to mention to a boyfriend that they received praise, will let him and his work dominate all conversations, will compromise all career goals and obligations for his.

Some women fall into a little girl routine when confronted with a difficult situation or when feeling intimidated. Again, it often happens unconsciously. You want to meet the boss, ask for a loan, or return a toaster oven that you've broken. Suddenly, your voice turns softer, your speech slower, and your eyes get a little dewy. You flash the authority figure (usually a male) a look of unabashed innocence and then quickly look down and maybe pout or blush.

Sometimes, tears are in order. A few years back, Jane Fonda couldn't get an elevator operator in Moscow to take her upstairs, so she started to cry until he reconsidered. Fake tears also helped her get seated in a restaurant. "If you're ever in a situation where you're not getting served or you can't get what you need," Fonda advises, "just cry." I pulled a similar stunt when I was studying in Paris. My first night in town I got locked out of my residence hall and desperately tried to get into the only one with an all-night concierge. I sat at his doorstep, whimpering, until he caved. It was a survival tactic, yet this sort of behavior hardly befits a nineteen-year-old college student—let alone a fifty-six-year-old former feminist activist.[23]

Clearly, women still play dumb or diminish their accomplishments because it works—because it makes some men feel big and strong (and it makes some women feel maternal). But that's not a good enough reason anymore. Liberal feminism requires equality of responsibility, and equality of responsibility requires being self-reliant—and not just when it's useful.

I'm not saying this is easy, and it does still have a significant downside. The day has not yet come when a single woman, after achieving something magnificent, will automatically think: because of this, I can get any man I want. Indeed, many women still feel precisely the opposite. Women often say that they feel punished romantically for succeeding professionally: every time they achieve, the pool of men who won't feel threatened shrinks proportionately. Yet the situation is not hopeless. As I discuss in chapter 4, men are being forced to evolve, albeit slowly.

Look, for instance, at how well many men have done with the obedience traits—submissiveness, subservience, dutifulness, and so on. There was a time not too long ago when many a man wouldn't even consider marrying a woman who didn't demonstrate the proper degree of servility. No doubt there are still plenty of men who want only women who are eager to obey. And no doubt there are still plenty of women, especially those with extremely low self-esteem, who assent to complete male authority in relationships and marriage.

But thanks to feminism, women today seem far less likely to accept a man's word as their command. Most remarkable perhaps is the change among older women whose subservience was already well established in the sixties.

Perhaps vulnerability was more deeply ingrained in women than obedience. Or perhaps women no longer find obedience as useful as they once did. Financial independence has allowed many women to hold overt power in their relationships (as opposed to using more indirect and, yes, manipulative means to fulfill their needs).

Being uncompetitive and unassertive is even less beneficial, so it's not surprising that many women seem to have quickly jettisoned these traits as well. Just forty years ago, the greatest ambition women were thought to have was removing that awful ring around the collar, and their ability to do anything more substantive in the world was believed to be limited by a natural passivity. Today, women have risen to the top of nearly every profession, and offices burst with women who are more competitive and assertive than their male colleagues.

None of this should surprise women who have been through the "popularity" gamut of most high schools, where the often vicious competitiveness can maim a young girl's self-esteem better than anything the patriarchy could concoct. It also doesn't surprise primate anthropologist Sarah Blaffer Hrdy. In her book *The Woman That Never Evolved*, Hrdy reports that although such female primates as langur, squirrel, and howler monkeys typically don't compete with the males, they do compete fiercely with one another, for access to resources, choice of mates, and high social status. On a daily basis, cooperative behavior between the females is far more frequent and visible than competition, but "every female is essentially a competitive, strategizing creature." Hrdy chides her colleagues for having always focused so intently on male competition that they neglected to notice what was going on among the females.[24]

Nevertheless, because the reproductive drive among many women may always be just as strong as, or stronger than, a drive toward worldly success, their ambitiousness may turn out to be more fluid than men's—rising in their twenties, ebbing in their thirties, rising again in their forties. Of course, we won't get an accurate assessment of this until the corporate world better accommodates itself to working mothers (through more pervasively offering—and supporting—such things as on-site day care, flextime, and home offices).

What shouldn't be overlooked, however, is that many women shucked off almost an entire layer of femininity with only moderate changes in cultural attitudes. Again, although both men and society need to continue to evolve to accommodate feminism, women can't wait around for that to happen—they must continue to work on their own, individual progress. This is crucial. Not only did these traits reinforce women's subordinate roles, they also assured women of second-class personalities.

I V

My final layer of traditional femininity consists of all the mannerisms, affectations, and details of appearance that women had to (and often still have to) follow from birth to be considered sufficiently female—from a slightly modulated voice to dainty movements and gestures to gracious discourse.

No doubt some of this layer is rooted in female anatomy. Women tend to speak more softly because their voices aren't deepened by mega doses of testosterone during puberty. They tend to take smaller steps because they have, on average, shorter legs. They tend to hold objects with more delicacy because they have, on average, a finer bone structure and musculature.

[But clearly much of the behavior that falls into this layer has been crafted and encouraged by society. Those smaller feet don't have to be crossed at the ankles; those dainty fingernails don't have to be long and painted; those smaller waists don't have to be corseted. This is especially obvious, of course, when you look at how vastly these behaviors differ across cultures. Among the Maasai and other African tribes, for example, decorated long hair is a fully masculine ornament; the heads of tribal women are covered or shaved.[25]]

[According to reigning feminist theory, the mannerisms and rituals of Western society developed to inhibit women physically as well as to reinforce their larger sense of passivity. It's no doubt the case that, to some extent, society subtly encouraged certain female behaviors to render women more effete. But did these traits develop *only* for this purpose—basically, misogyny—or did they also develop, at least to some extent, to enhance a certain beauty, grace, and elegance inherent in the female body?]

Many feminists would argue that there is no difference since the result was restrictive behavior. But there is a difference. More important, the fact that, whatever its genesis, much of the classical feminine style *does* add beauty, grace, and elegance to a woman's life would certainly help to explain why, during the eighties, many women began to reincorporate some of it into their lives.

More to the point, there's no reason to cast aside customs simply because they're associated with a less liberated era. Again, the line needs to be drawn at self-destructiveness, and the fact is, there's nothing self-destructive about crossing your legs at the ankles, walking and sitting with good posture, or moving with poise and grace.

[At the same time, much was missing from classical feminine style. For starters, confidence. Classical femininity looked pretty, but it often seemed to be externally imposed, mere decoration. Even the young Jacqueline Kennedy, much lauded for her elegant demeanor, was far too circumscribed by proper bearing to seem particularly confident or comfortable: in retrospect at least, her movements didn't appear to come naturally.]

The most proper archetype of femininity, arising in the Victorian era and reemerging in the fifties, also lacked sensuality. Stiff and robotic, she offered few hints of passion. This was not a coincidence. A truly feminine woman was supposed to represent an image of purity, not sexiness, and a blatantly sexual woman was hardly considered feminine.

Ironically, what many feminists have tried to replace classical femininity with also lacks confidence, sensuality, and individuality. In many women's studies classes, the dress code appears restricted to androgynous clothing and buzzcuts. In Susan Faludi's *Backlash*, sexy clothing like lingerie, miniskirts, and high heels are denounced as weapons of the patriarchy. In Naomi Wolf's *The Beauty Myth*, women are discouraged from losing weight and getting cosmetic surgery. And in *Femininity*, Susan Brownmiller frowns upon wearing makeup. Far worse, sexual harassment policies that prohibit compliments, flirting, and dating of colleagues implicitly view women's sexuality as a weakness, something that needs to be kept hidden and protected by government. In some feminist circles, it has become politically correct for gay males to be elegant and glamorous, but not for women.

Unfortunately, what some writers and singers—Lisa Palac (editor of *Future Sex* magazine), Madonna (in her first incarnation), Naomi Wolf (in her second incarnation), Sallie Tisdale, and some of the "riot-grrrl" bands—have tried to replace this feminist identity with is not much of an improvement. In attempting to show that they're just as sexual, as vulgar, as "bad" as the next guy, they've ended up exposing the most intimate and perverted details of their sex lives. Wolf informs us in the *New Republic* that her first orgasm was "pure heat and light." Palac tells *Esquire*: "I say to men, 'Okay, pretend you're a burglar . . . and you throw me down . . . and make me suck your cock.'" Thank you both for sharing.[26]

Of course, female sexuality is a tremendous power, and denying this denies an essential aspect of womanhood. (How women use this power is more complicated, something I take up in later chapters.) But this in-your-face model of womanhood (which *Esquire* aptly christened "do-me feminism") betrays just as much insecurity as the more repressed variety. It's certainly true, as Margaret Atwood has put it, that "equality means equally bad as well as equally good." But just because women are now free to be exhibitionists, to self-promote, to be vulgar, doesn't mean that they should do it—or that it should be celebrated. Real strength—even real sexual strength—doesn't need to be constantly exhibited and reinforced.[27]

Much has been made of women's attraction to the characters Demi Moore, Sharon Stone, and Liz Phair have been creating—1940s-type femme fatales with a postmodern, careerist spin. According to popular analysis, it is the exquisite "badness" of these characters that women find so compelling.

No doubt this is partially true. There are still stigmas and stereotypes to be broken, as the popularity of Roseanne also shows. But I don't think that's the main attraction of these liberated sirens. I think it has much more to do with their no-holds-barred toughness, their blatant selfishness, their serene emotional detachment—their masculinity.

At the same time, the ultimate femme fatale is also utterly feminine. Not in the repressed Victorian or girl-next-door mold, but in the sense of being sexually there, self-assured, and yet at the same time unapologetically "ladylike." The Bacall prototype may rob, steal, and kill, but she does so elegantly. Her refined exterior conceals a spine of steel.

I'm hardly recommending that women take up Sharon Stone

as a role model. But I think it needs to be said that just as ambition doesn't make you any less of a woman, grace and sensuality don't have to make you less of a feminist. Feminist theorists have spent an awful lot of energy in the past quarter century trying to throw out all aspects of the classical feminine style for the supposed sake of feminism. The feminist record needs correcting.

V

"You are in competition with only one person," Martha Graham once said, "and that is the individual you know you can become."

Women are no longer constrained by a mythology that allowed them only to be girlish or maternal, by a narrowly restrictive, socially accepted definition of femininity. Now every woman must design her own notion of what it means to be a woman and, one would hope, a liberated woman. The fundamental question for women is no longer, Who is the man you want to live with for the rest of your life? It is, Who is the woman you want to be for the rest of your life?

If it has been, as sociobiology suggests, the unconscious predilections of our female ancestors that determined the general course of masculinity, it is now going to be the very conscious choices of women that must determine their own evolution. Perhaps it is not a coincidence that the very traits our female ancestors looked for in their mates—emotional stability, independence, self-reliance, decisiveness, assertiveness, initiative, competitiveness—women must now develop in themselves.[28]

Women need these traits whether they want to become corporate raiders, full-time mothers, or some combination of the two. At the same time, however, many women may continue to feel a sharp tension between nurturing and ambition long after the corporate world gets its act together and men take on more childrearing functions. And, again, if the desire to nurture wins more often than not, this should not be seen as a blow to feminism. There are some things that feminism can't change. One is the fact that women represent the chief component of reproduction.

More important, there's no reason to bemoan this. The most significant contribution of the difference feminists has been their unabashed celebration of motherhood. Yes, their arguments could have been more nuanced and less politicized. Yet Gilligan and her colleagues have gone a long way to undermine the early radical feminist view of motherhood as unfeminist, as mere "breeding."

The fear has been that if we condone any aspect of traditional femininity—even the non-self-destructive aspects—women who aren't "sufficiently" feminine will continue to be seen as failures. By the general public, they very well might be, even after mainstream culture consistently offers a variety of styles of womanhood. But up until this point women have done an exceedingly good job of standing up for their own individual differences. There's no reason to believe that won't continue.

Three

◆

BEAUTY

I

IT WAS THE seventh grade, at a school where the superficial received a lot of weight. I was on the gymnastics team, standing behind the ever-blond, ever-perfect, ever-malicious Kathy Gilbert. Kathy and I had never spoken; she was popular, I was not. But right before she plunged into her flawless double handspring, she turned to me, apropos of nothing, and offered: "You know, you're really ugly."

I said nothing, and not just because she terrified me. I said nothing because I believed she had stated the truth, a fact, as obvious and immutable as her own exalted social standing. Kathy's remark stung, but only because she had the temerity to state aloud what I believed the world at large was keeping to itself.

It is surely one of the cruelest ironies of early adolescence that beauty begins to matter at precisely the time when you look your worst. Indeed, while much of the female contingent of junior high is being drained of anything that could remotely be called self-esteem, all are being assigned a place in the beauty hierarchy, a ranking that overrules all previous indicators of status, and one that will undermine any achievement to come. Overweight, gangly, and nerdy young men also receive their share of appearance abuse. But a teenage girl can be heir to no obvious defect, can be quite aver-age-looking in fact, and she will still be labeled deficient, defective, a failure.

Things don't seem to have changed much in this regard over the past twenty years. Although most young women today have mothers who work outside the home, and although attitudes toward these women have matured considerably, appearance still seems to rule, both in and out of the classroom. The vast majority of teenage girls say they are dissatisfied with their looks. Girls as young as nine go on crash diets. Their mothers, meanwhile, have been spending record sums on cosmetic products and services touted to keep them forever young and beautiful.[1]

Why, in the face of women's burgeoning autonomy, has a beauty hierarchy persisted with such determination? The standard feminist explanation is, again, cultural: youth, beauty, and thinness matter more than anything else because society tells us that they should. This message is reinforced daily by models and actresses who are almost by definition young, beautiful, and thin.

There is, of course, much truth to this. Imagery and implicit messages can obviously have an effect, subliminal or otherwise, especially on the young and insecure. And feminists have surely been right to argue that society's historical cultivation of a beauty ideal has been quite damaging to women. In the name of beauty, women have crippled their feet, broken their ribs, inflated their breasts, deflated their thighs, and lifted their faces and rears.

They've fainted from corsets too tight, fallen from heels too high, developed cancer from too much sun, died from too little food—often to find that the ideal they were trying to achieve had been revised.[2]

Indeed, the beauty ideal has gone through radical revisions over the years, sometimes changing more than once in a lifetime. The tall, blue-eyed, cellulite-free blonde who has tormented women for most of this century would not have gone over very well in, say, the seventeenth century (when big ripe bellies were considered attractive) or the early nineteenth century (when dimpled thighs and buttocks were in vogue).

In recent years, thanks largely to the feminist critique, notions of beauty have begun to expand beyond the Barbie standard. A few decades ago you'd have been hard-pressed to find even a brunette on the cover of a fashion magazine. Today, advertisers and editors will fairly regularly use not just brunettes, but women who are black, Hispanic, and Asian; even women over forty (Lauren Hutton, Isabella Rossellini) are now frequently interspersed among the nymphets. You can also find a far wider range of types, both facial (a somewhat crooked nose, eyes close together) and body (from gamine waifs to muscular jocks to curvaceous sirens). Several of the top models, especially Kristen McMenamy, are distinctive far more for their quirky features and attitude than for their beauty.

More important, there seems to be a far greater understanding among women today that they no longer have to adhere to a well-prescribed regimen to be considered womanly, or even beautiful. Women follow certain beauty rites and rituals but not others—and each woman chooses differently. Some women refuse to shave their legs and underarms but have no problem wearing lipstick and mascara and having their hair permed. Others refrain from makeup and jewelry but have their noses "fixed" and unwanted hair removed. Women today are also far less likely to change their entire wardrobes to accommodate the latest fashion.

Despite such apparent progress, in recent years the reigning feminist critique of beauty has taken on a "political" slant. The beauty ideal, claim many feminists, is not merely a cultural fixation with destructive side effects. Rather, it is a patriarchal ploy used both to control women morally and sexually and to earn profits for the "male-dominated" medical, cosmetic, diet, and fashion industries. The more progress women make, the argument now goes, the more society has forced women to abide by an increasingly strict and restrictive beauty ideal.[3]

In *The Beauty Myth,* Naomi Wolf argues that the recent rise in cases of anorexia is due to society's "material vested interest in [women's] troubles with eating. . . . Dieting is the most potent political sedative in women's history; a quietly mad population is a tractable one." In *Backlash,* Susan Faludi claims that misogynist fashion designers began pushing seductive clothes during the eighties (corsets, miniskirts, lingerie) to impede women's progress, attempting to reduce women to the status of passive sex objects. These feminists and others cite the recent increase in sales of beauty products and services as proof that the backlash has been successful.[4]

Some theorists take this argument yet another step, arguing that not only is a specific ideal of beauty constructed by society, but so is the very notion of beauty itself. According to Wolf and others, there is no quality called "beauty" that objectively and universally exists. Various academic feminists argue that the entire field of aesthetics is an instrument of "bourgeois hegemony."[5]

To disempower "beauty" once and for all, many of these feminist theorists argue, the "fashion-beauty complex" of advertising, women's magazines, and the fashion and cosmetic industries must be dismantled. The media must only use "real" women of all shapes, sizes, and colors, and Hollywood must end its love affair with pretty women. Only then will women be able to accept themselves the way they are and devote their time and energy to far more important matters.

If only it were that simple. Fortunately, beauty is not a myth, an arbitrary cultural convention, an ideological fabrication. Beauty is a reality, a gift of God, nature, or genius that, to some extent, transcends culture and history. Society has certainly exploited a

female obsession with youth and beauty, but society, ours or anyone else's, didn't create it. The real culprit is evolution: while men
have historically competed for women through bravery and brawn,
women have competed for men through displays of reproductive
fitness. Different cultures and eras have emphasized different features and body types, but physical female beauty has been a relatively stable commodity, and women's desire to attain it is buried
deep within their psyches.[6]

It is true that many women still destroy their bodies in the
name of beauty—smoking, starving, or vomiting to lose weight;
basking in the deadly sun; wearing toe-curling spikes; ingesting the
latest miracle potion promising eternal youth. And according to at
least one study, the number of women who view their bodies in a
less than loving way has more than doubled in the past twenty
years—nearly half of all women (compared with a third of men) say
they are dissatisfied with their bodies. Yet the explanations seem to
be far more complicated than the backlash analysis would suggest.
In fact, feminism itself may be partly responsible for the rise in
eating disorders.[7]

At the same time, feminism has surely allowed women to
broaden the venues for gaining self-respect, and has begun to break
society's nasty habit of equating a woman's worth with her beauty.
A woman sitting on the Supreme Court or on a corporate board
doesn't have to be beautiful to command respect; drop-dead looks
might even undermine her ability to be taken seriously.

What feminism can't do much about is society's general appreciation of beautiful women. Nor should it. Aesthetics and autonomy can happily coexist. Insisting that cosmetics and fashion are
tools of the patriarchy leaves women with two options: they can
either refrain from all traditionally feminine pursuits, and thereby
make themselves beauty martyrs; or they can engage in them, and
thereby be left with the view that they are victims of male oppression. Yet a woman can reconstruct her face, take two aerobics
classes a day, and wear corsets, bustiers, and fishnet stockings, and
still be a feminist.

Feminist theorists are hardly the first, of course, to denounce beauty in the name of a higher good. The Puritans believed that ornament and sensuality distracted women (and men) from their spiritual duties. A drab proletarian chic was practically an article of faith among the fellow-traveling set during communism's heyday and was picked up again, with variations, by privileged revolutionary students of the sixties.

Not only is damning beauty unnecessary to a feminist revolution then. It is also counterproductive. Much of what is touted as promoting beauty today—exercising vigorously, eating nutritionally, ingesting or applying various herbs and vitamins—is also good for one's health: the ironic truth is that many women don't focus as much as they should on their bodies. Blame and self-pity may feel comforting, but many of the problems our bodies encounter are our own fault. And it's not a coincidence that women who feel good about themselves physically tend to feel good about themselves emotionally. It's also not a coincidence that when women treat themselves well, they are not apt to allow others to treat them poorly.

There's also much women can do themselves to change their relationship with beauty. The fact that beauty is a reality makes it no less of a tyranny. Indeed, it makes it more so: some things will never change, no matter how much women achieve. Yet women can, for one, toughen themselves emotionally, so that they can withstand potentially hurtful remarks or societal messages. Hyper-analyzing fashion, advertisements, and sexual imagery, on the other hand, really doesn't help women very much on a daily basis. It also encourages a society-is-destiny view: women's lives won't change until society does.

Perhaps the ultimate feminist goal is to move beyond the injustice of beauty, to be able to appreciate its magnificence while ignoring its perversions, to be able to look at a beautiful woman with awe and only a tinge of resentment. That's hard work. Indeed, allowing beautiful women their beauty may turn out to be one of the more difficult aspects of personal liberation.

11

Scientists have always known that attractiveness matters. What they have been less certain of is precisely what constitutes attractiveness and why. Recently, with the help of digital technology, researchers have begun to quantify our beauty standards with astonishing detail. What we find *attractive* is the "average" female face, a face with perfectly symmetrical features (the left and right sides match). Researchers discovered this by superimposing photographs of women on a computer screen; the more photographs used, the more symmetrical the composite face; and the more symmetrical the face, the more attractive it was found to be. What we find *beautiful*, however, is this average face with certain features exaggerated: a higher forehead, fuller lips, shorter jaw, and smaller chin and nose. Clear eyes, clear skin, and a healthy head of hair have also been found attractive across cultures. Moreover, infants as young as three months gaze significantly longer at female faces considered attractive by adults than at those considered unattractive.[8]

These findings have no doubt annoyed many theorists, feminist and otherwise, who believe that all notions of beauty vary according to era and culture. But they don't surprise evolutionary psychologists. According to Darwinian theory, what men want most in women is fertility. The reason is simple: from an evolutionary standpoint, a man's main interest is in passing along his genes; an infertile woman is not a good match. Since a woman's fertility potential is not obvious (even to her), prehistoric man needed to develop indirect ways of evaluating it. Signs of general health were certainly important, but, since a woman's reproductive capacity begins to decline after age twenty-five, so were signs of youth: clear eyes, clear skin, lustrous hair, full lips, and so on.[9]

Evolutionary psychologists believe that symmetry is associated in our brains with health because, as Judith Langlois of the

University of Texas puts it, "individuals with average population characteristics should be less likely to carry harmful genetic mutations." A recent study at the University of Michigan would seem to substantiate this: the least symmetrical participants had the most physical complaints, from insomnia to nasal congestion. Less obvious, though, is why men go for tiny jaws and smaller chins. Neo-Darwinians speculate that since these and other features diverge in males and females during puberty, when our bodies are flooded with sex hormones, a tiny jaw may advertise a substantial supply of estrogen—that is, fertility. (By contrast, a man with a prominent, square jaw would advertise a healthy dose of androgens, indicating strength).[10]

At least this much seems clear: Hollywood and Madison Avenue did not arbitrarily create an obsession with female youth and beauty. Both have merely exploited male desires and, perhaps more important, women's competitive drive to satisfy male desires. And they've done a good job. According to a cross-cultural, cross-generational study of human mating behavior by evolutionary psychologist David Buss and a team of researchers, the importance men attach to women's beauty has risen in the past fifty years, as television and advertising (and, thus, beautiful models and actresses) have become increasingly prevalent.[11]

The study also shows that the emphasis men have placed on the youth and attractiveness of a potential mate has always been far greater than the emphasis given by women. Across cultures, men prefer mates who are at least two years younger, and the older men get, the younger they want their women to be. As far as attractiveness is concerned, men see it as important in a mate; women see it as desirable but not important. American college women in the fifties, for instance, rarely even listed physical attractiveness as necessary in a future husband, while men listed it as primary. David Buss explains that women have typically been far more concerned with the resources and commitment of a man than with his age or physical appearance: a man doesn't have to be beautiful or even symmetrical to make a good living and be a good husband and father. In fact, evolutionary theory suggests, women tend to find men *more* attractive as they get older because age typically corresponds with stability and responsibility.[12]

Men desire beautiful women not just for their presumed reproductive potential, however. Beauty is also a valuable social asset. Since a beautiful woman is in the best position to get a man with the most resources, a beautiful woman on a man's arm is believed to be an essential advertisement of those resources. And studies show that men in high-powered jobs tend to marry women who are considerably more attractive than the wives of men lower on the occupational totem pole. According to a 1993 study by the National Bureau of Economic Research (NBER), while a "plain" woman was just as likely to get married as an average or good-looking one, the mate of the plain woman tended to have less education and earnings. Moreover, the more men's income goes up, the more they seek younger and more attractive partners.[13]

This is not a pretty picture, but that doesn't make it any less real. At the same time, feminism has begun to change some of the details. For many men, beauty is still a priority in selecting a mate, but it's no longer the sole priority. According to surveys, men increasingly consider the future earning potential of women, as well as their intelligence and talents. Such calculations are part of what is called "assortative mating," and its effects are quite apparent in newspaper wedding announcements (especially those in the *New York Times*). Male doctors, for instance, increasingly marry female doctors, not female nurses. Even the high-profile "trophy" wives have undergone a transformation: although they are still young and beautiful, now they also have careers.[14]

Not coincidentally, this change wrought by feminism makes sense from an evolutionary standpoint as well. If one of men's key interests is status, then a successful—as well as beautiful—woman would add to the status of a successful man. (Of course, this assumes that successful men are strong enough not to be threatened by successful women, an assumption that is not always supported by reality.)

Feminism, in other words, is forcing beautiful women to get a life. It's becoming less acceptable for a woman to simply look pretty. There's no longer just a beauty hierarchy among women; there's also a personality hierarchy, a talent hierarchy, an intelligence hierarchy, and a savvyness hierarchy. This change is important not just for a woman's marriage and career prospects but for her emotional health. The flip side of the beauty reality is that beauty is ephemeral and that beautiful women are often unhappy. They worry about losing their looks, about not being fully appreciated, about drawing people for the wrong reasons. A striking woman who conducts symphonies may also have to pay this price for her beauty. But at least her self-esteem doesn't have to be based entirely on her aesthetic appeal.

Feminism has also enabled women, now more financially independent, to increase the importance they give to male appearance. It's not that women were ever uninterested in handsome men. It's that in the past a man's financial situation and prospects, along with his vigor and virility, added much to his attractiveness. Now that women are more financially independent, they may be less willing to settle in the appearance category. In the most exaggerated cases, we have uber-successful women like Elizabeth Taylor, Barbra Streisand, Cher, and Madonna choosing men who are terrifically handsome, younger, and (best of all) have served them in some capacity.

Feminism, in other words, is forcing men to notice their baldness, bulges, and bad breath. As a result, men are now spending $9.5 billion a year on face lifts, hair pieces, and liposuctions. They also now have to put up with increasingly "objectifying" ads glorifying the male anatomy.[15]

Nevertheless, beauty may always matter more for women than for men. Yes, this is unfair. And the fact that resources may always matter more for men doesn't mitigate the injustice: resources can be more easily acquired than beauty. But that's the situation at the moment; women can choose to ignore it, but they can't make believe it doesn't exist.

What now needs to be wrestled with are the questions that

arise from this truth. [Studies have long shown that beauty opens doors. From nursery school on, teachers, employers, and people in general believe that "beautiful is good"—that beautiful people are more intelligent, moral, competent, and likable. People also want to be around beautiful people because they are, well, beautiful. Beautiful women admit that opportunities often seem to just fall into their laps.]

What happens after beautiful women walk through the doors, however, may have already been changed by feminism.

[In *The Beauty Myth*, Naomi Wolf argues that the corporate world subjects women to a "professional beauty qualification" (PBQ), both to "checkmate power at every level in individual women's lives" and to "save magazines and advertisers from the economic fallout of the women's revolution." The PBQ keeps women focused on their appearance rather than on climbing the corporate ladder. It also prevents them from climbing that ladder: corporations use wages and promotions to applaud or punish women for their appearance.[16]]

Following Wolf's logic, women near the top not only would be the most beautiful, but also would spend the most time on their appearance to please their bosses. The National Bureau of Economic Research study adds some ammunition to Wolf's argument. "Plain" people do earn less—5 to 10 percent—than people of "average" looks, who earn less—3 to 5 percent—than those who are "good-looking."[17]

But the study also completely undermines Wolf's thesis. The economic advantages of beauty are larger for men (9 percent less for plain versus average) than for women (5 percent). Moreover, beauty enhances men's likelihood of being chosen for both clerical and professional jobs, while it helps women only for clerical positions.

In fact, beauty can be a great *disadvantage* for women in managerial positions. According to research done by New York University psychologist Madeline Heilman, while an attractive man is seen as more competent, tough, and decisive than an unattractive man, an attractive woman is seen as gentle, soft, and indecisive.

Again, women considered "attractive" or "sexy" advance quickly only in nonmanagement jobs.[18]

But you don't need to do a study to refute Wolf. Just ask a beautiful woman. Beautiful women say that their male colleagues often assume that they're not smart or that they constantly feel the need to prove otherwise. In many offices, especially in conservative cities like Washington, D.C., even wearing too much makeup and an overly glamorous suit will raise doubts about a woman's serious-ness. A quick look at women at the highest levels of power, from congresswomen to CEOs, also undermines Wolf's argument: while they certainly look more than presentable, these women hardly appear to spend an inordinate amount of time in salons.

This is not to say that beauty isn't an invaluable professional asset. Even more than money, beauty smooths over rough en-counters; beauty finesses. At the very least, people will pause to listen to a beautiful woman, even if she has nothing to say. But except in certain fields (such as modeling), it takes a lot more than beauty to hold down a job. Perhaps when male employers didn't think women were capable of anything more complicated than pouring coffee and taking dictation, they were satisfied with beauty. But it hardly makes good business sense for an employer to overlook competence today (especially when he or she can hire both beauty and competence). Looks may be a necessary condition for certain employers, but (as with certain husbands), they are no longer sufficient.

The NBER researchers attribute at least some of the pay dis-crepancy among the three categories to the fact that employers often hire better-looking people for high-visibility jobs, such as receptionists and salespeople. Is this such a bad thing? Modeling agencies are allowed to hire only beautiful women because that is considered an essential qualification for the job. But what about for, say, selling makeup?

During the seventies, feminists largely succeeded in relaxing the weight requirements for airline flight attendants. Since then, they have been fighting a losing battle to prevent television stations from considering a female news anchor's appearance a job qualification. But I wonder whether this sort of pseudo-paternalism is actually counterproductive. After all, we allow employers to discriminate on the basis of intelligence, talent, even charm. Why should beauty be put in a separate category?

[One thing is certain: beauty discrimination will continue no matter what the law says and no matter how much society changes. And that's because beauty sells.] Naomi Wolf knows this well. She allowed her own beautiful face (and well-coifed hair) to appear on the front cover of the British edition of *The Beauty Myth;* on the back cover of the U.S. paperback edition; on the back of her second book, *Fire with Fire;* and on the front of its paperback edition. Her books have sold well, and she is a frequent guest on talk shows and college campuses. If, as Wolf argues, the use of beauty imagery is really just a plot by the patriarchy's "clever economists" to get women to buy products and prohibit their progress, has she herself been a deluded pawn/victim—or just a savvy businesswoman capitalizing on one of her natural assets?

Yes, it's unfair that beautiful women have advantages in the public sphere. It's also unfair that some women are very intelligent, possess a rare talent, or have rich, well-connected families. Feminism can't do anything about this type of injustice: it can equalize only rights and opportunities, not individual endowments. What feminism can do is allow us to see that not only is beauty just one asset among many, but that women have the right and ability to develop their other assets. And perhaps by both valuing beauty and putting it in its place we can begin to do that.

I I I

Like wealth and connections, beauty is not a static quality: a woman can become more (or less) beautiful. And if she wants to, there's no reason she shouldn't try.

In *The Beauty Myth,* Wolf writes that one of the media's most damaging lies is that " 'beauty' can be earned by any woman through hard work and enterprise." Of course, the hyperbole of such a claim makes it untrue. But Wolf ignores the most important point: there's no reason women shouldn't believe that through *some* enterprise, they can make themselves more attractive. As Janet Radcliffe Richards points out in *The Sceptical Feminist*, "What is the great advantage in remaining as you are? . . . In education, manners, and morals people are all in favor of improvement. For some reason, however, there seems to be an idea that there is something very different about *natural beauty*."[19]

There's no reason women should feel guilty about wanting to look attractive, about spending time and money on their appearance—especially if looking attractive does serve some evolutionary role. Curiously, I rarely hear women complain about the time and even the money they spend on pampering themselves. In fact, quite the opposite seems to be the case: women eagerly await their visits to the hairdresser, the manicurist, the salon, the spa. It is their escape, their chance to focus exclusively on themselves—even better, to allow someone else to focus exclusively on them. Again, if a woman chooses to ignore beauty, that's her business. But doing so makes her no more a feminist than a woman who doesn't.[20]

Of course, not every woman can afford to pamper herself: the pursuit of high-tech beauty is not democratic. And even women who do have the money often can't fit a trip to the salon into their already overloaded schedules. Some see it as more of a "third shift" than a luxury.

Unfortunately, feminism can't do much about either of these situations. What it can deal with, though, is motivation. Even women who view pampering as an escape are often caught in an obsessive pursuit, not so much for beauty as for self-esteem. Of course, given the importance of beauty in both our social and work lives, it's unrealistic to expect it not to be part of women's sense of self. But women have control over how large that part is, and over whether they're trying to look "perfect" or merely as good as they can. By definition, seeking perfection is self-destructive, setting women up for frustration, resentment, and defeat: most of us will never look as good as we would like. Rationality begins at home. If we want society to stop equating our worth with our beauty, we need to make sure that we stop it ourselves.]

It is equally unfeminist to blindly follow the latest fad, diet, lotion, or potion, or to engage in certain beauty procedures solely to please a man. Some theorists argue that, given the constant touting of beauty products and services, this is inevitable. But it's not inevitable, even if women are endowed with a need to look attractive. According to a 1992 *Glamour* survey, 78 percent of the respondents said that the pressure to look good comes from within themselves; 89 percent said that they feel best about themselves when *they* feel they look great, as opposed to when a man (or another woman) tells them so. After all, we don't say it's inevitable that, given the media equation of high-powered engines with manliness, men will spend their annual salaries on the latest Porsche. Men are presumed to have the ability and the responsibility to make their own choices. Women are no different. And when they don't, there's only one person who can be blamed.[21]

The situation is more complicated, of course, when it comes to potentially risky products or procedures. Women often don't discover that a product is dangerous until after they've applied it, ingested it, or inserted it. In five years, will we find out that alphahydroxy acids, the latest miracle ingredient now found in nearly every lotion or cosmetic, causes skin cancer? Probably not. But that is one of the risks of living in the real world, and it's not at all useful to blame medical foul-ups on "misogynistic" scientists, as some feminist activists do. Government testing has to be as tough as possible, and activists should fight to see that it is. But after that, it's up to consumers to find out as much as possible about a product's risks and side effects, and women are just as capable as men of being rational consumers.

Beyond the issues of motivation and danger, though, can any more lines be drawn? Is there no difference between, say, coloring one's face and redesigning it?

Interestingly, many young women (and men) today are growing up in an environment where this question is really moot. To
women who engage in eyebrow-piercing and face-tattooing,
changing one's body, I would imagine, is not a moral issue (nor,
one could argue, an aesthetic one). As for the rest of us, yes, it's sad
that we think that a dramatic change in our bodies could make us
happy, and we can write lengthy, sentimental books about how sad
it is (as many have). But there's nothing inherently evil about nose
jobs or face lifts or tummy tucks. As Hillary Rodham Clinton, who
has gone through a number of minor makeovers herself, told *Elle*
magazine, "Cosmetic surgery may be just as important for someone's state of mind and well-being as any other kind of surgery."[22]

Actually, it can sometimes be more important. In the feminist
journal *Hypatia*, women's studies professor Kathy Davis reported
that women who undergo cosmetic surgery often refer to it as the
first time they are able to "do" something about their lives: "Cosmetic surgery may be, first and foremost, about being ordinary,
taking one's life into one's own hands, and determining how much
suffering is fair. . . . Should some women have to endure so much
more pain than other women because of their appearance?" It's
certainly true that a woman may have an inaccurate perception of
what her body "really" looks like. But the fact that others may find
her perfectly fine doesn't lessen her suffering.[23]

Still. What about the woman who has resculpted several parts
of her face, liposuctioned her body twice, and now has annual face
lifts? It is her body, of course, and she can do what she wants with
it. And perhaps after all of this home improvement she is finally
happy: no one should begrudge her that. Yet if she is going through
these procedures in an obsessive search for self-esteem, then she's
not using them to take control of her life; they in fact have taken
control of her.

What, though, about breast augmentation? Well before the
breast implant imbroglio, feminists had reserved special censure for
breast enlargement, arguing that breasts don't define womanhood
any more than motherhood does. This was, and is, a major point: a

woman without large breasts is still a woman. Even a woman without breasts is still a woman. Moreover, while it's probably fair to say that, in general, men like breasts (they apparently signal mothering potential), surveys do show that not all men like big breasts. Indeed, men like breasts considerably smaller than women imagine they do. But even if they did like large breasts, there's, again, a difference between wanting to look attractive in general and mutilating one's body specifically to satisfy one man's desires.[24]

Unfortunately, as the continued popularity of implants, Wonderbras, and other assorted breast enhancers clearly shows, this argument—along with the one about health risks—has not made much of a dent in women's breast consciousness. "Are my breasts too small for you?" the Bridget Fonda character asks the Matt Dillon character in the movie *Singles*. "Sometimes," he replies. So off she goes to a cosmetic surgeon and opts for breasts the size of cantaloupes. This being a movie, the surgeon eventually talks her out of surgery and into wanting a boyfriend who better appreciates her. [In the real world, far too many women stay with far too many men who seem to get off on making women feel inadequate.]

What's more sad than ironic is that, at the same time that so many women obsess about the size and shape of their breasts, they pay very little attention to their health. Less than 40 percent of women say they treat themselves to monthly breast self-examinations and less than a third of women over forty have mammograms as recommended—despite the fact that the cure rate for women with localized breast cancer is nearly 100 percent.[25]

According to the American Cancer Society, many women avoid monthly breast exams because of a fear of what they might find. Another reason is laziness, the same reason many women—women with fine health insurance policies—fail to get yearly Pap smears. These women know they're supposed to; there's plenty of information out there on the subject. And the 25 percent of women who smoke—not to mention the 20 percent of pregnant women who smoke—would certainly seem to know by now that lung cancer kills more than 64,000 women a year and that smoking while

pregnant can cause infant mortality, brain defects, and low birth
weight. Even tanning has received its share of negative publicity—
skin cancer is now more common than all other cancers combined.
Yet many women still feel they need to fry their skin to look
good.[26]

Women, it seems, can be quite self-destructive independent of
health-related messages—just as they can be quite rational amid
such presumably "negative" imagery as advertisements for mascara.
Meanwhile, *real* negative messages continue to do a great deal of
harm. According to the American Medical Association, for example, the tobacco industry's intensive efforts to promote smoking
among women is the primary factor influencing women to smoke.
Feminist efforts would be much better served in trying to counter
real harmful messages and promote healthful ones than in trying to
stop women from wanting to be beautiful. The problem, again, is
not a pursuit of beauty, but a mindless, self-destructive pursuit of
beauty. Sun exposure, after all, is quite "natural," but it can also be
quite deadly.[27]

I V

The fact that women can do themselves a great deal of harm by not
focusing on what they have control over brings us to the aspect of
the beauty ideal that has received the most attention in the past
couple of decades: svelteness. Fat was a prime topic of discussion
for women in the early years of the consciousness-raising movement, but it didn't officially become a "feminist issue" until 1978,
when psychologist Susie Orbach efficiently named her best-selling
book *Fat Is a Feminist Issue.* Orbach argues that women overeat or
undereat as a way to cope with society's sexist pressures; what
women need to do is understand the injustice of these pressures and
learn to accept their bodies as they are.

Today, many feminists have taken Orbach's analysis about five
steps further, arguing that the term "overweight" is meaningless,

that weight charts are concocted to adjust to the reigning beauty ideal and have little relation to health, and that the current cultural fixation on thinness stems from a desire to keep women weak, passive, and permanently enslaved to men. "A cultural fixation on female thinness," Wolf writes in *The Beauty Myth*, "is not an obsession about female beauty but an obsession about female obedience."[28]

Some writers argue that since fat was not only accepted but celebrated in earlier centuries, there's no reason it shouldn't be celebrated again, and they explicitly or implicitly encourage women not to care about their weight, not to restrict their intake of certain foods, not to worry about exercise. A sign in a woman-run restaurant in New Haven, Connecticut, reads, "Because all women are victims of fat oppression and out of respect for women of size, we would appreciate your refraining from agonizing aloud over the calorie count in our food."[29]

Well, it's certainly true that women have not done very well on the issue of body image. Women complain about their bodies constantly; anxiety over fat is no doubt a primary emotional preoccupation of most women. Eighty percent of women diet; 80 percent of participants in weight-loss programs are women. Girls are dieting at a younger and younger age; according to one survey, 50 percent of nine-year-old girls have already been on a diet. And women of all ages are more than willing to do whatever it takes to be thin, from starving themselves to using laxatives to vomiting.[30]

Nevertheless, the prevailing feminist argument concerning fat is not especially useful for women. First of all, it's wrong. The problem for the vast majority of American women is not that our thinness culture is too powerful; it's that it isn't powerful enough. Despite supposedly oppressive messages about slimming down, women, on average, *gained* nearly eight pounds during the eighties, placing more than a third of them in the category called "obese." (Men too gained weight during the eighties; slightly less than a third are now considered obese.) And this increase is not simply the result of the aging baby boom. While American consumption of fat has decreased over the past two decades, our consumption of sugars and carbohydrates has increased: our average daily intake went up about 300 calories.[31]

Women who are obese are four times as likely to die of heart disease and twice as likely to die of cancer as are women whose weight is below average for their age. Being even moderately overweight is associated with a substantial risk of premature death and has been linked to an increased risk of high blood pressure, diabetes, heart disease, and stroke, and to cancers of the colon, breast, and endometrium. One-third of cancer deaths and one-half of cardiovascular deaths are the result of too much fat. Obese women are at least twice as likely as thinner women to have babies with debilitating birth defects.[32]

As for the weight charts, those tabulated in 1990 are now considered too high, not too low, because they allow for a thirty-pound gain in midlife. The new 1995 charts reflect the belief that even a moderate weight gain after high school can be unhealthy.[33]

[Moreover, while one-third of a person's excess weight is considered to have a genetic basis, two-thirds is behavioral—bad eating and exercise habits that can be changed.] A woman may very well overeat because of sexism or abuse. But according to studies, she is far more likely to overeat because she's lonely, depressed, or anxious. Why women are more apt to try to substitute food for love and security is a complicated question, but we shouldn't overlook the fact that an underlying cause may be fear of independence, responsibility, and sexuality—in other words, fear of feminism.[34]

So, yes, fat is a feminist issue—but not in the way Orbach, Wolf, and others have argued. Far more important, fat is a health problem, a deadly serious health problem. Equating thinness with oppression is not only absurd, it's dangerous. Women who believe they are personally fighting the patriarchy by becoming overweight are both deluding and hurting themselves.

It's no doubt true that heavier women were better appreciated in other eras. Kate Moss would never have been asked to sit for Rubens. Indeed, according to evolutionary psychology, the most culturally variable standard of beauty appears to be a preference for slimness or plumpness. [Historically, body build has been linked to social status: in cultures where food is scarce, plumpness signals wealth and health; in cultures where food is abundant, thinness becomes a sign of status.]

But the desire for thinness today (in Western societies at least) goes well beyond social status. We now know how unhealthy fat and a sedentary lifestyle can be. Women's bodies were no more designed to sit and spread for ten to twelve hours a day than were men's bodies: our "gathering" ancestors engaged in daily, strenuous physical activity.

Unfortunately, you won't find much about overeating and underexercising in feminist literature. (There's not one mention of either in all 348 pages of *The Beauty Myth.*) Indeed, the emphasis in much feminist writing is on how ridiculous—and unfeminist—it is to care about fat.

Fortunately, though, in the past decade or so women's magazines (not to mention magazines devoted exclusively to health and fitness) have begun to offer women sage advice on how to treat their bodies. [And in the end, such counsel turns out to be, for most of us, quite simple: eat balanced meals, restrict consumption of high-fat foods, learn to eat only when hungry and stop when full, exercise regularly, etc., etc.] When most people do this, their weight decreases gradually to a healthy state.[35]

The difficult part, of course, is following the advice. It's far easier to go on a crash diet, take a pill, binge and purge, or simply blame the patriarchy than to learn how to eat well. And it seems particularly difficult for Americans to eat well. "We have no culture for eating," writes Aimee Lee Ball in *Harper's Bazaar.* "Our culture is one of excess. . . . We don't serve a few ounces of pasta, lightly sauced, before a nice veal chop. We serve a mountain of pasta, an ocean of sauce, a Brobdingnagian chop, and then we turn to the StairMaster for atonement." Bulimic-like tendencies to gorge and then starve, to obsessively count calories or routinize meals (my daily college diet: one-half plain yogurt for breakfast; eight rice cakes for lunch; one medium-sized bowl of popcorn for dinner) is far less common in France and Italy, where eating is as much an art as cooking.[36]

Not coincidentally, a healthy weight for most women does not make them look like Bridget Fonda. There's a genetic reason for why men have a far easier time losing weight than women (and thus less of a need for Weight Watchers or the latest fad). At puberty, the average young woman adds about thirty-five pounds of reproductive fat to her stomach, hips, and thighs (about 80,000 extra calories) so that she can sustain a pregnancy and then nurse a newborn.

It's also not a coincidence that the curves this extra layer of fat creates are what make the female body beautiful, what has inspired poets and painters throughout the ages to celebrate this beauty, what has historically caused men (and women) to dumbfoundedly stare. In fact, no matter what the reigning cultural ideal regarding plumpness, the hourglass figure—specifically, with a waist 20 to 40 percent smaller than the hips—has been considered by men to be the most attractive.[37]

Why? Most likely, again, the genes. Uncurvaceous women are certainly capable of bearing healthy children. But evolutionary biologists speculate that the hourglass figure was another signal to ancestral men of health and fertility. And it appears to have been a good one. Researchers in the Netherlands recently discovered that even a slight increase in waist size relative to hip size can make it harder for a woman to conceive. From an evolutionary standpoint, though, more important than a woman's curves is a woman's weight: a body fat content only 10 to 15 percent below normal can render a woman infertile.[38]

The fact that men like women slim yet shapely—far more shapely than women themselves desire—is consistently shown in studies. But you only have to look at the models in *Playboy* to see what men like. Even better, ask a man. It's highly unlikely that he'll describe his dream woman as having the slim-hipped, prepubescent male body that most women strive for.[39]

(And why do women strive for a body that would undermine not only normal reproductive health, but also their social lives? Probably because that's the body they find in advertisements and in the fashion magazines. Alongside the articles on healthy eating are photos of models who look distinctly unhealthy. Part of the problem is that many of these models have not yet reached voting age. That may be okay for teen magazines, but it's particularly ridiculous for magazines aimed at women, especially when the focus is on displaying work-oriented clothes. Rather than "conducting" a business meeting, these models often look as though they should be given lollipops and sent out to play.)

Naomi Wolf and other writers have rightly criticized the fact that the weight of models has dropped considerably since the fifties. Unfortunately, many have blamed this on a let's-starve-all-women-to-death conspiracy. (On every level, of course, this is absurd, most especially on the level of observable fact: the editors, fashion editors, and photo editors of women's magazines are nearly all female.[40])

While it's true that the body ideal has become slimmer during precisely the periods when more women are working or going to college—in the twenties and again in the sixties—the connection between feminism and thinness is a little more complicated than the backlash analysis would suggest. It could be argued, for instance, that working women are less bored or lonely. Or that thinness signifies their freedom—freedom to move about quickly in the public sphere. Based on several studies of the subject, Brett Silverstein, an associate professor of psychology at the City College of New York, believes that many women who work outside the home subconsciously adopt a less curvaceous, more masculine look because curvaceous women are considered less competent and intelligent than noncurvaceous women. Silverstein has also found that college women who report that their fathers did not believe them to be very intelligent have a keen desire to be slim.[41]

There would seem to be some truth to this argument as well, although it doesn't fully account for the fact that women went on cottage cheese and celery diets during the forties and fifties, and that women in general have become heavier in the past couple of decades. Whatever the underlying reason, the media, most especially the women's magazines, do have to take much of the blame for primarily showing prepubescent models.

This is not to say that magazines should have to use "real"—that is, overweight—women. What message would that be sending? That there's nothing wrong with being overweight? But there is. Moreover, according to *Glamour* beauty editor Lesley Seymour, focus groups typically reject magazine covers of "real-size" women. This is probably partially because clothes look better on tall, thin women. But I also think it has much to do with the reason women buy fashion magazines: because they present fantasy, because they are a legal, low-cost escape. Not surprisingly, whenever magazines have made a big show of using real women, the real women always turn out to be quite beautiful and shapely.[42]

Models don't have to be role models, but they can be inspirational. Looking healthy and attractive is important, but it would be even better if they looked healthy, attractive, *and* as if they really could be, say, international businesswomen. Women are still so desperately lacking in heroines that even a staged picture can be marginally inspiring. Lisa Fonssagrives, the great supermodel of the thirties, forties, and fifties, was renowned not merely for her extraordinary beauty, but for her serene intelligence, confidence, and sophistication, which the gifted fashion photographers of the time were able to capture. The models of today often seem devoid of not only a personality, but a life.

The fact that most models are so thin no doubt also helps explain why so many women abuse their bodies through food or the lack of it. But, again, it doesn't seem to tell the whole story. Cases of anorexia can be traced back as far as the thirteenth century. Researchers believe that many anorexics may begin to diet out of a desire to look like a model, but what turns dieting into a disease is far more related to underlying psychological problems, a biochemical disturbance in the brain, or most likely both. "The average person will not be induced into anorexia because they see Kate Moss," says Dr. Michael Strober, director of the eating disorders center at UCLA's Neuropsychiatric Institute. Strober has found that mothers and sisters of anorexics are ten times more likely to suffer from the disease than members of the general population.[43]

The typical anorexic is believed to be a perfectionist in her late teens and early twenties who comes from a middle- to upper-middle-class family where there is a heavy emphasis on achievement and physical appearance. Some young women use anorexia as a way to prove their independence from an often overprotective family. Other young women use the disease as a way to avoid responsibility, to ensure that their parents will continue to treat them like young children. Many anorexics also fear or feel uncomfortable with the physical aspects of being a woman: the disease offers a retreat from discovering a sexual identity at a time when women are finally allowed to do so. Indeed, anorexics aren't typically concerned with attracting men. They're focused on ridding their bodies of every ounce of fat; little else matters.[44]

These fears and an ambivalence about achievement may help explain a possible rise in reported cases of anorexia in the past couple of decades, especially among middle- and upper-middle-class women. Again, a connection between eating disorders and feminism may be there—but not in the way many theorists have characterized it.[45]

Perhaps as women become more secure in their equality, as fears of independence and responsibility begin to recede, and (yes) as magazines start showing more models with a little meat on them, the rates of all types of eating disorders will begin to drop. But what also shouldn't be overlooked is that many women may continue to have a greater need for love and security, and if that need isn't satisfied by a steady relationship, they may continue to turn to other, more self-destructive venues and substitutes.

Regardless, what will no doubt help is a continued emphasis on healthy eating and exercise, and the emotional benefits are just as important as the physical ones. Women who are in good physical condition exude a serene confidence, a self-possessed sexuality, that has far less to do with looking like Demi Moore than with feeling strong and in control. It's not just society's image of women that makes many women feel unsexy if they're fifty pounds overweight. It's also the fact that they're fifty pounds overweight. All the "self-acceptance" workshops in the world cannot overcome the connection between physicality and sexuality, between physical and emotional well-being.

It's not a coincidence that gaining control over your body often gives you control, or at least a sense of control, over your life. It's also not a coincidence that women who feel in control of their lives typically take better care of their bodies—and force others to take better care of them as well. Unfortunately, for many women the cycle works the other way: they hate an aspect of themselves, so they get depressed, so they do something worse for themselves (such as eat a carton of Häagen-Dazs), so then they can hate themselves even more. Many women treat the bodies of their children and husband better than they treat their own.

Actually, one could argue that it is far more of a feminist act to take care of your health than to, say, go to a political rally. "Yes, we need progress everywhere," Gloria Steinem writes in *Moving Beyond Words*, "but an increase in our physical strength could have more impact on the everyday lives of most women than the occasional role model in the boardroom or in the White House."[46]

V

If women haven't yet completely taken control of their bodies, they have begun to master their wardrobes. Thanks to feminist consciousness raising as well as the more general aesthetic rebellion of the sixties, women no longer assiduously "follow" fashion. While women may look to see what's "in," it appears that they no longer feel obliged to change their entire wardrobes to accommodate the whims of what "they" are wearing. And, not coincidentally, "they" no longer wear one set style per season. Even the once almighty hemline has been stripped of its power.

Of course, fashion magazines still make a big show of new trends, and many women still succumb to them like sheep—whether or not these trends make them look silly (baby doll dresses), dirty (grunge), or ugly (Prada's seventies line). Yet the streets are now filled with fashion anarchists: women don't wear the same styles en masse. Just as important, many women no longer appear to believe they have to mask their female bodies in order to be equal.

During the seventies, when sartorial taboos still needed to be broken (until 1975 women were required to wear dresses in many formal restaurants) and when women were still not being taken seriously, clothes became feminist statements. It was important in some circles to be able to say "I don't own a skirt." Overalls and baggy jeans hid the body well; makeup and jewelry were often shunned. And when women began to infiltrate the corporate world, they were wearing the very unfeminine, no-nonsense gray flannel suits.

Sometime during the eighties, though, many women seem to have grown sick of forced androgyny. They began to wear fitted suits with feminine blouses, slinky cocktail dresses, luxurious lingerie.

Feminist fashion critics like Susan Faludi argue that women began to wear these clothes as protective covering: women internalized a backlash against feminism and wanted to look less threatening. Faludi and others also argue that fashion designers are designing these clothes with the specific intent of impeding women's progress and stunting their sexual development. "Late-'80s lingerie celebrated the repression, not the flowering, of female sexuality," Faludi writes in *Backlash*. "The ideal Victorian lady it had originally been designed for, after all, wasn't supposed to have any libido."[47]

Well, it's no doubt true that, to some degree, women began wearing more feminine clothes because fashion designers and fashion editors decided it was time that they should: every fashion magazine nicely trumpeted the New Femininity. The idea that they did this to impede women's progress is a little hard to accept. Again, nearly every fashion editor is, after all, female, and there are increasing numbers of female designers. Moreover, unliberated women tend not to have their own money, and the fashion industry likes, more than anything, to sell clothes.

Throughout the next decade, the New Femininity was replaced by the grunge/gamine look, which was again replaced by the New Glamour (not too dissimilar from the New Femininity), which was then replaced by the seventies-redux look (the New Androgyny), which was replaced by the New Elegance (quite the same actually as the New Glamour). Yet, all the while, women continued to wear more feminine, sexy clothing.

Perhaps women are wearing more body-enhancing clothes because they no longer feel they have to hide their femaleness in order to be taken seriously. Rather than a renunciation of feminism, women's defiance of both "feminist"-inspired androgyny and whatever the fashion world is dishing up could be seen as a celebration of it, of women's desire to be both women and unique. (Not surprisingly, the fashion magazines were way ahead of everyone on this, touting the New Individuality for a time.)

This confidence, of course, is far from pervasive, as the frumpy attire women in Washington and other conservative cities feel obliged to wear demonstrates. But if the backlash analysis were accurate, women in these cities would be wearing to work the most frilly, revealing clothes.

Faludi writes that instead of lingerie, she prefers Jockeys for Her. Well, that's nice to know, but the fact is that women are no longer "Victorian ladies," and they are now *choosing* to wear lingerie from a wide range of options. If Faludi believes Jockeys are sexier than silk panties, that's her business. But women who disagree are not deluded victims, as she implies. (By the way, according to art and fashion historian Anne Hollander, sexy lingerie didn't make an appearance until the early twentieth century, just before the First World War; Victorian lingerie was "very, very plain.")[48]

Many theorists also argue that the only reason society considers things like high heels and corsets and miniskirts sexy is that they hobble women. No doubt for some men—the type who go for helpless women—this is the case. Moreover, there's probably some truth to the theory, as Hollander puts it, that "the look of pain and danger to the wearer is always an additional sexual fillip to any costume." But this is not (necessarily) misogyny. Hollander notes that high heels were worn by both sexes during the seventeenth and eighteenth centuries, the first two centuries of their use.[49]

I would imagine that most people—men and women—find these items sexy primarily because they either enhance or subtly reveal the beauty of the female anatomy. High heels, for instance, show off a woman's ankles, give her legs a longer line, and tilt her bust slightly forward. And there's nothing constricting or hobbling about silk nightgowns, seamed stockings, or angora sweaters, all of which are considered quite sexy.

Nevertheless, the fact that there *is* something constricting about (old-fashioned) corsets and something hobbling about stiletto heels can't be overlooked. Indeed, heels higher than an inch and a half can cause tendonitis, bursitis, inflammation, stress fractures, and arch strain. Women have more problems with their feet than men do. This is where the feminist line should be drawn—at actual physical harm.

Another prominent feminist theory suggests that overtly sexy or feminine clothes are inherently exploitative because they draw attention to women's sexuality. Well, when their sexuality was all women had to offer the world, these clothes were surely problematic. But that's no longer the case. Again, women today who choose to wear sexy clothing may be showing a healthy degree of control over their sexuality. Why many feminists would prefer to see women wearing shapeless androgynous clothing—or equally desexualized earth mother attire—is not clear. By definition, asexual clothing exempts women from even having a sexuality.

Equating sexy clothing with the patriarchy leaves women with no choice but to cover up their bodies. In fact, following this logic, the sexier the female body, the more it should be covered up.

This type of feminist thinking would fit in well, of course, in many Middle Eastern countries, where exposure of the female body is considered shameful and where women choose their clothing according to male dictates.

What this analysis completely misses (or, more disconcerting, gets) is the sense of power women derive from wearing sexual clothing. They strut when they put on clingy dresses, sheer black stockings, and (unfortunately) heels. And they strut not just because they're fulfilling stereotypes. They strut because sexuality is a form of power, a strength, an asset, which some men have always exploited just as much as women and which is nothing to be ashamed of. The difference now is that it's not women's only power.

Actually, what we should be doing is celebrating the fact that women, unlike men, probably won't have to give up their sexuality or their sumptuous clothes in order to have economic and political power. Back in the fifteenth century, men's clothes were even more splendid than women's. But throughout the centuries, men increasingly restricted their clothing choices until they were left with one outfit: the dark suit. No doubt there will always be sartorial lines that professional women can't cross—as well there should be. But women's ability to choose from a variety of styles, fabrics, and colors is surely one of the great benefits of the manufactured side of femininity.

Moreover, unlike facial features, style can be democratic (just look at the hideous taste of so many rich women). Not only is fashion not a "patriarchal tool" used to control women, but it can now really be a form of self-expression, of pleasure, of beauty in which all women can engage. And if women are in fact returning, as seemingly every month's fashion magazines suggest, to a time when women paid more attention to the details of their wardrobes, when they "dressed" for lunch and wished to look well groomed and glamorous, this wouldn't undermine feminism in the least. No one said equality had to be boring.

VI

What, though, if a woman pays attention to her clothes, her body, her skin and hair and makeup—and actually *likes* the effect? What if she believes she looks beautiful and loves herself because of that? In the past this was called vanity and thought to be a sin. Today it's considered rude and thought to be unsisterly. Women are encouraged to be proud of their professional success, their children, their charitable work. But God help the woman who stands before a mirror and says to her friends, "I look pretty good today, don't you think?"

Movie stars now topple over one another to be photographed without makeup, and top grossing models happily confide that they never thought of themselves as attractive. Much of this is no doubt progress. Even models no longer want to be thought of as just a pretty face. Yet something has been lost in the transition. In our desire to fully value women, we've managed to devalue not only beauty, but pride in one's appearance. Just as girls pick up cues that beauty is the most important thing, they also notice that they're not supposed to think so.

I'm hardly advocating mindless self-promotion. But our bodies comprise a rather large part of who we are. It would seem that there has to be some sort of middle ground between the narcissism of Wollstonecraft's era ("Taught from their infancy that beauty is woman's scepter, the mind shapes itself to the body, and, roaming round its gilt cage, only seeks to adorn its prison") and the self-abnegation of today.[50]

Allowing women to openly appreciate their beauty won't undermine one of the greatest triumphs of feminism: increasing the value of imagination, intellect, and personality so that a woman can be admired solely for her dignity and character. Beauty isn't always sexy these days, especially when it's lacking in confidence and intelligence. Indeed, it is often remarked that, in contrast to Americans, European women are "naturally" elegant and glamorous. One reason could be that, regardless of their facial geometry, many European women radiate a certain toughness, independence, and savvy; they emit what used to be called a "sense of themselves."

Appreciation of beauty also won't undermine a woman's ability to boost her self-esteem through her imagination, intellect, and personality. But self-esteem can also come from without and work its way in—and there's nothing wrong with that. European women often appear more elegantly turned out because they also have a better appreciation of aesthetics and sensuality, an appreciation that is deeply embedded in European culture: what applies to art and food also applies to personal style.

In the United States, unfortunately, an underlying hostility to aesthetic standards—given further credence by ideological feminism—doesn't really allow a woman to derive much satisfaction from her appearance. Her beauty may get her business contacts and rich boyfriends and give her a topnotch place in the beauty hierarchy, but—unearned and potentially destructive to others—it's not supposed to be a source of pride, let alone power.

In the past, it was typically believed that a woman couldn't be both smart and beautiful: a beautiful woman was thought to have no brains or no need for brains. The current thinking inadvertently perpetuates this: a brainy woman should have no need for beauty. But a liberated woman has to be able to love her body as well as her mind, even if her body is beautiful.

Of course, allowing beautiful women their beauty reinforces not only the reality of beauty but the unfairness of the beauty hierarchy. But the alternative hardly seems worthy of a mature, confident feminism. Moreover, as the other hierarchies grow in relevance and as women grow in emotional strength, they will probably learn to confront the beauty hierarchy on their own terms, weakening its tyranny in the process. As Eleanor Roosevelt put it, "No one can make you feel inferior without your consent."

Four

♦

SEX

I

I DON'T REMEMBER actually learning the rules of romance. They just seem to have appeared one day, sturdy and inflexible, in stark contrast to the emotional flux of my early adolescence. They bristled with gravitas; ignoring them could jeopardize my dating career, which was already bleak enough. A girl didn't call a boy socially, rule number one declared, let alone for a date. If a boy called her, a girl had to wait before calling him back. When he asked her out, she had to say she was busy. Only when he persisted could she accept.

The older I got, the more rules there seemed to be. There was the never-go-to-his-bedroom-alone rule. The never-let-him-touch-your-breasts rule. The never-let-him-touch-you-down-there rule. Finally, as I approached the latter half of high school, the never-go-all-the-way rule asserted itself as the ultimate badge of good-girl-ness, of a girl who wanted to marry and marry well.

By this time, though, it was also the latter half of the seventies, and feminist ideas had finally started to infiltrate my tradition-bound suburban community. Feminism, my friends and I soon realized, did not just mean that we got to have a career; we also got to have sex. And both were to be pursued with the same degree of boldness. We were supposed to call guys, ask them out, and take them to bed, preferably all in the same evening. Virginity was something to get rid of; promiscuity, a matter of principle. The emblem of our potential sexual freedom became Erica Jong's "zipless fuck"—a quick and torrid encounter in which no telephone numbers, not even names, were exchanged. Courtship was dead.

I haven't kept close tabs on all my high school friends, but a lot of women who came of age with feminism have had no trouble discovering their assertive natures at the office. Many women in their twenties and thirties not only live and breathe their work, they've become ball-busting dynamos, ordering their male colleagues around with a Pattonesque assuredness and swagger.

Yet when many of these same women come home, they often quite literally sit by the phone. They may call men socially, but rarely for a date. When a man calls, they typically wait a bit before calling him back. When he asks them out, they may very well say they're busy. Only when he persists do they accept. And this social reserve often carries over to the sexual realm, where women are far more apt to tie sex to strong feelings than to seek out torrid affairs.[1]

What's going on here? Why are women today living an apparent contradiction? Well, many women I've talked to—from power lunchers to full-time moms, from radical leftists to radical conservatives—report that they tried the zipless, antiromance route and found it wanting. These women say they never quite got the hang of asking men out. Unlike giving orders at the office, a more dominant romantic role never felt quite comfortable. And many men seemed even less able to adjust. While most of them were quite flattered to receive a call from a woman, many had this funny little habit of running when pursued.

Women also report that casual sex (not to mention promiscuous casual sex) usually made them feel vulnerable, depressed, degraded—just plain lousy. And while most guys were quite pleased with the sex-is-a-sure-thing aspect of the sexual revolution, many women found that sleeping with a guy on a first or second date was a sure way of not having a relationship. Many guys didn't even seem to like women who were too experienced. While in bed with a friend of mine, a man pouted, "You've obviously done this before." Sex, many women discovered, was not something they could do more of or get better at in order to achieve equality.

Given this state of romantic affairs, it's really not all that surprising that *The Rules* became an instant self-help bestseller. *The Rules*, of course, is simply a bound version of pre-seventies courtship practices. Although the authors go much too far—recommending, for instance, that women never even *return* a man's calls, and that women should essentially be seen and not heard when first dating—the book appears to have provided women with permission to act in a more comfortable manner.

Nevertheless, most women don't seem to be readopting *all* traditional romantic and sexual behaviors. Women born after 1960 typically have their first sexual encounter by age seventeen and have an average of three premarital partners. The prayers of the religious right notwithstanding, chastity has made only a negligible comeback. Many women seek out sex for fun, adventure, or relaxation. They sleep with their friends, with married men, with near-strangers. And increasing numbers of women watch or read pornography and buy an assortment of sex clothes and toys; even male strip joints are developing a following.[2]

Clearly, women like sex. They like sex just as much as men like sex. In fact, they have probably always liked sex just as much as men have. But before the sixties, you might not have known this.

Social controls on women's sexuality were so tight that it was widely believed women had little interest in sexual activities. "The majority of women (happily for them) are not much troubled with sexual feelings of any kind," asserted William Acton, a popular medical authority of the mid-nineteenth century. Remnants of this view survived until the 1950s, and even today certain social conservatives seem to wish it were still the case.[3]

Feminists, meanwhile, have been all over the place on the subject. Some (ironically) have agreed with the conservative view that the act of intercourse is distinctively male: women are far more interested in love and affection. Others, notably Catharine MacKinnon and Andrea Dworkin, have taken this analysis a step further, arguing that intercourse is inherently a violation of a woman's body: under patriarchy, sex and rape are barely distinguishable. Most feminists, however, seem to believe that there is no such thing as male sexuality and female sexuality—women and men have basically the same sexual drives and desires. Such parity isn't obvious only because patriarchal controls continue to obstruct women's real choices.[4]

It's no doubt true that stubborn social attitudes are responsible for some of women's sexual reserve today. Women who call men are still considered desperate; those who sleep around, sluts. "I'm as tough as a man at the office," complains the Demi Moore character in the movie *Disclosure*. "Yet I'm supposed to want to lay back and be fucked at home." And, no doubt, fear of AIDS has played a role in forcing women (and men) to circumscribe their sexual options.

Yet what's becoming increasingly apparent is that the forces of nature, of evolution, can't be ignored in the romantic and sexual realms. Birth control and legal abortion have effectively separated sex from reproduction from a technological standpoint, but the psyche of the average woman doesn't seem to have caught up. The evolutionary need of our female ancestors to entwine sex with love, or at least with commitment, may still be deeply ingrained in many women today. So may be a desire to test a man's ability to provide resources and make that commitment through courtship rituals.

New research by feminist-minded Darwinians has begun to offer us even more clues about what's going on today. Anthropologists and ethologists have found that other female primates possess not only a robust sexuality but an assertive and strategic one as well. At the same time, most primates are hardly promiscuous: they are quite discriminating in their mate choices. Scientists speculate that, before puritanical social controls were introduced, our female ancestors were also sexually desirous, sexually assertive—yet quite choosy.

Now that the social controls have been lifted, women appear to be left with two sets of contradictory behaviors. They are assertive at the office, yet far less so in the romantic realm. And they have strong sexual desires, yet tend to resist fulfilling them if the situation isn't right.

No doubt sexual behaviors—of both men and women—will continue to change. Perhaps women will "evolve" to the point where they think of sex as nothing more profound than a game of tennis. We can only speculate. But what does again seem to be the case is that the closer some behaviors are to reproduction—to the survival of the species—the harder they may be to change. Unlike competitiveness (and like nurturing), women's romantic and sexual behaviors appear to be far more rooted in biology than in culture.

No matter what happens, I would argue that it's actually better for women to continue behaving in their seemingly contradictory ways. Not because being sexually discriminating is more "moral," as religious conservatives maintain. But because it's more rational—it's in women's best interests. It's also more rational, I would argue, for women to engage in some of the rituals of traditional courtship and to demand chivalry of men. Choosiness, courtship, and chivalry may give women different roles in the romantic arena, but, significantly, the same—or greater—degree of "power." Each can happily coexist, in other words, with feminist ideals.

What does undermine feminism is women pursuing self-destructive sexual behaviors, refusing to take responsibility for their sexuality, or failing to match their actions with their beliefs.

Women who have sex because they are too timid to say no, who have sex out of self-loathing or desperation, who use sex to gain self-esteem—these women are hardly "sexually liberated."

Ironically, the most prominent feminist theories regarding date rape would deny women responsibility for their sexuality. The neo-Victorian strain of feminism, based on the theories of MacKinnon and Dworkin, holds that it is acceptable for women to willingly sleep with men one night and then cry date rape the next morning, the next month, or even the next year, and that psychological pressure is just as coercive as physical force.

Worse, the champions of such views have been quite successful in institutionalizing new codes of sexual behavior. Most notorious, of course, is the thirteen-page sexual-consent policy known as the Antioch rules, which require men at the college to obtain verbal permission before touching a woman's hand, breast, whatever. ("If you want to take her blouse off, you have to ask. If you want to touch her breasts, you have to ask.") Aside from being prudish and paternalistic, these mandates are completely unrealistic: they deny the very basic biological underpinnings of sexual behavior.

The broader desire to recodify sexual behavior in some way, however, is not entirely without merit. It stems from the legitimate belief that much of the old set of social controls were oppressive and the perception that, especially in our multicultural society, a new set of standards is needed. While we never want to return to the days when social controls nearly annihilated women's sexuality, society will always set standards, and women now may as well have a part in creating them.

But any new set of standards can emanate only from the choices of individual women (and men), not from any administrative body or institution. Even feminists should not be in the business of dictating a politically correct form of sex. The only thing a liberated woman "should" feel sexually is strong and independent: by definition, a liberated sexuality cannot be imposed externally.

Before the sixties, women had the power to say no, and many women used it quite wisely. After the sixties, women were given the power to say yes, and many women used it quite unwisely. Women should now feel they have the power to say yes or no. But only when women understand—and choose—for themselves when it's best to say which can they truly be called sexually free.

I I

Women and men do different things during sex. They also do different things after sex, especially if sex leads to conception. Throughout their reproductive life spans, women produce a somewhat fixed supply of about four hundred mature ova; men produce billions of sperm, which are replenished at a rate of roughly twelve million per hour. If one of those sperm meets up with one of those eggs, a woman may end up carrying a fetus for nine months, nursing for up to two years, and, more often than not, rearing the child for another fifteen. A man can deposit his sperm and run.[5]

For men, in other words, sex can be a low-cost matter. And having frequent sex makes evolutionary sense for men: the more sex partners, the more chances to pass their genes into the next generation. But for women, a nine-month minimum investment is not only time- and energy-consuming, it also forecloses other potentially better mating opportunities: having frequent sex is an evolutionary waste of time. Moulay Ismail the Bloodthirsty, the seventeenth-century king of Morocco, is believed to have left 888 direct descendants; a wildly successful woman might leave—at the outside—two dozen offspring.[6]

Because each act of conception is critical for women in evolutionary terms, Darwinians believe that our female ancestors were highly selective about their mates. They were (unconsciously) more attracted to males who had not only good genes, but also ample resources and a willingness to commit to a long-term relationship. "Over evolutionary time," writes psychologist David Buss, "those women who expressed these desires experienced greater survival and reproductive success" than those who didn't.[7]

This choosiness on the part of women has traditionally been viewed by Darwinians both as "coyness" and passivity: females patiently waiting for males to approach so they can invite them in or kick them out. It has also been traditionally believed that since frequent sex for women would not result in a large number of conceptions, our female ancestors would have had no reason to have developed a strong sexual drive or to be sexually assertive. Whatever sexual desire and enjoyment women do show is considered merely a by-product of male sexuality, allowing females to put up with sex. In his *Evolution of Human Sexuality*—a bible for many Darwinians—anthropologist Donald Symons calls intercourse a "female service" designed exclusively to satisfy the needs of men.[8]

While neo-Victorians like Andrea Dworkin (and clueless men) might agree, this view of female sexuality didn't sit well with many anthropologists and biologists. After all, women have just as much of an evolutionary need to pass their genes on to the next generation: they should also want to have sex and like it. Moreover, the female service theory doesn't account for the sexual appetite of women, who, unlike other mammals, are capable of having sex on virtually any day of the month at any time of the year. If female sexuality were geared only for conception, anthropologist Sarah Blaffer Hrdy wanted to know, "what is all this nonreproductive sexuality about?"[9]

Hrdy found that, in fact, other female primates—orangutans, chimpanzees, langurs—engage in a great deal of nonreproductive sex as well. Indeed, among many primates, females engage in sexual activity at times when conception is unlikely or with more partners than is necessary for conception. Moreover, in most of the species she studied, the females actively seek out sex.

Hrdy speculates that an assertive female sexuality, combined with a lack of conspicuous ovulation and near-constant receptivity to sex, allows female primates—and allowed prehominid females—to facilitate a specifically female sexual agenda. Our female ancestors probably mated with more than one male at a time so that each male—not knowing if a child were his—would act paternally toward all of the mother's offspring. A female might also use a loyal mate as the caretaker for her kids but then have an affair with a "superior" one for the sole purpose of acquiring his genes.

Hrdy's studies and theories have since been confirmed by other research. Researchers have found, for example, that female savanna baboons form "special friendships" with one or more males other than their primary mates; these friends protect them against harassment and provide them with extra resources.[10]

However, while female primates are not exactly passive and monogamous, they are not indiscriminately promiscuous either. "Prehominid females . . . were possessed of an aggressive readiness to engage in both reproductive and nonreproductive liaisons with multiple, but *selected*, males," writes Hrdy. "What happened next is, and probably will always remain, shrouded in mystery."[11]

Actually, there are clues to the mystery, clues that further bolster Hrdy's arguments. At some point in history, the majority of the world's cultures felt a need to secure strong control—from chastity belts to clitorectomies—on women's sexuality. If women didn't possess strong sexual desires, why would that be necessary? Feminists have typically argued that all sexual controls stem from misogyny. But it's not that simple. If women are indeed sexually assertive—and, just as important, if men can be sexually aggressive—men had legitimate worries of paternity: well before genetic testing, a man had no way of knowing whether a child was his. Sexual controls not only made women more subdued—both sexually and otherwise—but they also gave men the peace of mind that their efforts and risks were for their own offspring.

These theories are still the subject of much controversy, even among Darwinians. But it's been thirty years since the last layer of sexual controls on Western women began to be removed, and they are beginning to show a sexual manner not too dissimilar from the other primates. This does not appear to be a coincidence.

III

If sexual selectiveness is deeply ingrained in the female psyche, so may be a basic pattern of courtship. That would explain why aspects of this pattern—for instance, males wooing females with gifts of food and other delicacies—turn up not only in a wide variety of human cultures, but throughout the animal world as well. The male common tern presents a fish to his lover, the male roadrunner a lizard, the male chimpanzee a morsel of baby gazelle. (The American male human, a Domino's anchovy pizza.)[12]

It would also explain why this pattern continues to thrive in Western societies, even after feminists in the early seventies sentenced it to sexist oblivion and many women themselves tried to dispense with it. Of course, the fact that many women *were able* to dispense with it, even for a short time, shows that culture has had much to do with, at the very least, its preservation. Moreover, many women today continue to buck the traditional romantic rituals—they call men, ask them out, pay for the pizza.[13]

But the degree of discomfort many women say they feel without these rituals, compared again with the ease with which they order men around at the office, would seem to suggest that courtship has a strong biological basis. It also may show that, contrary to feminist analysis, *women*—or, perhaps more likely, their parents— may have had as much to do with perpetuating some of these rituals throughout the ages as men, precisely because it was in their best interests to do so.

Courtship is typically thought of in terms of hunt, pursuit, and capture, a conception that leaves women completely passive and powerless. And on the surface, that certainly appears to be the case: man approaches woman; man starts conversation with woman; man asks for woman's phone number, and so on.

But apparently, that's not exactly how it happens. After eye contact has been made, according to cross-cultural research, it is usually the *woman* who will attempt to initiate an encounter through a well-established sequence of "nonverbal solicitation behaviors": smiling, lifting her eyebrows and gazing with her eyes wide open, then dropping her lids and tilting her head down to one side, then looking away, sometimes covering her face and giggling. In American singles bars, women will initiate encounters by touching a man briefly, asking for help, caressing him, etc.[14]

Now, it would be somewhat of a stretch to call any of these behaviors assertive, and they certainly seem far more suitable to Jane Austen's heroines than to liberated women of the nineties. But what they show is that women do seek men out, though they do it in a less than direct way. As Diane Ackerman puts it in *A Natural History of Love*, "We think of men as the great seducers in mating dramas, but women do much of the choosing." Indeed, it has also been found that a woman is far more inclined to initiate contact and sexual activity with a man during ovulation—in other words, when she is most fertile.[15]

Nevertheless, female initiative during courtship does typically end after those first smiles and eyebrow lifts. At this point, it's typically been up to men to offer women a drink, a dance, a future date.

It is this second stage of courtship that underwent the most reform during the seventies. Women approached men, asked them for their phone numbers, called them up, asked them out. And many women continue to do this, to the delight of both themselves and many men.

But many women were not happy doing this. And they weren't happy not just because many men don't respond well to being pursued. No doubt ordinary fear of rejection plays a role: women say they dread picking up the phone and putting their egos on the line. But why do they seem to dread it so much more than men do? Is it merely a lack of experience or emotional fortitude? Why then have many of these same women taken easily to a more dominant role at work?

Again, courtship rituals may be more ingrained in women, and thus harder to change, because they are closer to the exigencies of reproduction. According to anthropologist Helen Fisher, traditional courtship has historically served as a perseverance test, allowing women to figure out if men are strong, confident, and assertive enough to commit to a long-term relationship, pass on good genes, provide well for future offspring, and ward off predators.[16]

Today, of course, women no longer desperately need men to acquire resources or ward off predators. Moreover, many women at various times in their dating careers are not looking for commitment. Thanks to feminism, women can now pursue different sexual "strategies"—both short term and long term—just as men do. Women who just want to have fun don't have to concern themselves much with a man's long-term potential.

Yet at some point, most women start looking for a husband, and there still seem to be many advantages to using courtship as a test of a man's marriage potential. Not coincidentally, in his cross-cultural studies David Buss has found that, in searching for a mate, women still put the greatest value on qualities that seem to indicate the ability to both commit to a long-term relationship and help provide for a future family—ambition, industriousness, dependability, stability, support, love, and so on. Indeed, women worldwide still value good financial prospects in a potential mate roughly twice as much as men do. And it doesn't seem as though feminism is going to change this: women who are financially successful themselves place an even *greater* value on mates with high social status and earning capacity than women who are less successful.[17]

Courtship, of course, is hardly a surefire test of a man's strength of character, as a history filled with crafty lotharios well shows. Many men have been quite adept at faking their resolve, either to get a woman into bed or to the altar; seduction and deception often go hand in hand. And many women have historically been incapable of seeing through male chicanery. Moreover, an overly rigorous courtship test could fail the shy or more reserved man who has always had trouble in the wooing department but would make a great boyfriend or husband. A lot of successful marriages might never have happened were it not for a woman's romantic assertiveness.

Yet what courtship can often effectively do is winnow out ambivalent men. And for whatever reason—feminism, the sexual revolution, a natural promiscuity, nihilism—there seem to be more men today who in some way dread the prospect of marriage. Ambivalent men tend not to say or do anything that could remotely suggest they were interested in the long haul; slow romantic build-ups bore them. Courtship allows women to focus on themselves while their men learn how to focus on women. Courtship also forces women to keep their feelings in check until the appropriate signals have been sent; excessive neediness spoils the test.

Nevertheless, waiting for a man to make all of the moves can be frustrating and infantilizing, especially for women who are used to asserting and fulfilling their needs in every other area of their lives. But this voluntary restraint has to last only until a "relationship" develops, which (for better or worse) is typically quite soon.

Perhaps it's better to look at courtship as the conscious exercise of female choice. According to Darwinian theory, males have historically competed not only for food and other resources but also to satisfy the mating preferences of females: men may have built the physical foundations of civilization, but it was only because savvy women chose men who were virile and confident enough to do so. Today, women can deliberately choose not only these qualities, but also sensitivity, support, and sweetness.

Yes, in some ways courtship is a game, and we're all supposed to be beyond games. Indeed, it's even more of a game now that we are no longer forced to play it. Yet for women looking for a long-term mate, courtship is far more a matter of self-preservation than a ruse. Men and women are reproductively different and always will be. Failing to understand and respect how those differences appear to have shaped our psyches and thus continue to play a significant role in our social lives can cause a lot of unnecessary hurt and confusion. The presumed benefits hardly seem worth it.

IV

A man's sexual persistence may have been just as important to our female ancestors as his romantic persistence: those who chose sexually persistent males may have done better at genetic proliferation than those who didn't. This would go a long way to explain why, in the vast majority of sexual encounters, it is still the man who leans over and plants the first kiss, attempts the first caress, ventures the first fondle. And if sexual persistence is deeply ingrained in the male psyche, it is probably ingrained in the female one as well, which would explain why many women say they can become aroused only by men who are a little assertive—not aggressive or violent, just assertive—in sexual encounters.

Of course, sexual assertion has been even less of a foolproof test of a man's true character than romantic assertion; slimy men also have an instinctual need to spread their seed. Yet weak, unconfident men typically have trouble making the first sexual moves, and men not interrupted in a relationship typically have trouble delaying gratification. All of which may at least partially explain why women persist in saying—or more likely indicating—no when they really mean "give me a minute," "try tomorrow," or "maybe in a week." Some women have no doubt continued this charade out of concern for their reputations: they don't want to appear too "easy." But many may also use this device to slow down an encounter—to see if a man is confident and committed enough to persevere.

Shouldn't we try to change this? Well, to what end? To prove that women can be just as assertive sexually as men? But we know that they can be. Indeed, many women prefer taking the sexual initiative some or most of the time, especially once they're in a steady relationship. Moreover, a position of sexual reserve is not necessarily lacking in power.

But don't women lose credibility when they say no and then go "further" five minutes later? In the most literal sense, yes. But let's not forget that, throughout history, the vast majority of men have been able to tell the difference between the two types of nos: the one that says "get off of me, you creep" and the one that says "try again later."

Yes, women need to take responsibility for their words as much as for their actions. But pushing a man's hand away without a detailed explanation is not lying. You can't force women to say "I'm not ready at this exact moment for you to put your hand down my pants, but I'm more than ready for you to put your hand up my shirt" any more than you can force men to ask permission to touch, kiss, bite, whatever. Sex is primal, intuitive, anarchic, mysterious, and more than anything, achingly personal. It can't be reduced to political deconstruction—and it doesn't need to be. Moreover, too much talk at an inappropriate time can deaden not only a mood but a relationship.

One of the most worthwhile contributions feminists have made in the past few decades has been trying to convince the public that a woman can be raped by someone she knows. According to anthropologist Peggy Reeves Sanday in *A Woman Scorned: Acquaintance Rape through the Ages,* at least half of reported rapes throughout history have involved people who knew each other. Unfortunately, some juries still refuse to believe that a woman can be raped by a co-worker, boyfriend, or husband, just as some still believe that a woman who wears a miniskirt is asking for it or a woman with a "past" can't be telling the truth. Many district attorneys, particularly in smaller jurisdictions, refuse to even prosecute these cases, believing them unwinnable.[18]

Nevertheless, we are not in the throes of a date rape epidemic. As Kate Fillion reports in *Lip Service: The Truth about Women's Darker Side in Love, Sex, and Friendship,* the surveys used to support a date rape crisis—particularly the survey that gave birth to the now infamous statistic that one in four women has been a date rape victim—have been misinterpreted. Most of the "rapes" have involved unwanted sex, not unavoidable sex. That is, women were verbally pressured or persuaded to have sex, not physically forced into it. Moreover, much of the unwanted sex involved women who were not completely excited about having sex at that particular moment but went along with it to please their long-standing lovers. As Fillion puts it, this is not rape, it's a relationship—and men do it too.[19]

The researchers did find many women who had had unwanted sex on a date. But as Fillion reports, many of these women did not make their lack of interest clear. Not one of the women slapped the man, asked him to leave, or even walked away from him.

The problem, in other words, is not so much women saying no when they would prefer to say yes, but women saying yes when they would really prefer to say no. According to a study by sociologist Susan Sprecher of Illinois State University, more than half of the female college students had said yes to sex even though they didn't want to (equally surprising: 35 percent of the males did this too). Some of this emotional weakness can no doubt be blamed on the fact that we're still in a transitional period. Many women of my generation were taught to be compliant and avoid confrontation in social situations. As a friend describes her college experience: "Sometimes it was easier to fuck than to say no."[20]

And some of the problem can no doubt be blamed on the fact that feminist ideas have still not penetrated many areas of the country. There are women who say yes to sex quite simply because they don't know that they are able to say no.

But, again, explanations are not excuses. Yes, it's certainly true that, as clinical psychologist Mary Koss, who conducted the one-in-four date rape surveys, puts it, "It's the man's penis that is doing the raping, and ultimately he's responsible for where he puts it." But women are hardly free of responsibility. Unfortunately, at the urging of some feminist activists, the law is beginning to treat women as though they are. While it's crucial that women no longer have to "earnestly resist" a rapist as they did before the seventies, some states have nearly eliminated the requirement that a rapist use physical force. Thus, a woman can consent to sex one night and the next morning say she was "psychologically coerced."[21]

Other states now require the accused to prove that the woman explicitly said yes to sex. These changes are creating, according to a Cato Institute analysis, a criminal liability regime in which "all heterosexual sex is like statutory rape unless affirmative, explicit verbal consent given in a clear and sober frame of mind can be demonstrated." As Katie Roiphe puts it in *The Morning After:* "The idea that only an explicit yes means yes proposes that women, like children, have trouble communicating what they want."[22]

Meanwhile, the problem of women saying yes when they mean no may be getting worse. The 1995 Sex in America survey found that more than a third of the younger women said that peer pressure had made them have sex for the first time, compared with only 13 percent of those from previous generations.[23]

Conservatives are certainly right to argue that, prior to the sixties, this type of insecurity would rarely have gotten a woman into a bed she did not want to be in. Curfews, chaperones, and single-sex dorms contributed to an atmosphere in which peer-pressured sex was less likely to happen. Of course, the stakes were also higher. Before the wide availablility of birth control, an hour of sex could mean a lifetime commitment to a child—a powerful check against the libido.

But universities are unlikely to reinstate these particular types of controls—nor should they. Women don't need curfews any more than they need a new set of romantic rules. Real sexual liberation cannot be imposed through administrative mandates, from the right or the left. Moreover, the problem of women having sex when they don't want to is hardly limited to college. What women of all ages and socioeconomic brackets need is to understand more thoroughly their sexual rights and responsibilities.

Instead of vainly trying to reconceptualize courtship, feminist activists could better put their time and energy into, for instance, reinvigorating the traditional consciousness-raising group. Women don't have to use explicit words to communicate their desires, but they do have to make certain that their desires are properly communicated. The first step, of course, is understanding what those desires are—a process of self-awareness that all of the rules, laws, and mandates in the world can't expedite or replace.

V

Just as there are still women who consent to sex under the influence of sexist socialization, there are also those who consent to sex under the influence of what they assume to be feminism. Indeed, many women still don't seem to understand where the sexual revolution ends and feminism begins. Should they have sex merely for the experience? Is a well-rounded sex life crucial for autonomy? Should women engage in S&M, read hard-core porn, cheat on their husbands, pepper their conversations with profanity—all to show that women are sexually equal?

Fortunately for many women, the answer is no. Liberal feminism couldn't care less about what women actually do in bed. All feminism cares about is that they're doing it voluntarily and that they are having a good time while they're doing it. And the reality seems to be that many women have less of a good time when their sexual interactions don't include love, or at least a great deal of affection.

In one of the early segments of *Melrose Place*, the character Alison gets picked up at a bar by a brainless stud. He walks her home and at the door says something like "Aren't you going to invite me in? I can't just walk away from you right now." He kisses her. She giggles. You know what's coming. "Oh, all right," she sighs. "But just for a few minutes."

Suddenly it's the next morning. She wakes up with "love" in her eyes; he's hurriedly dressing. "You were wonderful last night," he oozes, assuring her with big plans for the evening; then, he splits.

Though this scene has been played out a thousand times both on screen and off, it is still brilliantly painful to watch. Not surprisingly, the young stud never shows up at the bar where they're supposed to meet. So Alison shows up at his office the next day. "I thought it would be easier on you this way," he explains. "It was fun, that's all." She throws a vase of water on his head.

Now, the guy appears truly slimy. But it should also be noted that, in this situation, he owed her nothing. He did not force or even pressure her to have sex. It is not his fault that he viewed the evening as a one-night stand and she saw it as the beginning of a relationship.

What's impossible to know is whether Alison really liked the guy or whether, because she had sex with him, she *needed* to like him and, more important, needed him to like her. Anyone with single female friends knows how common this particular need is, how many women long for the emotional aspect of an encounter to immediately catch up with the physical. Sex still makes many women feel quite vulnerable, in need of a great deal of emotional reassurance. No matter how hard they try, many women have trouble treating casual sex casually, viewing it as merely "fun."

In fact, studies still show a huge discrepancy between the way women and men view sex. According to a 1994 survey by David Buss and David Schmitt, men say they would have sex with an attractive woman after knowing her only one week; women say they need to know a man they find attractive for several months. Within the next year, men say they would like six sex partners; women, one. Men's sexual fantasies more often include strangers, multiple partners, or anonymous partners.[24]

The survey did not find, it should be noted, that women have less interest in sex; it found that their interest was tempered by the situation. Another indication of this attitude has been found in women's responses to various types of pornography. Measurements of genital blood flow show that in watching pornography women become as physiologically aroused as men. And, like men, women show no physically discernible sexual arousal to scenes of pure romance. Yet women *rate* the romantic scenes as equal to, or sometimes more arousing than, the sexual ones.[25]

Finally, there's the dramatically different sexual lifestyles of gay men and gay women: gay men tend toward promiscuity, gay women toward monogamy.

Evolutionary theorists aren't surprised by any of this. It was not only important for our female ancestors to pick the best and brightest mates. It was also crucial that they would want to wake up with them the next morning. No doubt culture has reinforced women's need to connect sex and love. But it didn't create it. Most women currently in their twenties did not grow up believing that love is their sole goal in life, and yet it seems that many still find it just as difficult to separate sex from intimacy as their older sisters or even their mothers did. This despite the fact that, for the past twenty years or so, much of culture has been sending precisely the opposite message.

And yet, if we are to accept Hrdy's speculations, the connection of sex and love for our female ancestors was never absolute: they took lovers at times for the purpose of obtaining resources, better genes, protection, or no doubt solely for pleasure. And there are certainly many women today who engage in casual sex and at least *say* they feel completely content. Like the sultry Sabina in Milan Kundera's *The Unbearable Lightness of Being*, they take what they want from a man and then tell him to go home at four A.M., feeling no emotional dissatisfaction.

Actually, it may turn out that women still use extracurricular lovers for better genes, though perhaps not consciously. One study in Britain found that women tend to have affairs during ovulation, when they are most fertile (and, not coincidentally, more easily aroused sexually). Another British study found that women typically have affairs with men who are higher in status than their husbands. And surveys find that women require a higher level of physical attractiveness in their casual lovers than in their permanent mates. This all reinforces the "sexy son" hypothesis: women want their sons to have the good genes of their lovers.[26]

Nevertheless, the vast body of evidence shows that far fewer women than men commit adultery and enjoy casual sex. Will this change? Evolutionary psychologists don't think so. Should we try to change it? Well, it does have its downside. Some women so strongly connect sex and emotional assurance that they sleep with men to feel loved, to feel wanted, to feel alive; sex becomes something they do when they feel bad about themselves. For others, sex represents an annoying dilemma: their desire to have sex is strong, yet they know if the emotional setting isn't right they'll feel horrible afterward. As a result, sometimes they have sex anyway and feel lousy the next day; and sometimes they refrain and wonder what they missed.

Yet for women who are interested in having a relationship, their complicated sexuality offers a wonderful self-correcting mechanism, which, if heeded, could serve them well. In addition to offering many women emotional peace, refraining from sex can give them a great deal of power. Conservatives have always said this, of course, but in the past this power didn't really do much for women: they were still forced to trade sex for economic security. The thought of women withholding sex for power still unsettles many feminists. Power, they argue, shouldn't be allocated by gender. Besides, this is still only an indirect (i.e. manipulative) power. Yes, it is—and this is the real world, where indirect power pervades every situation and interaction. Moreover, if women and men have fundamentally different reproductive needs, then it would make sense that they would also have different types of power in the personal realm. Indeed, many men effectively exploit this difference—withholding affection to seek a semblance of control. I'm hardly advocating that women make this type of adversity connection the basis of a relationship. But I think it's important that women understand the differences—and that many of those differences may not change.

Another reason for sexual discretion is the double standard. It still reigns. Many men still lose respect for women who sleep with them right away. Some evolutionary psychologists believe a madonna/whore dichotomy is deeply ingrained in male psyches. While men are compelled toward promiscuity on the one hand, they also need to ensure that the offspring they are investing in are *their* offspring. So men learned, as Robert Wright puts it, to "shower worshipful devotion on the sexually reserved women they want to invest in" and, at the same time, to "guiltlessly exploit the women they don't want to invest in, by consigning them to a category that merits contempt."[27]

It's not exactly clear where Wright is finding all of this "worshipful devotion," but perhaps it will return if more women allow several dates to pass before they allow a man into their apartments, let alone into their beds.

Wouldn't this merely perpetuate the double standard? Not if women subject men to a slut test as well. Economically independent, women can now have as little respect for indiscriminate men as men have traditionally had for promiscuous women.

What doesn't seem at all necessary is a return to chastity. First of all, given our later marriages, it's completely unrealistic. Moreover, as even conservatives have to admit, sex is an important part of a relationship—you can be compatible with someone in every way except sexually. Indeed, surveys show that sexually incompatible couples are more likely to look for satisfaction elsewhere or get a divorce. Sex before marriage is especially important for women since there are still plenty of men who haven't quite caught on to the idea that sexual pleasure is supposed to be mutual. But it's also for the benefit of men—women are individuals in bed, too.[28]

VI

Just because many women find men's sexual assertiveness in the bedroom rather pleasant doesn't mean they necessarily enjoy it everywhere else. Take, for instance, the often continual barrage of commentary—from "Hey, sexy" to "Bet you taste as good as you look" to explicit descriptions of the observer's sexual prowess—that many women are hit with the minute they leave their homes. It can be rather hellish, especially during the warmer weather when more men are out and less clothing is on.

Of course, women can't expect to wear skimpy clothing or a tight dress and think that no man is going to want to look. Men are going to want to look. And many women want them to look. Indeed, what one woman sees as harassment another can take as a compliment. Some women like this sort of attention so much that they seek it out, eagerly searching for a lingering male glance as they cruise down the street.

Nevertheless, street harassment is a problem for many women. As feminists have argued, it can limit women's mobility, and there is sometimes a fine line between harassment and assault. Moreover, it has become worse in the past few decades, a fact that is typically attributed to men's fears of women's independence. No doubt that may have something to do with it, but it seems that the far larger problem, as conservatives argue, is society's general lack of "civilizing" forces. Indeed, one of the numerous ironies of contemporary feminism is that there was less street harassment before chivalry was condemned by feminists as degrading to women.

It was during the sixties that feminists began to argue that the semiformalized practices of holding open doors, pulling out chairs, and helping with coats was demeaning, reinforcing women's inferior status. Not coincidentally, chivalrous attitudes and behavior proved to be perhaps the easiest to change in men. They may still refrain from changing diapers and leave toilet seats up, but by God you'll never catch *them* opening a door for a woman.

Of course, as part of the whole "pedestal package," chivalry was clearly no bargain for women. But what many feminists seem to have forgotten is that chivalry developed in order to encourage respect for women, not condescension.

Chivalry, along with courtesy in general, first arose during the Middle Ages as part of an effort to tame coarse warriors of the knightly class. A set of codes of correct behavior soon permeated society, becoming the basis for manners in general and the proper treatment of women in particular. Chivalry required men to *think* about women, to become more attentive to their demands and needs.

Today, without any sort of polite constraints against uncouth behavior, many men are revealing the cruder side of their natures. Leaving aside the harassing commentary, the profanity, and the belches, many men (and women) show no desire to accord another person, not even a woman with three kids and two bags of groceries, any sort of consideration, let alone respect. Even women who are elderly or obviously pregnant often have trouble getting a seat on a bus or subway.

In response to such boorishness, some feminists now want to establish a new code of speech and behavior—but this time they want government and universities to institute it. Yet these proposals—campus speech codes, criminalizing street harassment, expanding the definition of sexual harassment—undermine two of the primary tenets of liberal feminism. They unnecessarily politicize a part of our personal lives: government has no business curtailing the speech and nonviolent behavior of its citizens. Moreover, by seeking to protect women but not men, they undermine the notion of equal treatment under the law.[29]

Actually, an unwritten code of etiquette enforced by peer pressure would again be far more effective in recivilizing men than would any law. Of course, on one level, a new set of social standards may seem no better than government dictates. It was society, after all, that imposed the strictest controls on women's sexuality in the past. It would be best, of course, if we didn't need either, if people—based on their own sense of personal morality—simply acted civilly and rationally toward each other all the time. But we've seen how well that's worked.

More important, it is unlikely that an updated code of etiquette would hurt women or undermine women's equality: manners can enhance freedom as well as limit it. Having a man open a door for a woman does not imply she can't (necessarily) open it herself. Having a waiter pull out a woman's chair doesn't mean he believes she is inferior. Having to lug heavy grocery bags home while a sturdy man whizzes by is hardly a badge of liberation.

Chivalry corrects for the weaknesses of men, not women. A

man who holds open a door for a woman is less likely to make a derisive comment about her breasts. A man who helps a woman on with her coat is less likely to force her clothes off at the end of a date. Both courtship and chivalry train men to act like gentlemen, an unfortunately dated concept that seems to go a long way toward capturing what many women today desire in a man.

Feminists typically recoil at the idea of restoring the word gentleman to a place of esteem, believing that both the words lady and gentleman are not only sexist but elitist. Yet as many "sophisticated" men have well demonstrated in the past thirty years, money and education hardly guarantee courteous behavior. Moreover, asymmetrical social practices—like asymmetrical sexual practices— are not inherently misogynistic. A man can see a woman as his equal yet still treat her differently than he would treat a male buddy.

Our different reproductive strategies, in other words, are probably always going to produce a great deal of tension between women and men. We can either feed that tension through anti-male rhetoric and policies, or try to subdue it through expectations of the best from both sexes. What we can't do is make it disappear. Which, in the end, I would think even Catharine MacKinnon would have to agree is a good thing.

◆

LOVE

I

"N O   M A T T E R   H O W   many other careers we've had or wanted," declares Bette Davis in *All about Eve*, "in the last analysis nothing's any good unless you can look up just before dinner or turn around in bed and there he is. Without that, you're not a woman."

In 1950, when this film first appeared and the careers of most women were still largely restricted to finding a husband, the vast majority of female moviegoers probably agreed with Bette Davis. Nearly fifty years and a major revolution in social roles later, the vast majority of women, I would bet, still agree. No matter how many careers they've had or wanted, most women today want to fall in love. And get married. And have kids. And stay home with their kids at least part of the time. Perhaps they don't feel like less of a woman without a man in their bed, but given the subject matter of most self-help books, talk shows, and therapy sessions, they certainly appear to feel less than ecstatically happy.

This is not the way it was supposed to be. In the early seventies, many radical feminists declared romantic love to be a myth, constructed by our misogynistic society to induce women to marry and serve men. Shulamith Firestone argued that the patriarchy taught women to develop an emotional need for men, and then named it "love." Marilyn French called love a "lie to keep women happy in the kitchen so they won't ask to do what men are always doing." Ti-Grace Atkinson proclaimed that love had to be "destroyed." "A woman without a man is like a fish without a bicycle" went one refrain. "Feminism is the theory; lesbianism the practice" went another.[1]

According to this feminist analysis, marriage was also created with the express purpose of controlling women's sexuality and exploiting her unpaid labor. Some feminists have even considered motherhood a manufactured "institution" designed to enslave women. Reduced to lovesick "breeders," women are being duped into giving up their political and social power in exchange for some allegedly higher moral purpose.

Feminists have certainly had reason to find romance and marriage problematic. In the first "marriages," the myth goes, man secured a wife by dragging her from a cave. Over time, man progressed to purchasing a wife, to compensate her father for his loss of labor. In ancient Greek society, a wife became her husband's chattel and could be lent or sold. Early Christians offered dowries to marry off their daughters. Arranged marriage became the norm in many societies and survives in various parts of the world today.

If love wasn't always present in marriage, obedience was. That is, a woman's obedience to her man. Wifely obedience was not only mandated by the Bible, it was enforced by most governments. In early America, under the vestiges of common law, a husband and wife were considered one entity, and the husband was that one. A man could legally beat and rape his wife and force her to return home if she ran away.

At the end of the eighteenth century, Mary Wollstonecraft called marriage "legalized prostitution." A century later, Charlotte Perkins Gilman labeled it an "economic contract": men needed women to raise the children and keep house, and women, lacking rights, education, and opportunities, needed men to live.[2]

The economic terms of the marriage contract began to loosen throughout the twentieth century, but they weren't radically rewritten until the seventies, when women began to take advantage of their newfound opportunities. Nevertheless, many if not most marriages were still, ostensibly at least, structured on the hierarchy of husband-rule. Moreover, while many women were no longer completely financially dependent on men, many were still emotionally dependent, making men the centerpiece of their identities and existence.

So a new feminist critique of love and marriage was in order, and, to some extent, the one formulated during the seventies served a number of useful purposes. The economic contract (for the middle and upper classes at least) has been noisily put to rest: women no longer need to marry in order to eat. Love can now be the basis of marriage, and equality the basis of love. Feudalistic husband-rule has nearly been relegated to the status of sitcom humor, and we are finally witnessing the rise of the "new father," one who is more directly involved with housework and the care of children.

Yet, at the same time, the way many women deal with love doesn't seem to have changed much since the first consciousness-raising groups of the late sixties. Many women—in all socioeconomic brackets—remain too dependent on men for their complete happiness. They still put up with verbal if not physical abuse; still lose their identities when in a relationship; still marry who they want to be. Many women say they don't feel fully "alive" unless a man is in love with them.

Clearly, women could use a more sophisticated analysis of love and marriage than they are receiving from the self-help books and daytime talk shows. Unfortunately, they're not getting it from feminist thinkers either. Most continue to focus far more attention on the amorphous "patriarchy" than on actually helping women deal with the individual men in their lives. One brand of feminists is still busy trying to "degender" motherhood and deinstitutionalize love and marriage. At the 1995 World Conference on Women in Beijing, American activists attempted to replace each mention of the word *mother* with *caretaker*, contending that all men can "mother" just as well as women. These feminists argue that equality won't reign until just as many men stay home with the children as women. Some also consider the traditions associated with romantic love—engagement rings, big weddings, taking a man's last name—hopelessly regressive because of the (ostensible) symbolism of ownership.[3]

Meanwhile, another strain of feminists has been trying to re-value motherhood by arguing that all women, whether they have children or not, share an exalted "maternal thinking," a talent that makes women morally superior to men. And some feminists of both schools have taken to defending—even celebrating—single motherhood, arguing that it is a woman's ultimate right and test of autonomy.

It's easier, of course, to talk about love as a cultural phenomenon than as the mystical, elusive, highly individual emotion that it is. Indeed, love probably ranks as one of the most incomprehensible aspects of human existence. Nevertheless, observations, both scientific and anecdotal, suggest that certain generalizations are possible. One is that love, like sex, doesn't respond well to political programs. Another is that romantic love—the passionate spiritual-emotional-sexual attachment between two individuals—is not a myth, a construction of Western civilization, a noose around every woman's neck. Romantic love can be found in nearly every known society, and perhaps even in the animal world.

To be sure, arranged marriages and other societal interference have prevented romantic love from flourishing in many cultures. And women's daydreams about love have no doubt been artfully exaggerated and exploited by advertisements, the bridal industry, and Hallmark cards. Yet romantic love survived throughout the ages because it is deeply embedded in our psyches. In fact, it is considered an important part of our evolutionary package, spurring women to seek and hold on to good providers for their children and motivating men to want to become those providers.[4]

As the past couple of decades have shown, equality and romantic love can happily coexist. Equality and self-abnegating obsession, however, cannot. There is a huge difference between not being fully happy without a man in one's bed and not being able to function without one. While we can't expect all love troubles to disappear in a feminist world, emotional independence is crucial to anything that can remotely be called autonomy.

The traditional family also needed reform, not annihilation. Just because it existed before the sixties doesn't mean it has to be discarded; indeed, the "nuclear" family has survived precisely because it works. Equality also doesn't require that men stay home with the kids in equal numbers to women. Even if it turns out that it's in the best interests of children that mothers—and not fathers—stay home for the first three years or so, the rights of women would not (necessarily) be jeopardized.

Again, there's little reason at this point to fear sexual difference in our private lives. Women are the ones who have babies. Only when we truly accept the implications of this fact will motherhood again be given the respect it deserves. And only when motherhood is truly valued will the corporate world be forced to make the necessary accommodations to two-career families.

Feminism has provided women with the chance to have lives full of sublime opportunities as well as ridiculous conflicts: how can I give each of my three children quality time while leading the United Nations delegation to Bosnia? The trade-offs, as a result, may always be more difficult for women. Society can help mitigate the pain of these trade-offs, but it can't eliminate them. In the end, biology will to some extent always be destiny for women—just as it has been for men. Yet that very same biology—love, maternity, nurturing—can offer women inordinate pleasure. Ignoring this reality is as unfeminist as ignoring any other aspect of womanhood.

I I

In 1986, a team of researchers from Harvard and Yale dropped a media bombshell. College-educated women over thirty, they discovered, had only a 20 percent chance of getting married. Women over thirty-five, a 5 percent chance. Single women over forty were more likely to be killed by a terrorist than to wear a wedding band.[5]

Fortunately, there turned out to be a major flaw in the study's methodology that had drastically skewed the data. Women over thirty actually had about a 60 percent chance of being wed; over thirty-five about a 38 percent chance; over forty, about 20 percent.[6]

The corrected story, though, failed to attract nearly any media attention, as Susan Faludi astutely observes in Backlash. Yet in her exhaustive chronology of the "marriage crunch" nonstory, Faludi offers a very predictable analysis of why the original study caused single women across the country (and the world) to work themselves into a tizzy. Why did it upset so many women, women who, more likely than not, had put off marriage because of a career, who were, financially at least, rather independent?[7]

Faludi, like other feminist writers before her, dismisses women's reaction to the survey as the product of a political and cultural "backlash" against feminism. The media and society in general, she argues, have stoked the flames of women's anxiety over men by sending out messages declaring how miserable single women are and how marriage is women's only hope for happiness.[8]

Well, it's certainly true that there are still far too few images on television and in the movies of content and confident single women, women who want men but don't need them. It's also true that single women, especially as they ease into their thirties and beyond, are still invariably subjected to such helpful hints as "You really ought to settle down, don't you think?" "You know, you're not getting any younger." "But *why* haven't you met anyone?" And my personal favorite: "Maybe there's hope for you yet."

Nevertheless, it's hard to believe that women's continued desire to fall in love and get married is primarily the result of social messages, however annoying they may be. Actually, a researcher at Yale University found that in 1993 just 23 percent of female TV characters were full-time homemakers, compared with 60 percent in 1955.[9]

According to evolutionary theory, romantic love has served as an inducement for women and men not only to want to have sex (and thus reproduce) but to want to wake up with the other person the next morning (and thus care for the children). And scientists are beginning to discover direct evidence of a woman's biological need for a steady man in her life. Male "essence" (sweat) has been found to regulate menstrual cycling. Moreover, during ovulation women are able to smell male scent most strongly. As a result, women may be more susceptible to sexual arousal and even infatuation when they are most fertile.[10]

If a psychological need for love is firmly rooted in female biology, it's not that surprising that women—no matter how independent they may be—would feel the absence of a man as significant and find the prospect of dying alone quite upsetting. Denying this reality is not particularly useful. It can also make a woman feel as though there's something wrong with her for wanting a man in her life: she's merely another hapless victim of our misogynistic culture.

However. There's clearly a healthy need for love and an unhealthy need for love. And while it's dangerous to generalize about love, it unfortunately seems that many women still fall prey to the unhealthy one.

An overdependency on men was supposed to have disappeared as women gained identities of their own. And for many women today, it did disappear; life no longer begins when they get married. Some view their dating years as an adventure, a time to test out different types of men like flavors of frozen yogurt; others talk about being "defiantly single." Many women don't even think about a serious relationship or marriage until they reach their thirties.

Yet a lot of women—from burger flippers to investment bankers—still seem to date and marry more out of a need for emotional security than for love. For some, no matter how much good is going on in their lives, they feel like a failure if they are not involved in a relationship. Others—with high-profile, high-paying jobs—run to a man whenever they feel the slightest bit insecure. And once in a relationship, many women—confident, independent, successful women—quickly latch on to a man, subordinating their lives to his.

Feminism, it seems, can offer women only the prospect of a more balanced life; it can't force women to be more balanced. Ironically, success and responsibility may actually make many women *more* needful of emotional reassurance, as well as assurance of their sexual attractiveness. (Men, by contrast, often need to pull away when work isn't going well or they're feeling insecure.)

For some women, though, the problem seems to go far deeper. In *Revolution from Within*, Gloria Steinem draws a distinction between love and "romance." While love is real and solid and stems from a deep friendship, Steinem argues, romance exists in the realm of fantasy, typically beginning across some sort of chasm, thriving on separation, and growing weaker with closeness.[11]

Of course, love, like everything else, seems to rest on an ambiguous continuum; the lines between healthy and unhealthy are often quite blurred. And, again, any categorization risks the danger of being too pat. Nevertheless, Steinem's distinction is useful, though there seems no need to give the term "romance" such a pejorative connotation. I would contrast love with obsession. Love is not blind or irrational; obsession is. While love stems from strength and is a response to one's highest values, obsession stems from weakness, from desperate need.

Steinem and others also argue that, without feminism, real romantic love is impossible: true love can exist only between equals. Thus, it's not love and autonomy that are incompatible; it's obsession and autonomy.

Interestingly, scientists are now beginning to locate the actual biological process of romantic love in our brains. They believe that it typically occurs in two stages. During the first stage—what's being called infatuation—both women and men report feeling dizzy with excitement, anticipation, and anxiety. This can't eat/can't sleep/can't think high is created, researchers have found, by a surge in the neurotransmitter phenylethylamine (PEA), which is typically responsible for feelings of elation and exhilaration. When a relationship stabilizes somewhat, the second stage—attachment—has arrived. At this point, endorphins begin to kick in, producing feelings of calm and security. Researchers now also believe that people who go from one bad relationship to another—so-called romance junkies—may be seeking to capture and maintain a PEA high.[12]

Perhaps people who fall into and stay emerged in obsessive relationships are also in need of a PEA high. Indeed, scientists have begun to conclude that depression and all of the obsessive-compulsive disorders—from anorexia to workaholism—have a similar underlying biochemical profile that can often be treated with antidepressants. Are women more prone to this profile than men, or are the outlets just different—for instance, men turn to gambling and women to shopping? It's unclear at the moment. But discounting the biological basis of these behaviors doesn't help women very much.[13]

The broader point is that not only will women love with or without the help of the "patriarchy," they will often love too much. Thus, the unqualified celebration of women's greater "connectedness," made by some relational feminists, is just as detrimental to women as a categorical denial of it. Yet whatever the cause of obsessive love, it is still up to women themselves to get out of it: again, no explanation can be turned into an excuse. Women are going to stop allowing love to consume them, infantilize them, and destroy them only when they accept that this behavior is their responsibility and, to some degree, in their control—whether that means merely enforcing emotional self-discipline or seeking help before a problem escalates. Romantic love was designed to bring women (and men) great happiness, not wrenching anxiety and pain.

I I I

However needy many women are emotionally, though, many men aren't that far behind. Indeed, an argument can be (and has been) made that men are actually far *more* dependent on women emotionally, but women are so much better at nurturing that men rarely feel unloved. This would at least partially explain why men are more apt to get depressed (and kill themselves) after the breakup of a marriage than are women.[14]

Moreover, while women are typically unsubtle about their emotional needs, men like to hide theirs through displays of unneediness. As a result, we have women's near-constant complaints about men—about their inability to express emotions, to be romantic, to commit. Women complain that they often have to tell a man what he's feeling, that it's a rare man who is truly sensitive to their needs and supportive of their goals, who doesn't constantly have to be the center of attention. Women say that they often find themselves shrinking their personalities down to a size they think a man can handle, allowing him to be the witty one, the star, allowing his life to take precedence.

These complaints aren't anything new, of course; women were saying the same things thirty years ago in the first consciousness-raising groups. Ironically, the legacy of the seventies' Sensitive Man has added a new category of complaint to the list: the man who is so self-involved that his *lack* of action becomes extremely hurtful—the passive abuser. Yes, the Aldaesque new man can be sensitive to feelings, but they often turn out to be his own.

Men say they are sick of hearing these complaints. Women want men to be like women, they argue, and it just isn't going to happen. But that hardly seems to be the case. For one, women say they're not sexually attracted to effeminate men. Moreover, it's not male strength that's the problem for many women, but male weakness—men too weak to be considerate, sensitive, and sweet, too weak to allow a woman equal status. "Why can't he act like a man?" has become a not uncommon lament.

Unfortunately, the reigning feminist line on masculinity—that it is nearly worthless—doesn't allow for these sorts of distinctions. Some feminists argue that masculinity, like femininity, has been entirely a product of social construction: males receive messages of machismo from infancy telling them to repress their feelings and to be arrogant, domineering, and obnoxious. Other feminists seem to believe that all males are born aggressive, violent, and misogynistic; it's only the degree that differs.

The implication of either analysis is that (a) men are universally unappealing, and (b) they're not going to change unless society or male biology gets a complete overhaul.

This is not particularly helpful.

What first needs to be taken into account are the evolutionary roots of male behavior. Men, like women, are more prone to certain traits and less prone to others because of the survival and reproductive needs of their ancestors. A ready ability to take risks and show aggression was crucial to hunting for food, competing for mates, and protecting one's children. At the same time, revealing feelings or sensitivity and vulnerability could jeopardize more than merely a macho affectation.

Today, it's not that many men don't *experience* feelings of love, caring, and compassion. It's just that these feelings aren't as readily accessible for many men as they are for most women—figuring them out and then expressing them requires greater effort. Indeed, brain studies show that men use a more primitive part of the limbic system (the part of the brain responsible for emotions) than do women. This emotional handicap has obviously been reinforced by culture, to the point where many men feel that expressing feelings of any kind weakens them.[15]

But even though these unattractive traits have biological roots, they are hardly universal and, as the past couple of decades have shown, certainly seem capable of change. And it's not going to be an overhaul of society that induces this change but men themselves. Those who aren't wise to this may find themselves increasingly without women.

At least that would be the hope. For this to happen, though, women have to be able to say: "I don't want to be treated this way." They have to feel confident and independent enough to walk out, to be alone on a Saturday night.

"Are you strong enough to be my man?" croons Sheryl Crowe, capturing, it seems, the mood many women are in. "Lie to me; I promise, I'll believe . . . but please don't leave." Unfortunately, she probably got that right too. Many women today may desperately want strong men but often aren't up to living without a man until they find one.

Feminists can continue to write volumes about the patriarchy's exploitation of women, but the primary problem for most American women today isn't how "society" deals with women, it's how individual men do—and how women let them get away with it. Not much more will really change until women, in their individual relations with men, demand it. Women can no more allow the men they are romantically involved with to manipulate them, use them, or even treat them insensitively than they can allow themselves to be physically abused. Yes, this is blaming the victim. But sometimes the victim needs to be blamed so she'll stop being the victim.

The easiest way for a woman to change a man, of course, is not to choose one that needs to be changed in the first place. Much has been written about the foolish choices of smart women, but apparently most women at least *try* to choose wisely. As I discussed

in chapter 4, women still look for traits (ambitiousness, industriousness, dependability, stability) that advertise a man's level of commitment and resources, both present and future potential, far more
than men do.[16]

Does continuing to place a high priority on resources and
long-term commitment prevent women from fully dispensing with
the old economic contract of marriage? "We are still looking for
forms of security, strength, and social approval that we no longer
need—and thus missing love," writes Steinem. But there's no reason
love and economic security can't go hand in hand—and they often
do. Moreover, no matter how independent and successful a woman
is, commitment and resources are still rather crucial to a marriage
and family. A more feminist marriage contract would hold that a
woman doesn't need a man to survive; but her children very well
might.[17]

Actually, it often seems that women don't have a choice about
whether to make economic security a high priority. Many men
can't even think about a commitment—or even a relationship—
until they have come into their own careerwise. The highest proportion of never-married men have the most erratic employment
history or the least education. Moreover, men who are both strong
and successful themselves seem to be far less intimidated by strong
and successful women; indeed, those are precisely the women they
are now desiring. Unfortunately, these men are still relatively rare.
The highest proportion of never-married and divorced women are
among the most well educated.[18]

While women today want men to fully support their goals and
dreams—want, in short, to be treated like equals—they also still
appear to want romance (flowers, cards, candlelight dinners) and a
good deal of affection. Many women have found that acting like
buddies all day and then hopping into bed at night—being, essentially, friends who fuck—doesn't turn out to be as emotionally fulfilling as many radical feminists had hoped. Women complain that
they get more compliments from street harassers than from their
boyfriends.

You can understand how this seeming contradiction on the part of women—wanting to be treated both as equals and as, well, women—could confuse men. And what exactly does it mean today to treat a woman like a woman? Femininity has, after all, become highly individualized. Perhaps women don't want men to forget that, underneath the high heels or combat boots, the daintiness or aggressiveness, lies a female sexuality: women want men to respond to them not just as human beings, but also as sexual beings—and not just while in bed.[19]

Admiration of a woman's femininity does place her, temporarily, in a somewhat passive position: she becomes a sexual object. Does this matter? Well, it did when her only source of self-esteem came from her lover's eyes, when she couldn't gaze back. But that is no longer the case. More important, women's desire to feel sexually desirable does not emanate from the publishers of *Playboy* or the producers of pornography. It is deeply embedded in their need for sex and romantic love, and there's no reason to make them feel guilty about it.

I V

The culmination of this desire to mate, to fall in love, is the pair bond, what we call marriage. Marriage is not just a construction of Western society, nor merely, or even primarily, a means to control women and serve the needs of men. A form of marriage has existed in every known human society and even among certain other species of primates. Unfortunately for women, the most common form of marriage has been polygyny, where the husband takes more than one wife. Monogamy has been the rule in only 17 percent of human societies, leading many anthropologists to believe that Western-style marriage is actually a means to control men.[20]

Curiously, during the seventies, some radical feminists tried to do away with not just the blatantly negative aspects of traditional marriage—male domination, the sexual double standard, the gen-

der-based division of labor, and so on—but with the entire concept
of monogamy, by supporting such notions as group marriage and
open marriage. Today some radical feminists still hold that the
Western-designed institution of marriage—joining a man and a
woman in a social and legal bond for the purpose of emotional
intimacy, sexual expression, and (if desired) reproduction—is inherently exploitative and oppressive.

Yet marriage reform has been not only possible but quite successful: husband-knows-best marriages have been steadily declining
in prevalence and acceptability, and men have begun to contribute
more to domestic life than just taking out the garbage.

The idea of a completely egalitarian relationship is, as Camille
Paglia and others have pointed out, unrealistic: we are hierarchical
creatures—one person will always have *some* degree of power over
the other. But with the vast majority of married women in the
workforce, power between individual women and men may now be
far more a matter of personality or emotional or sexual need than of
gender politics. A woman can earn twice as much as her husband
and, if her emotional need for him runs too deep, still be his domestic slave—and vice versa.

So an egalitarian marriage requires emotional independence.
Does it also require financial independence? It's certainly true that,
as conservatives have long argued, women ruled many a household
in the past, even when they didn't have a cent to their name.
Nevertheless, as history also well shows, there's often a very fine
line between economic dependence and a suppliant, subservient
relationship.

At the moment, of course, any theoretical discussion about
whether married women should work outside the home is strictly
theoretical: with stagnant wages, rising housing prices, and soaring
college costs, two paychecks are now nearly essential for most
families.

But the economic situation may change. And if it does, it will
be interesting to see if the results of a 1995 survey by the Families
and Work Institute are borne out. According to the survey, only 15

percent of women say they would work full time if they had enough money to live comfortably. The rest would either work part time, care for their families, or do volunteer work. And the numbers aren't so different for the eighteen-to-twenty-four-year-old cohort: only 22 percent say they would work full time if given the choice.[21]

To college-educated women on the career track, these numbers may seem more than a little shocking. Yet it's important to note that these women may not be saying that they have a complete aversion to work in the public sphere; all they may be saying is that at certain times they may have other priorities. Regardless, if only 15 percent of women do end up working full time outside the home, this still shouldn't be viewed as a blow to feminism. Indeed, under a liberal feminist society, all women could spend their days needlepointing "Home Sweet Home" samplers—as long as their choices are being made freely.

At the same time, it's always worth pointing out the benefits of working in the public sphere, especially now that child-rearing occupies such a relatively small fraction of a woman's life. As Charlotte Perkins Gilman observed in *Women and Economics* more than a century ago, working outside the home is also "an exercise of faculty, without which we should cease to be human." Many full-time mothers exercise their intellectual faculties by reading up on the latest child psychology, volunteering at libraries or nursing homes, or involving themselves in local community politics or activism. But without any of this, a decade of full-time housewifery has the potential to turn adult brains to mush, causing women with college degrees to talk about oven cleaning with a rather scary intensity.[22]

Actually, according to the evolutionary psychologists, women weren't designed for years of full-time housewifery, especially in secluded suburbs far from friends and extended family. Our female ancestors had various jobs—gathering, farming, toolmaking—and were part of a close-knit community. Not surprisingly, studies consistently find that the most mentally healthy women are those who both are married and work at least part time in the public sphere.[23]

And who, no doubt, have husbands who have gotten over their fear of dust rags. Women still do more than two-thirds of the domestic chores—even if they're working full time and even if they make more money than their husbands. Too often it's the woman who must do it, or it doesn't get done. Women still report that they notice a mildewy bathtub far more frequently than their husbands do.[24]

It's hard to believe this situation won't dramatically change. Especially if it's still true that, as sociologist Arlie Hochschild noted in *The Second Shift* more than a decade ago, one of the primary reasons women are divorcing men is that the men won't do their share of housework. On the other hand, if—because of biology or culture or most likely both—the average woman is more "sensitive" to peeling paint or droopy plants, many women may have to get used to always being, at the very least, the initiators of home improvements. And they may want it that way. According to a 1995 Virginia Slims poll, more women than men (67 percent versus 56 percent) believe a woman should be in charge when it comes to housework and childrearing.[25]

There's also some evidence that suggests women are divorcing men who aren't emotionally supportive. Women continue to report giving more than they get emotionally in marriages; more men than women consider their spouses as their best friends. If women (on average) truly are better at intimacy, women may continue to find that their husbands can't quite provide all of the emotional sustenance that their mothers, sisters, or female friends can.[26]

Actually, this may not turn out to be all that unfortunate. No matter how good their marriages, no matter how successful their careers, women need to maintain a strong community of love and support—a personal, chosen sisterhood. A husband is, after all, just one person; and the divorce rate is, after all, still hovering at 50 percent.

The larger point is that women may always in some ways act more "wifelike" than their husbands. And their husbands—especially if they are bigger and stronger and can more *easily* change a flat or move the refrigerator—may always be more husbandlike than their wives. This should hardly be cause for despair or hand-wringing. As long as the "power" is relatively equal, there's no reason women and men can't have somewhat different roles in the home.

V

These differences may always be even more pronounced when children enter the picture. The facts of human life are such that because women and men have different responsibilities before a baby's birth, they have different needs and desires after a birth. A mother's initial investment in her offspring (nine months of pregnancy, a year or so of breastfeeding) is far greater than a father's. Moreover, during our two-million-year hunter-gatherer past, women had the job of raising the kids (as well as gathering, farming, and so on) while their husbands went off to kill gazelles and antelopes. Natural selection had by this time seen to it that men would also come to care about their offspring. But during this critical period in our evolutionary history, women were far more involved in the rearing of children than their husbands.

In the centuries since, this division in parental roles has obviously been reinforced by culture, in some periods more strongly than others. Feminists often point to preindustrial times when fathers were more intimately involved in childrearing. In the past few decades, the New Father has emerged, at times able to coo and cuddle like the best of mothers. And the next thirty years of feminism may bring more dramatic changes.

At this point, however, the differences between the way women and men view childbearing and -rearing are still quite profound. It is rare, for instance, to find a man—even a sensitive New

Father type—who will express a desire to have children with any sense of anxiety, or even urgency. Meanwhile, even some of the most driven and successful career women often talk about children in desperate tones. The biological clock is not a figment of the conservative imagination. It is a very real—and painful—part of the lives of most women, especially as they cross the thirty-year mark—not coincidentally, when studies show fertility begins to appreciably decline.[27]

Again, we're talking averages here. The capacity to nurture should not be confused with a desire to nuture. Many women have happily turned a deaf ear to the ticking of their reproductive clocks; the number of women age thirty-five to thirty-nine who are childless, by choice or otherwise, has doubled in the past thirty years—it is now up to 20 percent—and it may continue to climb. And yet, despite birth control, abortion, and feminism, it's difficult to imagine a time when *most* women still wouldn't want to become mothers. Women who put off childbearing until it's too late to bear a child often face considerable emotional turmoil. Minimizing this problem, as Susan Faludi and other writers have tried to do, is hardly in the best interests of women.[28]

The intensity of the bond formed with a young child, especially a newborn, also seems to be stronger among mothers than fathers. And scientists have begun to figure out exactly how evolution tried to ensure this intensity. During labor, breastfeeding, and physical contact with her child, a mother releases oxytocin, a peptide hormone that is believed to facilitate bonding.[29]

Dismissing the importance of the maternal bond, as some feminists have done, seems not only unnecessary, but potentially quite harmful. Studies show that a child needs to develop solid attachments, a secure base, before she can explore the world. At the moment, there is no evidence that a child needs to bond with her mother more than her father; she apparently will bond with whoever is more attentive and caring. Yet the average mother, given her biological and psychological makeup, will probably be more sensitive, nurturing, and responsive to a child's needs than the average father. It is not merely socialization that causes a mother to be more apt to hear a child cry than her husband, to feel a greater urge to run back to a screaming child left with the babysitter. More than a century ago, in arguing for government to remove the "arbitrary barriers" placed on women's development, Margaret Fuller noted that mothers would probably still "delight to make the nest soft and warm. Nature would take care of that."[30]

Again, this is not to say that a father can't be as nurturing as a mother, or in some cases even more so. Some men are naturally very nurturing; others become so when necessary. But if it turns out that women (on average) can mother better than men, it certainly doesn't do women—let alone children—any good to ignore this.

Many feminists argue that real equality won't be achieved until as many men as women are willing to stay home with the kids. In *Kidding Ourselves: Why Women Won't Achieve Equality Until Men Really Share Parenting*, Rhonda Mahony admonishes women for taking fewer math and science courses and pursuing fewer graduate and professional degrees. These women, she argues, are ensuring that their income will be smaller than their husband's, and thus easier to forgo.[31]

Well, it's no doubt true that more degrees, especially in business, usually mean more money, which may make a woman's career more valuable than her husband's. But as long as women have the right and opportunity to pursue as many degrees as they want, it doesn't matter how many men stay home with the kids. Indeed, it doesn't matter much to feminism if, fifty years from now, fewer women than men still want to pursue the highest spots, still choose jobs with flexible hours and less responsibility in order to have more time to raise the kids. Focusing on these women or on women who choose to take time off from work to stay home with their kids detracts from the real problem: women who don't want to—or, more likely, can't—take time off to raise their children.

A corporate world more sensitized to the needs of two-career families—offering more options like workplace-based day care centers or flextime—can certainly help. But it may very well be that, because it is women who give birth, life will always demand more exacting trade-offs for women than for men. Restructuring the working world and promoting more community-based support systems will certainly lower the costs of these trade-offs, but they can't eliminate them.

A woman's reproductive system will continue to intrude upon her life in other ways as well. Women will always get monthly periods, which may be temporarily disabling. Women will probably always be primarily responsible for contraception. Women will always be the ones who have the abortions. Women will always have to contend with the ticking of a biological clock. And women will always have to go through nine months of gestation and possibly a year or so breastfeeding each time they have a child.

Women can look at all of this—at their biology—as a curse, an injustice, a nuisance. And it certainly can be. Women who do everything possible to minimize the effects of their reproductive systems on their lives are no less female than women who have eight children, though it may take a while before much of society agrees.

But women can also look at their biology as a great pleasure, a gift, a source of power. And women who do this are no less feminist than those who forgo childbirth. Indeed, it's hard to make the case for the corporate world to fully value motherhood if women themselves don't—if they view their periods as a source of shame, their pregnant bellies as ugly, if they apologize for wanting to stay home with their kids until kindergarten. A true appreciation of motherhood doesn't make women superior to men any more than it makes them inferior. It simply offers the starkest example of the fact that, while women are inherently equal to men, they are also fundamentally different.

V I

If we're going to truly value motherhood, though, we have to acknowledge a couple of unattractive things. One is that many women have children for the wrong reasons. The other is that not all women make good mothers.

Children are not pets. You don't get one to combat loneliness, to raise your self-esteem, to escape a boring job, to save a marriage. They're not just another possession to be acquired at the right age like the VCR, the Jaguar, or the home in the Hamptons.

This is where the conservative "family values" message reveals the extent of its shallowness. Now that we really can choose when and with whom to reproduce, children can finally be viewed as the product of profound love between a man and a woman, as a choice to be made under the best circumstances. Contraception and, if necessary, abortion don't guarantee this somewhat utopian notion, but they certainly can facilitate it.

This is also where the feminist analysis of single motherhood reveals its politicization. In the past decade or so, many feminists have taken to not only defending single motherhood, but actually celebrating it. They have argued that there are a variety of ways to raise children, all potentially very good. Any criticism of single motherhood, they claim, is nothing more than an attack on women, especially poor, black women.

Well, yes, single motherhood, divorced fatherhood, grand-motherhood, adoptive fatherhood, gay motherhood—all can be better than a nuclear family with a history of incest, wife-battering, child abuse, or neglect, than a home without love and kindness. And that is why the divorce laws have to remain as liberal as they are.

At the same time—all things being equal—an ideal family would still consist of both a mother and a father. It's hard to get around the fact that study after study shows that children raised in one-parent homes have two to three times more behavioral and psychological problems than children in traditional families. Most of these problems result from the poverty in which the vast majority of single mothers live—the rate of child poverty is six times higher for children living with single mothers than for children in two-parent families.[32]

But what about the single mothers who have money—the Murphy Browns? The percentage of women with professional or managerial jobs who become single mothers has tripled in the last decade, now more than 8 percent of all mothers. What do you say to a woman who is inching toward forty, has been through a series of unsuccessful relationships, has a good job, a nice bank account, and wants desperately to have a child before it's too late? At another time, she would be married right now either to someone she wasn't in love with or to someone who treated her poorly. At the moment, she'd rather be alone. She'd rather give all of her love and devotion to a child than to a husband who doesn't deserve it.[33]

The choice is obviously hers, and there are plenty of single mothers who have successfully raised children. But it doesn't do anyone any good to deny the possible problems. As Maggie Gallagher, a single mother and author of *The Abolition of Marriage: How We Destroy Lasting Love*, puts it, "Children not only need a father, they *long* for one, irrationally, with all the undiluted strength of a child's hopeful heart. . . . We have to stop pretending that all choices are equally good—that single motherhood is just an alternative family form and that fathers are just another new disposable item in the nursery." Whereas a mother's love is considered unconditional and all-protective, a father's love is more distanced and often has conditions attached to it. "From mother's love, a child learns how to love," writes Diane Ackerman in *A Natural History of Love*. "From father's love, a child feels worthy of love."[34]

Ironically, single motherhood may undermine efforts to change masculinity. According to psychologist John Munder Ross, the presence of a father can secure a boy's basic sense of masculinity, thus freeing him to take on some more feminine traits and behaviors. Some studies have found that boys learn the limits of aggression from the kind of rough but controlled play they enjoy with their fathers.[35]

Isn't it also somewhat inconsistent to suggest that fathers are irrelevant to single motherhood, yet in two-parent families, they must be involved in childrearing on a fifty-fifty basis?

Some feminists also celebrate single motherhood as a way of showing that women are now completely autonomous. But being able to raise a child by oneself is hardly a testament to autonomy. Autonomy implies the ability to be self-reliant, not self-indulgent.

Far worse than single motherhood, though, is bad mother-hood. Both feminists and conservatives have been loath to admit that there is such a thing as a bad mother. The emphasis from all ideological sides has been on how bad fathers can be. And there's certainly much evidence to substantiate this. But as psychologist David Celani puts it: "We all assume that mothers love their chil-dren. Unfortunately, many mothers who were raised poorly by their own families do not develop a strong bond with their child. They may pretend to be involved, but many are indifferent. And the child can sense this very, very easily."[36]

Bad mothering spans socioeconomic brackets. As the seem-ingly weekly horror stories show, bad mothers can beat or drown or starve their children. Bad mothers can also care more about their careers or their pleasure than their children; they can take out all of their resentments and dissatisfactions on their children; they can hit their kids for no reason and look at them with contempt.

Nothing else that happens to these kids for the rest of their lives—sexism, racism, whatever—will ever affect them as much as bad mothering. Insufficiently mothered adults never fully grow up and can suffer from everything from chronic depression to an in-ability to be intimate.

Elevating motherhood, in other words, really means elevating childrearing. The decision to bring another life into this world is one of the most important a woman today can make. This is one of the primary reasons for keeping abortion legal as well as for finding out which lifestyle would best accommodate a child's needs. Arguing one without the other betrays a greater regard for ideology than for children.

V I I

Does a marriage contract based on love and choice suffer if more women than not continue to take the name of their husbands, if they continue to immerse themselves in all of the trappings of traditional weddings, from wearing an expensive engagement ring to being "given away" by their fathers?

Well, you could view all of this as symbolizing a husband's "ownership" of his wife, and no doubt that was at least partly why these customs developed. But customs persist for a variety of reasons that have little to do with gender politics. Besides, there's no reason why at this point we can't redefine the symbolism, to signify, say, unity. Unity need not mean a single entity, nor even a "merging" of souls or loss of identity. It can simply mean the desire to link independent lives, to form a bond that can be broken only at great cost.

In the end, it's perfectly "natural," perfectly healthy for women to dream about love, marriage, and children, to want them all to be a pivotal part of their lives. The danger is in ever again allowing any one of them to be the whole of their lives, to represent the entire extent of their identities. Only a woman who has fully developed herself—intellectually, emotionally, spiritually—can make rational choices about her life, as well as about the lives of her children.

Self-development, though, doesn't have to occur independently of men and marriage. Indeed, many women—in stark contrast to men—find it easier to concentrate on their careers once they feel secure emotionally. We may wish that this would not be the case, and in a couple of generations it may no longer be the case. But for many women today, who may desire responsibility as much as they fear it, a man may still bring the emotional stability needed (paradoxically) to become more autonomous. The more important point at the moment is that women do continue to strengthen themselves. After all, a woman's first—and last—love still has to be herself.

POWER

I

- A veteran congressional lobbyist in her fifties dresses in a tight leopard-skin getup whenever she cases Capitol Hill for her corporate clients. Male members of Congress tend to greet this striking brunette with such lines as "You gorgeous thing." She then proceeds to lobby with her ribald humor and her chest, rubbing it against the appropriate arm. Her efforts, apparently, rarely go unrewarded.

- Several successful Washington journalists are known for wearing low-cut dresses and high-stacked heels on assignment. They are also known for being able to extract huge amounts of information from male congressional staffers. The theory is that they make men think, "I can sleep with this woman if I talk to her long enough."

• When interviewing for a position at a new firm, an advocate for a liberal public interest group repeatedly alluded to the senators she had slept with on junkets in the past. She apparently believed these accomplishments represented her best credentials.

• At a reception, a woman approached a congressman she barely knew and started eating coquettishly off of his plate. She was looking for a job.[1]

I heard these and numerous other such stories a few years ago while researching sexual harassment in the hallowed halls of Congress. The issue, I found, is a little more complicated than a bunch of old codgers fondling unwilling young nymphets in their private Capitol hideaways. Some of the nymphets, young and otherwise, are quite willing to be fondled. Indeed, some seek out such fondling, hoping it will advance their personal or professional careers. Others have simply mastered the art of aggressive flirtation, ably providing men of power with the delicate stroking their egos crave.

Whether this mode of doing business is more prevalent in Washington, where access means everything and congressional offices are filled with men who couldn't get dates in high school, I don't know. Yet, it's probably safe to assume that every field has its women who treat their sexuality as legitimate professional currency, as a bargaining chip. It's probably also true that most women, at some point in their working lives, have put their sexuality to good use—even if it's just by making themselves as attractive as possible.

The subject is not one that women like to talk about. A primary goal of feminism, after all, has been to enable women to earn power in the public sphere using their minds, not their bodies, to be workers who happened to be women, not women who happened to be working.

Yet as anyone who has ever primped before a big interview or meeting knows, a mind-body distinction is not always easy to draw. Where minds go, so do bodies. And a woman's sexuality is still, for better or worse, of far greater value in the marketplace than a man's. It's also the case that a woman's values, tastes, and personality aren't going to dramatically alter the minute she steps through her office's double-glass doors. A woman who is reticent and retiring in her private life, for instance, rarely becomes a gregarious glad-hander between nine and five. And a woman who places a higher priority on spending time with her family than on establishing her career is not going to take a job that requires late nights at the office or extensive travel.

At the moment, because of both their potentially lucrative sexuality and their potentially disruptive reproductive capacity, it may be more difficult for women than men to separate their minds from their bodies, their professional identities from their personal ones. Whether this matters is a complicated question. It's also one of the most important facing women today.

According to the principles of liberal feminism, at least one point is clear. The government and corporate world must *judge* women exclusively by their minds and their merits. Feminism is rooted in gender blindness, in viewing women and men as individuals who deserve equal treatment under the law. If women wish to engage in hazardous industrial work, military combat, or bartending until dawn, the government has no right to stop them. As Justice Ruth Bader Ginsburg argued in the 1996 Supreme Court case that opened up military academies to women, "Generalizations about 'the way women are,' estimates of what is appropriate for *most women*, no longer justify denying opportunity to women whose talent and capacity place them outside the average description." No matter what the differences between the sexes turn out to be, schools, tests, and standards must remain gender neutral.[2]

Ironically, while Ginsburg and other equity feminists have

spent most of their careers trying to secure legal equality for women, another group of feminists—the gender feminists—has spent the past decade or so trying to unravel it. Under the guise of making the legal system more woman-friendly, a new breed of feminist legal theorist has been somewhat successful at replacing the "reasonable person" standard of inquiry with a "reasonable woman" standard: the assumption is that women are universally more sensitive than men and therefore universally view situations differently. Now these feminists are trying to replace such allegedly "patriarchal" legal principles as neutrality, objectivity, rationality, and rights with such allegedly feminist notions as subjectivity, "connection," "context," and personal experience. Meanwhile, some feminist activists, notably those of the National Organization for Women, have gone so far as to support a government mandate requiring that powerful institutions—from Congress to the judiciary to corporate boards—be (at least) 50 percent female.[3]

Although gender feminist theories are turning up in laws, policies, and court rulings regarding sexual harassment, domestic violence, and date rape, it's probably safe to say that most women who consider themselves feminists don't agree with this rather original form of preferential treatment. Equity feminism will probably prevail. Still, a pure equal-treatment approach to women in the public sphere is not without its complexities. Consider, for instance, the issue of pregnancy. Only women get pregnant. Yet to avoid discrimination, equity feminists during the late seventies succeeded in classifying pregnancy as a "disability," to be treated in the workplace with the same degree of attention as, say, tendonitis. In 1993, Congress passed the Family and Medical Leave Act (FMLA), which entitled both male and female workers to twelve weeks of unpaid leave. But the act covers only workers at companies with fifty or more employees: most women work at smaller companies.[4]

Should Congress simply broaden the act? Or would women and children be able to gain more coverage by establishing a separate, federally guaranteed maternity leave, while still entitling men to a more limited child care leave? In other words, is this type of purism—at this point—more symbolic than substantive?

Even more complicated are the issues surrounding pregnancy—career interruptions, part-time work, flextime. While the corporate world has to treat women as equals in terms of hiring, promotions, and pay, how is it supposed to react to the different choices most women are making? Can it be made sophisticated enough to treat women as both equal and different? Do we ourselves understand what that means?

These issues aren't, unfortunately, going to be neatly worked out any time soon. What's crucial, though, is that the essential individuality of each woman doesn't get lost in the process. No matter how similar women are to one another and no matter how different they turn out to be from men, presumptions can never be made about a particular woman's skills, choices, values, or identity.

For this reason, it's no longer useful for feminists to continue to exhort women to move out of "pink-collar" jobs (child care, teaching, bank telling), even if they are low-paying and barely valued. It's also counterproductive for various feminist writers (Carol Gilligan, Suzanne Gordon, Nel Noddings, and others) to argue that, for the sake of women and feminism, the workplace needs to be "feminized": compassion and cooperation must replace competition, selflessness must replace self-interest, consensus must replace hierarchy.[5]

As I've been saying throughout this book, women may very well turn out to be—on average—more nurturing and less consistently ambitious than men. Yet we really don't know how this will ultimately translate into women's choices and behavior in the public sphere. Whatever the outcome, it's certainly not the job of feminists to tell women which career choices and behaviors are more "feminist." The point of feminism is to achieve a world in which women are treated (and treat themselves) as both individuals and adults. And an adult is assumed to be able to make not only her own choices but her own rational choices.

What often gets lost in all of the discussions about the problems women face today in the public sphere is the fact that we've traveled a tremendous political and social distance in just thirty years. What also gets lost is the fact that our problems, compared with those of women a hundred years ago, are relatively minor. Women are not "oppressed" in the United States, and they're no longer (politically at least) even subjugated. What they very well might be, though, is overwhelmed and confused. Fine-tuning feminism can seem almost as daunting as creating it.

I I

The first thing we need to understand about power is that not all women want it. In fact, most women today—even most women in their twenties, who grew up with feminism in full swing—are still choosing jobs with minimal responsibility, flexible hours, and limited travel, jobs that are either in the unfortunately named "pink ghetto" or in the expanding service sector. Eighty-five percent of elementary school teachers are women; 93 percent of nurses; 98 percent of secretaries; 97 percent of child care workers; 90 percent of bank tellers; 99 percent of dental hygienists. Meanwhile, women comprise only 5 percent of senior managers at Fortune 1000 companies.[6]

This is not to say that the past couple of decades haven't seen a dramatic shift in the education and career choices of women. In 1993, women earned 35 percent of all MBAs (up from 4 percent in 1972), 42.5 percent of all law degrees (8 percent in 1973), 38 percent of all doctoral degrees (18 percent in 1973), and 39 percent of all medical degrees (8 percent in 1970). The most popular academic major for women in 1992 was business, accounting for 20 percent of the bachelor's degrees awarded to women. The number of women majoring in English or education is half of what it was in the early seventies.[7]

Still, the education and career decisions of women graduating from college today are nowhere near the same as those of men. In 1992, women earned 75 percent of the advanced degrees awarded in education, 70 percent in public administration, 65 percent in English literature, and 63 percent in ethnic and cultural studies. Men, meanwhile, earned 86 percent of the degrees in engineering, 75 percent in physical sciences and science technology, 65 percent in business management and administrative services, and 60 percent in mathematics.[8]

Feminist economists typically blame this state of affairs on "channeling" and discrimination. From the earliest age, they argue, girls are still being socialized to view marriage and mothering as their grandest ambitions and to see themselves as capable only of a job in the caregiving professions or other "soft" fields. Parents and teachers discourage girls from taking math and science courses, which would lead them into higher-paying and higher-status careers. At their jobs, women receive little encouragement and instead face continual sexism, discrimination, and sexual harassment, which keep them in corporate "staff" jobs or send them back to more comfortable all-female pursuits. The fact that they still have to do the bulk of the childrearing and housework when they get home only compounds the problem.[9]

There is, of course, some truth to this argument. Many parents and teachers still have lower expectations for girls than for boys. Studies show that teachers call on boys more often in class and encourage boys but not girls to call out answers. These studies have been criticized for ignoring the fact that not only do girls get better grades than boys, but more girls go on to college. But such criticisms miss the point. Grades mean very little if a girl can't talk in class, and it hardly matters how competent, knowledgeable, or skillful you are in your job if you can't express yourself. Moreover, schools (especially public schools) should in no way be actively discouraging girls from taking advantage of their opportunities.[10]

In addition, many employers are still less inclined to hire or promote women because they (rightly) believe that women are more likely to take off when starting a family. Studies also show that more subtle discrimination remains quite pervasive. Bosses and colleagues still more often call women by their first names, still often assume that every woman is a secretary or an assistant, still exclude women from social events where business is transacted. And women still suffer from a dearth of strong, savvy role models, both in the real world and on celluloid.[11]

The playing field, in other words, is still not level. Yet a great deal of progress has been made, enough so that the channeling argument no longer seems to be telling the whole story.

First of all, discrimination is not as bad as it's made out to be. It often takes twenty to thirty years to climb to the top of the corporate ladder, and there weren't too many women starting the climb twenty or thirty years ago. Even so, the 5 percent figure (of female senior managers at Fortune 1000 companies) is more than a twofold increase since 1981, and women now constitute nearly half of all managers. A 1992 study found that while more women than men expected to be part of their company's senior management team, far fewer aspired to be CEOs (14.1 percent of women, compared with 44.6 percent of men). What women are doing, however, is starting their own businesses, at a faster pace than men. Women now own more than six million businesses—one-third of all U.S. companies and 40 percent of all retail and service firms.[12]

Even the gap in pay has nearly closed: women with the same level of education and experience as men typically receive the same pay—and sometimes more. A 1996 *Working Woman* survey found that, on average, women earned 85 percent to 95 percent of what men in similar positions earned. Women between the ages of twenty-seven and thirty-three who have never had a child earn 98 percent as much as men.

It's true that, in the aggregate, women are still earning 74 cents for every dollar earned by a man. But this has far more to do with career choices than with discrimination. One in four women who earned doctoral degrees in 1992 did so in education, which has a mean monthly income of $3,048; one in five men who earned doctorates did so in engineering, which has a mean monthly income of $4,049. Less than one in eight women who held a degree in 1990 earned that degree in business management and less than two in one hundred in engineering. Like it or not, a degree in business or engineering is worth more in our current marketplace than a degree in education.[13]

The channeling analysis also doesn't account for the fact that many women simply don't want to work sixty-hour weeks, travel on a moment's notice, or bring work home on weekends. According to studies by the Women's Education and Research Institute (hardly a bastion of conservative thought), employed mothers are significantly more likely than fathers to want to stay at their current levels of responsibility and to say that they would trade job advancement to work part time, work at home, or have control over their work schedules. Four-fifths of mothers who work part time do so by choice. The WERI has found that, on average, mothers would prefer to work 32.5 hours a week—5.8 hours less than the number they actually work. (By contrast, fathers would prefer to work 41.2 hours—6.7 hours less.)[14]

Again, I don't want to minimize the influence of stalled socialization, discrimination, a less than accommodating corporate world, and men who won't touch diapers. Indeed, much could be different in the next generation. But I think it's time to begin assuming that most women are at least aware of their options and are making choices based on personal and economic preferences.

I grew up in a very traditional middle-class suburb, where our mothers were waiting with milkshakes and brownies each afternoon when we came home from school. Early on, I felt a desire to have a different kind of life from my mother's, a desire that was nourished neither by my parents nor by my teachers but by books and (embarrassingly enough) TV shows like *That Girl* and *Mary Tyler Moore*. I had always assumed that most of the girls in my school felt the same way. As it turns out, the majority may have worked briefly after high school or college, but they soon settled down to have children and now either don't work at all or work part time in low-responsibility jobs. Meanwhile, I know quite a few women who grew up in communities full of high-achieving mothers but who have nevertheless chosen far less ambitious paths for themselves (much to the dismay of their mothers). Clearly, individual preferences are now playing a greater role than socialization for many women.

The issue is not that women, as a sex, lack ambition or competitive drive. As I discussed in chapter 2, it seems that women have always been ambitious and competitive, but for hundreds of years these traits were considered unfeminine and were suppressed (turning up in backstabbing, gossip, and contests over waxy shine and fingernail length).

Now that ambition is far more accepted (though still rarely applauded) for women, we are beginning to get a glimpse of what it will look like. And at the moment, it seems that the bell curve in ambition is slightly different for women than it is for men. The ambitions of most women appear to be tempered, to various degrees, by their desire to nurture. Many women may turn out to have an ambition lull during their prime childbearing years. Or many women may have two equally strong drives, neither of which they can fully satisfy.

It's still much too soon to say. But we should keep in mind that not all men are ambitious and competitive either. Many—in all socioeconomic brackets—view work as something to do only to make enough money to live comfortably. And increasing numbers of fathers (now up to 10 percent) are staying home with their kids full time.[15]

Continuing to urge women, even implicitly, out of the caregiving professions is not only condescending, but it also further denigrates the very jobs that need to be better valued. And they need to be better valued not just to raise their low salaries, but because they happen to be some of the most important work a woman—or a man—can do.

Would more men want to become caregivers if the status and salaries were higher? Probably. There was a 24 percent increase in male nurses between 1991 and 1995, when a nurse shortage caused salaries to shoot up as high as $60,000 a year. Still, only 7 percent of our two million registered nurses are male. Elementary and kindergarten teachers make as much as high school teachers; yet men constitute more than 47 percent of high school teachers, but only 16 percent of elementary teachers and an even smaller percent of kindergarten teachers.[16]

Certainly, men in caregiving fields suffer from a stigma problem as much as a status problem: a male child care worker is still considered a trifle suspect. But, again, it doesn't do anyone any good to discount biology. More women than men may always be more likely to gravitate toward these fields not just for the flexible hours, but also because they would prefer to spend their days taking care of children, the elderly, or the infirm.

If we don't fully acknowledge—and accept—the choices working mothers and potential working mothers are making, how can we expect the corporate world to become more attentive to their needs? Yes, the needs of working fathers must also be considered. But at the moment it is still mothers who are far more likely to take advantage of such options as flextime, home office, and part-time jobs.[17]

Of course, acknowledging these realities can also be used against women who are making other choices, which is why many feminist activists hit the roof a decade ago when Felice Schwartz, the former head of the consulting group Catalyst, wrote in the *Harvard Business Review* that most corporate women prefer jobs in middle management during their childbearing years. These activists excoriated Schwartz for trying to put women on a "mommy track" with lower status and pay, even though all she did was state a fact and urge employers to take full advantage of these hardworking and dedicated employees.[18]

How to get the corporate world to better accommodate mommy trackers without discriminating against fast trackers is feminism's current conundrum, one that isn't going to be solved any time soon. What is far from useful is obsessively focusing on numerical equality and magnifying the problem of discrimination.

Counting women like beans or, worse, setting quotas for them undermines not only their choices but their individuality. Many of us may wish that women would make different choices. But if those choices are made voluntarily, on a level playing field, and with as little discrimination as possible, then they're really none of our business.

I I I

While we're adjusting to the fact that some women may not want too much power in the public sphere, we may as well also get used to the idea that many women want a great deal of it. And many women want power for reasons that don't always suit everyone's tastes. Some women want power solely to be able to buy expensive clothes, big houses, and elegant cars. Others want power to make political decisions that don't exactly chime with the reigning politically correct agenda. And many women (even some outspoken feminists) don't always acquire power or wield it in the nicest way. They act like, well, men with power have historically acted— they're ferociously competitive, domineering, demanding, and, often, quite selfish and pigheaded.

   Some people, especially some feminist theorists, are bothered by this. A strain of feminism has typically held that when women finally have the opportunity to hold power, they will change the nature of it, use it only for good, altruistic, "feminist" purposes, and wield it compassionately. The duty of women, said Frances Willard, head of the nineteenth-century Women's Christian Temperance Union, was to "make the whole world homelike." A hundred years later, Carol Gilligan writes in *A Different Voice:* "Women's culture of nurturing and caring and their habits of peaceful accommodation could be the salvation of a world governed by hypercompetitive males and their habits of abstract moral reasoning." In many women's studies classes, women who have acquired power under the patriarchy are disparagingly referred to as "women worthies."

Even in *Fire with Fire: The New Female Power and How It Will Change the Twenty-first Century*, Naomi Wolf qualifies her endorsement of female power and greed with the condition that it be used only for the good of the women's movement.[19]

Many more feminist theorists and activists have believed that when women achieved political power, they would, without question, toe the establishment feminist line on all issues. This did not happen. So writer Polly Toynbee labeled former British Prime Minister Margaret Thatcher a "surrogate man." Gloria Steinem called Texas Republican Senator Kay Bailey Hutchinson a "female impersonator." And Naomi Wolf described the foreign policy analysis of former United Nations Representative Jeane Kirkpatrick as being "uninflected by the experiences of the female body."[20]

Well, to begin with, for better or worse, there is nothing inherently unfeminist about wanting power and money for entirely selfish reasons. Ambition, competition, and hierarchy are also not inherently unfeminist. In fact, they are considered quite "natural" for females. Even if women—on average—turn out to be slightly more cooperative, compassionate, and caring at the office than men, that doesn't justify any sort of a forced "feminization" of the corporate world. If it's going to happen, it will happen of its own accord.

And there's little evidence at the moment that it's going to happen. Indeed, it's probably not a coincidence that women at the top of all fields are typically direct and focused, know what they want, and don't let emotions get in their way. Consider just the most well known women of power—Ruth Bader Ginsburg, Hillary Rodham Clinton, Tina Brown, Barbra Streisand.

Some feminists argue that women today *have* to adopt traditionally male mannerisms to achieve anything and that when more women reach the top there will be a far greater variety of leadership styles. There may be some truth to this. Yet as Kate Fillion reports in *Lip Service*, studies show that when women are assigned the role of "boss" or "leader" in experiments, they typically conform to masculine stereotypes, expressing more direct eye contact, more authoritative orders, fewer questions, fewer supportive and affirming comments, and less anxiety.[21]

Of course, in a large variety of jobs—especially those (not coincidentally) in traditionally female fields—traits like caring and compassion are and should be quite prevalent. But a law firm is not a day care center, and there's no feminist reason to try to make it into one.

In the past decade, law schools have become embroiled in a debate about whether to change some fundamental aspects of legal pedagogy, including the Socratic, or case study, method (randomly grilling students on particular cases), for the sake of their female students. Women at law schools began pushing more earnestly for change in 1994, when Lani Guinier, a professor at the University of Pennsylvania Law School, published a report in the *University of Pennsylvania Law Review* stating that although women were coming into law school with the same qualifications as men, they were not performing as well once they were there. Guinier argued that law school pedagogy alienates women, who learn differently from men. Women, for instance, tend to deliberate before speaking, while men raise their hands and open their mouths immediately. "Why is speed better than depth?" asked Guinier. "Why is it better to be quick-witted rather than thoughtful?"[22]

As I said earlier, from a young age women certainly appear to speak less in class. But we don't know exactly why this is so. No matter what the cause, law school is not the place to begin to coddle women. Both speed and depth are crucial for lawyers—or at least for as many women lawyers as men lawyers. So is analytical thinking, another trait considered by some to be inherently "male" and therefore oppressive. Ruth Bader Ginsburg, Sandra Day O'Connor, Marcia Clark, and thousands of other women benefited quite well from traditional legal pedagogy, whether they came to law school with their quick wit and analytical skills or not. Women who go into highly competitive fields, be it law, journalism, politics, or investment banking, *have* to be highly ambitious and assertive—in addition to being highly intelligent and talented. Perhaps those daunted by the prospect should choose other professions.

Even more than in private life, an abundance of "relational" traits can actually be quite destructive in the corporate world. Oversensitivity, indecisiveness, passivity, timidity—all do little for a woman, whether she's a CEO or a nurse. Indeed, it would be far better if women didn't apologize as much as they do, if they didn't feel crushed by criticism, if they didn't downplay their authority or accomplishments, if they would learn how to brag, to bullshit. There's a reason men have retained their ability to be well in control of their emotions: such control is a great source of power.

It's also far from apparent that an office run on a "web of relationships" would be any more fair, just, or productive than one run on competence and objective criteria. The word favoritism comes immediately to mind. A writer friend who deals with numerous feminist groups calls their typically nonhierarchical organizational style "feminist collective disease"—nothing ever gets done. Worse, women in overly cohesive environments, such as on Capitol Hill or in corporations in Japan, find it far more difficult to report sexual harassment or discrimination.

Of course, women who adopt the male persona too well are often treated to lovely labels like "bitch." Streisand has been called a bitch, and so have Hillary Clinton and Ruth Ginsburg (to which the justice reportedly responded, "Better bitch than mouse"). Some women with power really are bitches, just as some men with power are arrogant bastards. And there's no reason anyone should refrain from saying so. Yet it is precisely because female strength is still confused with female nastiness that these issues have to be negotiated by women on their own terms, at their own speed. The task of feminism is to make women into neither bitches nor mice, but self-defined human beings.[23]

I V

If there's nothing inherently unfeminist about a woman who wants to build casinos or own a football team, there is also nothing inherently unfeminist—or unwomanly—about being a Republican, a libertarian, a National Rifle Association member, a Zen Buddhist. Feminism is the ideal of equal rights and opportunities for women. Only if a person doesn't believe that women deserve those rights and opportunities (including, I would argue, the right to an abortion) can she or he legitimately be called unfeminist. How women achieve their rights and opportunities is open to debate, and what they do with them afterward is a matter of personal choice. Women, like men, come in different ideological stripes.

What is unfeminist—quite sexist in fact—is making assumptions about women's political views, contending even implicitly that all women have the same opinions. In 1990, the National Organization for Women tried to organize a "women's party," as though all women would agree with every specific plank in the thirty-nine-page platform (for example, "Establishment of a full-employment economy with a guaranteed annual income provision"). Even after the 1994 elections, when nearly half of women voted Republican, NOW and other groups embarked on a "Fight the Right" campaign to try to canvas the supposed "women's vote."[24]

There's nothing wrong, of course, with trying to get women to vote or trying to get women to vote for liberal politicians. The problem arises when feminist activists aren't up front about this and when they talk as though all women are as leftist as they are—and if they're not, it's only because of socialization, a domineering husband, or "backlash" messages from the media.

No doubt some women still find it easier to yield to the political views of their fathers and husbands than to make up their minds independently (though no one knows what levers they ultimately push behind the curtain). But I think at this point we should assume that most women are making their own political decisions. According to surveys, female voters do tend to support a slightly greater role for government in domestic affairs and a slightly lesser role for the military, which has meant that since 1980 they have tended to vote Democratic. And in 1996, women gave President Clinton the largest gender gap in the nation's history—45 percent voted for Clinton, 37 percent for Bob Dole. But that hardly translates into a "women's political voice." Moreover, other demographic divisions, such as race, income, religion, and marital status, are of far greater relevance than gender. Most important, there is no correct feminist politics to which women must adhere in order to be "true feminists."[25]

Even those activists who really do want to elect "more women" and not "more leftist women" do women a disservice by focusing so assiduously on gender and not on competence. There is no question that female lawmakers—of both parties—have given greater priority to feminist and family-related issues than male lawmakers, and they may continue to do so. But that doesn't mean that women voters will—or should—like the solutions these lawmakers propose. And the fact is, a male politician may have a more rational solution to one of these problems than a female politician.

Moreover, gender-first political strategizing can undermine a woman's qualifications. "We'll come of age," said Jane Danowitz of the Women's Campaign Fund during the 1992 election, "when we realize that a mediocre woman is as good as a good man."[26]

The dilemmas are obvious and ridiculous. Is it better to vote for a pro-choice man or an anti-choice woman? Whom are you supposed to vote for in a two-woman race?

This last issue was played out in the 1992 New York Democratic Senate primary, when Elizabeth Holtzman, Geraldine Ferraro, and Robert Abrams avidly competed. Holtzman was subsequently skewered by some members of the feminist establishment for daring to engage in (fairly legitimate) negative advertising against Ferraro, most likely costing both of them the primary to Abrams. Not only was Holtzman—as a woman—not supposed to say nasty things, but she was especially not supposed to say them about a "sister." According to the *New York Times*, Letty Cottin Pogrebin, a founder of *Ms.*, accused Holtzman of "betraying" feminist goals by trying to beat Ferraro.[27]

There is every reason to believe that the number of women in Congress, state legislatures, and the judiciary will continue to grow: the number of women who run for office and win has increased steadily each election year. But if women never reach 51 percent parity because enough qualified female candidates aren't choosing to run, feminism won't be undermined and women won't (necessarily) be ill served.

The same applies to women writing political commentary. Women should be given space or airtime because they have something interesting to say, not because they're women. Incompetent women in any profession hardly promote the cause of equality, and they certainly don't inspire as role models. It's obvious to anyone who has ever worked at a political publication (including me) that the reason women journalists and pundits write more about "softer" social issues than hard political analysis has far more to do with personal preference than with discrimination. This may change or it may not. Either way, it's hardly earth-shattering.

Gender-first feminism has also created such a hypersensitive atmosphere that it often seems as though any (liberal) woman who has been criticized or victimized in some way is considered a heroine, and the perpetrator is automatically denounced as sexist. The coronation of Anita Hill probably represented the pinnacle of this perverse paternalism. All commentary suggesting that Hill had no business making her accusations ten years after the alleged events, especially after following Clarence Thomas to another job, were summarily dismissed as "backlash"—even though polls showed that the majority of women believed this.[28]

A paternalistic stance is especially unfortunate when it comes to possible ethical transgressions. Achievement of true equality, of course, requires that women must be held to the same standard of ethics to which we hold men. But when politicians like Carol Moseley Braun are charged with wrongdoing, the accusations are nearly stifled by counteraccusations of sexism and (in her case) racism.

Perhaps the woman who has most skillfully deployed the "backlash" defense has been Hillary Rodham Clinton. To avoid answering questions concerning her involvement in the Whitewater fiasco, Clinton has continually attributed her media attention to antifeminism: "Having been independent, having made decisions, it's a little difficult for us as a country, maybe, to make the transition of having a woman . . . sitting in this house." The backlash defense has also been deployed whenever questions have arisen concerning her self-invented role as First Lady. People who raise these questions, wrote Katha Pollitt, are "no great fan of real feminists": the men doing the criticizing "fear for their jobs"; the women are simply "jealous."[29]

No matter what the truth behind various charges and criticism, women both in and out of the media glare have to be able to take the heat. Hillary Clinton would have been a far better role model for women if she had actually practiced feminism—by standing up to her accusers and answering their charges—instead of cynically using feminism as a defense.

Part of the reason women often get away with inferior scrutiny of their behavior is that they are still perceived as being morally superior to men. Ironically, in recent years various female candidates have tried to profit from this sexist stereotype. The message from these candidates was not (or not just) "Vote for me because I'm a woman and therefore more politically correct." It was "Vote for me because I am a woman and therefore more honest." Other female candidates have tried to exploit the entire "superiority" package, asserting that they are more compassionate and pacific and therefore better able to deal with those homey, domestic concerns—health, education, and welfare.

The fact that this strategy could prove counterproductive in the long term appears to have eluded them. If female politicians excel in domestic policy issues, does that mean they're naturally not so good at foreign policy? And wouldn't this strategy also mean that there might be other traits—say, strength, resolve, rationality, logic—that are not particularly common to female politicians? These traits are usually considered important for presidents. How will innately pacific politicians be able to defend a woman's right to serve in combat, let alone lead the country into war? Pollsters already say that voters generally find it easier to vote for a woman for a legislative job like senator than for an executive post like governor.

Women politicians may very well turn out to be less inclined to initiate force, as women in general tend to be far less violent than men. On the other hand, most of the women who have ever had the opportunity to lead a country—from Golda Meir to Indira Gandhi to Margaret Thatcher—have been just as, if not more than, ready to resort to force.

The gender-first strategy illuminates again the conundrum of viewing women as both equal and different. While the solution may be a generation away, we can begin by keeping the emphasis, as much as possible, on each woman's individuality. If a female politician believes that she personally is more compassionate and pacific than her opponent, she should say so. Attributing those traits to her biology undermines not only her own unique qualifications but the individuality of every other woman.

V

If liberal feminism holds that the corporate world must focus primarily on merit, not gender, what are women supposed to do with their sexuality, their womanliness, at the office?

During the seventies, many women tried to deal with this question by, essentially, neutering themselves—wearing androgy-

nous power suits, speaking in affectless tones, eschewing all potentially flirtatious mannerisms. During the eighties, many women decided that this forced androgyny was no longer necessary,
showing, in my opinion, that they finally were beginning to feel
confident enough to reveal (within reason) the fact that they are
women.

But the problem itself has hardly gone away. In fact, as
women continue to wear more body-enhancing clothes to work as
well as move up the ranks, it has probably become more pronounced. What, exactly, should be the parameters of a woman's
sexuality at the office? To what extent should she engage in sexually tinged banter? Should she have a fling with a colleague? a
client? her boss?

There are no correct "feminist" answers to any of these questions. Although we're talking about the public sphere, these are
personal, not political, issues, which each woman has to figure out
on her own. Unfortunately, sexual harassment laws and policies,
rooted in the extreme theories of feminist legal scholar Catharine
MacKinnon and others, are increasingly undermining the ability of
women to do so. Sexual harassment law was originally confined to
"quid pro quo" harassment: a boss demanding that an employee
sleep with him (or her) in exchange for a job, a promotion, a raise.
In the 1986 case *Meritor Savings Bank v. Vinson*, the Supreme Court
ruled that an employer could also be found liable for sexual harassment if his (or her) office promoted a "hostile environment," conduct "sufficiently severe or pervasive to alter the conditions of [the
victim's] employment and create an abusive working environment."
The Court also found that "voluntariness," in the sense of consent,
is not a defense against a sexual harassment charge.[30]

Since then, courts as well as university and corporate policies
have continually broadened the hostile environment test to include
anything that makes a woman "uncomfortable" about sexual issues;
pinup calendars, dirty jokes, flirting, compliments—all have been
found to be sexually harassing. Fearing liability, employers have

begun to discourage consensual sexual relations in the office, especially between (male) supervisors and (female) assistants, and universities have done the same between professors and students.[31]

The numerous problems with these laws and policies have been exhaustively discussed by now. They encroach upon the rights, especially the (admittedly nebulous) right of privacy, of both women and men. They unnecessarily create a sterile, oppressive atmosphere. They treat women like children who have trouble knowing and communicating what they want, who can't fully take care of themselves. They also turn women into overly sensitive, prudish victims—just as the old obscenity laws had, which is why feminists worked so hard to abolish them during the seventies. Indeed, courts are increasingly using something called the "reasonable woman" standard to try sexual harassment cases; this standard assumes that women and men have different "perspectives" regarding various behaviors. As one court put it, "conduct that many men consider unobjectionable may offend many women. . . . The sexblind reasonable person standard tends to be male-biased and tends to systematically ignore the experiences of women."[32]

This conception of sexual harassment suffers from another problem as well. It views women's sexuality as a weakness, as something that can cause women harm, as something that has to be hidden and controlled. It also assumes women don't have much in the way of sexual desires of their own and would never use their sexuality for professional gain.

Well, the fact is, women do have sexualities, and often assertive and strategic ones as well. As a result, sexual tension is as much a part of any office environment as professional jealousy. Has been, always will be. And along with sexual tension comes flirtation—compliments, teasing, innuendo—from both men and women. No doubt flirtation can escalate into sexual harassment. But on its face, it hardly promotes a "hostile environment." Indeed, most people—women and men—probably think this kind of interaction makes many offices bearable, especially since the office is often their primary social venue.

I've heard women, married and single, who work in all-female offices complain that they miss male sexual attention. This is nothing to be embarrassed about. Women's need to attract and be attracted to men doesn't stop at the office door. Indeed, women admire men's minds and lust after their bodies in the office as well as out; there's no reason men can't do the same. The problem is not sexual banter, but unwanted and egregious sexual banter.

There are also going to be office romances whether they are banned or not—and many of these are going to be initiated by women. Ironically, the "consent" theories of Catharine MacKinnon and others don't allow for this type of sexual agency. According to MacKinnon, a woman can't truly consent to sex in a patriarchal society because of an inherent "imbalance of power" in heterosexual relationships.[33]

Well, it is no doubt true that *some* women sleep with their bosses or colleagues because they aren't strong enough to say no, because they fear they'll be fired, because they don't know the law, because they don't know that they don't have to. And these are the women that feminist activists need to find and help. But that is no reason to disparage the lucidity or will of every other woman who works.

In fact, to have any sort of objective discussion about sex at the office, we need to acknowledge that some women readily accept the most venal form of sexual harassment—sleep with me if you want a job, a promotion, a raise—in order to further their careers. Moreover, these women will probably always exist, no matter how feminist society becomes. Sex can be a great and quick leveler for women; just as some will probably always sell their bodies for money, others will do so for power. We might not like this, and we might try to minimize the situations that lead women to think this is their only option, but women have as much of a right to do this as to, say, feed the homeless.

What women don't have a right to do is use sex strategically and then, when the relationship sours, claim sexual harassment. This is what appears to have happened a few years ago in a well-publicized case in Philadelphia, where the murkiness of the Supreme Court's ruling in the *Vinson* case enabled the woman not only to sue but actually to win the suit. Kathleen Frederick, a forty-year-old former associate at a top-drawer law firm, accused Richard Glanton, a high-powered senior partner, of promising to help her troubled career in return for sex. Frederick claimed she had sex with Glanton three times. "I was trying to preserve my job," she explained. "I realized I had been basically forced to prostitute myself to save my job and career."[34]

When she finally broke off the alleged affair, she said he no longer referred work to her, her performance suffered, and she was ultimately fired, three months later. Glanton, meanwhile, denied ever touching her, and the firm said she was fired for incompetency and "bizarre" behavior (including making anonymous calls to the husband of another associate, telling him his wife was cheating on him).[35]

The jury issued a confused verdict, finding Glanton guilty of harassment but saying that it wasn't quid pro quo: the firing did not stem from the ending of the alleged affair. (The jury also rejected Frederick's husband's contention that he was entitled to damages for loss of his wife's companionship during the affair.)[36]

The verdict isn't surprising, though, given the murky nature of the law. In *Vinson*, the Supreme Court decided that the standard was the *ultimate* unwelcomeness of the harassment, not the victim's immediate reaction. Just as a woman can sleep with a date and cry rape the next morning, the Court appeared to be saying, a woman could sleep with her boss and cry sexual harassment the next business day. What the court should have done is draw a clear distinction between consenting to sex when there is an explicit threat to your job (quid pro quo) and consenting to sex when there isn't. Glanton may have promised to help Frederick's career in exchange for sex, but he didn't threaten to fire her, demote her, or decrease her salary—and there is a big difference.

Complicity on the part of some women in no way excuses the inability of some men to distinguish between those who crave their sexual charms and those who don't. Rather, it means that sex between *willing* partners—no matter the circumstances—is a private matter and should be kept that way.

The questions that concern most women, though, involve not sex itself, but things that stop just short of sex. I'm not talking here about the most innocent forms of flirting—smiling, laughing, and teasing. I'm referring to, say, an account executive at an ad agency who tends to look at her clients seductively, touching their arm when she laughs, making suggestive comments about their body or hers. She has no intention of sleeping with any one of them. And she happens to be, in fact, one of the most talented young people in advertising today. Shouldn't she stop this kind of behavior?

Well, again, theoretically yes. Feminism has offered women the ability to be judged on their competence, not their feminine wiles. But we don't live in a theoretical world. We live in a world where one rarely gets anything on merit alone. Some level of manipulation is implicit in all business relations—in all relations period. Is it worse to trade on your ability to toss off double entendres than on your ability to collect high-powered friends?

Moreover, we can't get around the fact that a woman's sexuality is far more valuable in the world of interpersonal relations than a man's. To be sure, many men use their good looks, charm, and charisma to great advantage in the workplace. Some of these men are also smart and talented; others are not. Yet the situations are not parallel. I don't mean to suggest that *all* men are going to be receptive to female seduction. But I don't think it would be too gross a generalization to suggest that more men—married or single—than women would be. It's a rare (heterosexual) man who doesn't pay more attention to an attractive, openly sexual woman than to an unattractive one.

If we accept that women other than prostitutes have sexualities at work and that some level of sexual manipulation is going to be a part of all business transactions, we seem to be left with the question: to what degree should women exploit their sexuality? I'd like to say that women should neither use it nor hide it. But I'm not sure how utopian that is. I guess it really comes down to an issue of integrity, of self-respect, of being, essentially, able to live with oneself. It may, in one sense, be quite *rational* for that lobbyist in leopard skin to rub her breasts against the congressman du jour: she gets the job done quite efficiently. But does she like the person she has become?

The question also involves viewing one's sexuality as a strength, not a weakness. Contrast, for instance, Sharon Stone's use of her femininity in *Basic Instinct* with, say, the sugary sweet, innocent helplessness we typically associate with the Southern belle. Or with women who pull out their little girl, damsel in distress personas whenever something bad happens or they need to get something. Or with women who are, consciously or not, so uncomfortable with their sexuality that they try to erase it through eating too much or too little. Compared with any of these, I'd rather see women who are at home in their bodies, who understand the power of sexual tension, who would rather use it to their advantage than have it used against them, who have no intention of either being— or playing—a victim.

Feminists are right to argue that sexual harassment is more often about power than sex; the intention is to intimidate and bully, and it can be quite successful. Women who flirt aggressively are playing off of the inherent weakness of sexual desire. Their sexuality becomes a power as (potentially) strong as sexual harassment. I'm not saying this is an appropriate way to conduct one's life, but women should certainly be aware of their options.

The lines between sexuality as weakness and sexuality as strength are not, of course, easy to draw. No doubt some women deploy their charms, as Molly Haskell wrote, "less to advance a career than to allay the fears of men. . . . A certain kind of flirtatiousness becomes a form of dissembling, a mask to hide one's brains and ambitions." Many men in the corporate and political worlds demand high levels of feminine solicitude, responding only to women who first provide sufficient verbal stroking.[37]

Nevertheless, most women, I would imagine, know when

they're acting like little girls and not women—just as they know when they're placing more emphasis on their swiveling hips than on their competence. And this is a good thing, because, again, there can never be a feminist rule book entitled "How Women Should Use Their Sexuality Responsibly in the Public Sphere."

More important, there can never be a rule book written by the government or any other authority telling women (or men) how they should conduct themselves. Politicizing (real) sexual harassment has, in general, done a world of good in sensitizing men (and women) to a problem that was previously either dismissed or mocked. But in the name of feminism, many feminists have successfully promoted policies and legal reforms that undermine women's freedom and privacy. Some of these same feminists have been very good at coining such pro-choice bumper stickers as "Keep your laws off my body." If only they fully understood the implications.

V I

If the term "political power" assumes that all women have the same values, and "professional power" assumes that all women have the same goals, it seems that the only power that can legitimately be discussed is personal power, the ability to make choices that satisfy one's yearnings.

Personal power has a far better name—"autonomy," a word that was often used during the early days of the Second Wave. But as the feminist emphasis has increasingly shifted to the "patriarchy" and away from women themselves, the word has nearly lost its relevance in feminist discussion.

Autonomy means the capacity for self-direction and self-regulation. As it happens, some psychologists now consider autonomy and self-esteem to be essentially inseparable. An autonomous woman is not waiting to be rescued, by a man, a job, or a certain number of seats in Congress. Her primary source of approval resides within herself—no matter what she decides to do with her life.

With the basic rights of feminism acquired, the opportunities nearly completely open, and the playing field closer to being level, most women, I believe, are finally ready to work on achieving autonomy. Yes, huge systemic barriers still inhibit the freedom of many women, and government and the corporate world need to continue to work on solving the problems created by both sexism and equality. But we need to keep in mind that there are also systemic barriers that inhibit the freedom of many men. And there probably always will be. Many of these barriers are far more a problem of socioeconomic class than of gender.

Unfortunately, like self-respect and (at least in theory) seats in Congress, autonomy can't be granted or bestowed. It must be earned. Becoming fully autonomous, achieving personal power, may prove in the end to be harder than achieving any other aspect of feminism. Because, of course, women are only human.

Seven

◆

SISTERHOOD

I

SOME TIME AGO, I had a friend I'll call Nena. Tall and thin with cool retro glasses, Nena lived in my then-boyfriend's group apartment. The three of us would hang out a lot; Nena and I would frequently indulge in a mutual fetish for obscure vegetarian cafés. When I would complain about the lack of romance in my relationship, she would spout antipatriarchal proverbs at me: men were to be used and discarded at will, she'd tell me; don't let them interfere with the greater feminist fight.

One day my boyfriend and I decided we should each see other people. The next day he told me that one of his other people was going to be Nena. What a coincidence. Especially marvelous were Nena's apparent professions of long-standing love for my former lover. Clearly, I had missed something significant in Nena's lectures. Men are the enemy—until you fall in love with one. And then the enemy becomes any woman who gets in the way.

Since then, I've been far more alert to women who treat other women with less than sisterly affection. And while Nena may have been more hypocritical than most, she seems to have plenty of company. A bright, beautiful art historian I know ignores or mocks her female friends whenever men are around. A successful editor continually belittles the work of other women in her field. A stunning, superbly talented dancer who can have her pick of men chooses the husband of her far less attractive best friend. A high-powered law partner never invites her firm's other female attorneys to any networking functions.

If sisterhood hasn't transformed women in their personal lives, it hasn't had much more success in the political arena. Less than a third of all women call themselves feminists and feel part of a self-consciously unified "women's movement." Critiques of "orthodox" feminism have permanently shattered the illusion that all feminists—let alone all women—speak in the same voice. Women don't tend to vote a narrow "women's" agenda, and they don't vote for candidates just because they are female.[1]

Even among women who call themselves feminists, the notion of an all-embracing sisterhood has lost some of its appeal. Many have complained that the concept ignores essential differences in race, class, age, ability, and sexual preference. Indeed, while most feminist writers and activists still stress a common political agenda, younger feminists in particular now subdivide themselves along increasingly idiosyncratic lines—a bulimic Asian bisexual, an alcoholic, Catholic single mother, and so on.

This is not the way it was supposed to be. The ideal of sisterhood, of a unique solidarity among women, was supposed to transcend all cultural differences and unite women against a common enemy—patriarchal society. As women's collective consciousness rose and the pillars of patriarchy began to fall, this public female bonding was supposed to pervade women's personal lives as well. Women were to begin to see men, not other women, as the source of their problems, and all vestiges of female competition, jealousy, and backstabbing were soon supposed to vanish.

The fact that women were never able to achieve a pure political or personal sisterhood is not a great surprise to scientists who have studied other female primates. It's also not a great loss.

There was, of course, a great need for women to consciously band together throughout the past century and a half. Without both the First and Second Waves of feminist activism, women would never have gained their essential rights and opportunities, and the revolutionary changes in relations between the sexes would never have occurred. Moreover, some type of organized feminism continues to be necessary, both to push for the legal reforms that are still needed and to guard the gains that have been made. There will probably always be a need for feminist activists to establish battered women's shelters and rape crisis centers, to help organize women against employers who discriminate, and to raise women's consciousness about their rights, both personal and political.

Yet the idea of a rigid political sisterhood—of a "women's movement" with a distinct ideological agenda—has become not only anachronistic but counterproductive. Again, women do not represent a homogenous political class; they are individuals with their own beliefs, opinions, and values. Moreover, the women's movement of the 1990s is especially counterproductive: its theorists and activists are stuck in an ideological rut, scrutinizing every aspect of a woman's life with a preconceived political formula and prescribing ready-made political solutions. Yes, men are often the source of women's problems. But they're also often the source of the solutions to those problems—sharing housework, ending discrimination and harassment, paying child support. The effort now should be not to alienate men, but to get men to see that a fully feminist society is in their best interests as well.

Also undermining the individuality of women is the concept

of a personal sisterhood, the theory that women should feel "at one" not only with their female friends and family members, but with every other woman on earth. Female friendship is not automatic. Even with their real friends, women need to be careful not to let intimacy stifle autonomy.

Women don't "owe" other women anything more than a respectful appraisal of their characters. Artificial sisterhood is not only a crock, as Nena demonstrated. It is also not especially empowering.

I I

In *The Women*, Clare Boothe Luce's 1936 satire on women who lunch, five thirtysomething women spend their days gossiping, sniping, conniving, and backstabbing—all under the guise of caring for one another. While the play has been criticized as overtly misogynistic, it did capture the stereotype of the time: all women secretly hate each other.

Forty years later, in the early seventies, that stereotype still reigned, and feminist theorists were blaming it on sexism. By forcing women to compete for male approval in order to survive, many theorists believed, the patriarchy created hostility and jealousy between women. It was a political necessity, therefore, for women to bond intimately with each other, and a political faux pas to create any sort of tension with another woman. All competition between women for men—or even jobs—was considered unsisterly.

In the late seventies, more "relational" feminists added their own twist to this theory. Not only *should* all women like one another, but they already do. Women can't help but be empathetic and connected, especially to other women. Competition between women (and between women and men) is thus unwomanly.

Twenty years later, has feminism changed the way women relate to one another? Well, women still break dates with women to go out with men. But they often seem extremely embarrassed about it, sometimes even asking the other woman for permission. And women still gossip about other women. But gratuitous cattiness is often noted if not frowned upon. Time spent with female friends doing other things besides talking about men, looking for men, and shopping (to look good for men) is no longer automatically viewed as wasted. And it's getting to be something of a cliché that women return from social functions saying the only people worth talking to were the other women.

Yet women don't seem to have developed a natural affinity for all of womankind. Indeed, women size each other up just as men size each other up, and they're now competing not only for men, but also for top-draw salaries, wardrobes, and country houses.

Feminist theorists now tend to blame romantic competition between women on the fact that they are still socialized to "need" male attention, and professional competition on the fact that it's still a "man's world": there are so few spots for women; the journey is so difficult, etc., etc. "Career women intent on beating the competition are disinclined to let sisterhood stand in their way," says Ellen Willis. They note with dismay the irony of feminism allowing women the ability not only to work but to compete with each other more mercilessly than ever.[2]

An arduous professional struggle has undoubtedly played a role in the way many women today deal with female competition. It's difficult not to feel hints of jealousy or resentment when a young upstart seems to be following the same career path with much less effort or strain. It's often even more difficult to find the motivation to help her out.

Nevertheless, feminism hardly seems capable of wiping out competition between women—nor would we want it to. First of all, female competition may be quite natural. According to research by anthropologist Sarah Blaffer Hrdy, other female primates do bond, "but they do so imperfectly or incompletely. They cooperate self-ishly, and there is a perpetual undercurrent of competition."[3]

Moreover, men are necessary for reproduction, and competition for the best man is as much a matter of insuring women's genetic legacy as it is a matter of self-preservation. And now that most women want and need jobs as much as they want and need men, it makes perfect sense that women wouldn't spend too much time considering the sex of their rivals. Indeed, this was part of the goal of feminism. Perhaps most important, competition can push a woman to do her best work, which is not a bad way to build real self-respect.

However. There's a huge difference between healthy competition for men and jobs, and sniping, scheming, and backstabbing; between trying to look and do your best and betraying your best friend.

No doubt some of the ugly sort of competitive behavior still stems from traditional feminine socialization. While men are able to do very active things to compete for women—score a touchdown, get a good job, display a sense of humor—women are still often most rewarded for putting their energies into making themselves beautiful. There's a lot of energy left over for trying to destroy the competition, and historically the only means allowed have been underhanded.

Socialization and lack of formal power, though, may not be entirely to blame for even this. Hrdy found that the primary mode of competition among other female primates is indirect—ignoring another mother's infant in their care, for example, or subtly pressuring a lower-ranking female away from a succulent lobelia plant.[4]

Nevertheless, at this point I think we can fairly assert that the type of malicious manipulative behavior that Clare Boothe Luce satirized in her play, the less than admirable antics that would often in the past have been excused as "typically female," are less a product of patriarchy or biology than they are of individual personality.

Various writers have tried to get at the sources of this behavioral quirk by drawing a broad distinction between a "woman's woman" and a "man's woman." In an insightful essay on female friendship in *Esquire*, Elizabeth Kaye writes that women's women "seek sustenance from other women," whereas men's women "seek sustenance from men." The former you can trust absolutely; the latter, never.[5]

However, as Kaye herself argues, most women are a combination of the two, so this doesn't seem to be a particularly helpful way of arranging the problem. Nor does simply saying that women who see every other woman as a threat, who can't feel genuine happiness at the success of another woman, are insecure. All women (and men) are insecure. But some women keep their insecurities to themselves, while others allow their insecurities to make them bitter or vindictive.

Kaye observes that negative competition between women has less to do with who is prettier or more successful in general than with individual turf wars. "Most women, accustomed to playing roles, reflexively assign roles to other women, so that one is touted as the wisest and another as most attractive and another as wittiest," writes Kaye. It's hard for a woman to feel "genuine warmth for any women who might be contesting for the same prize." But, again, women can feel envy and not act on it.

In the end, there will probably always be malicious women who backstab, just as there will always be malicious men who backstab. Which is why women shouldn't have higher expectations of other women just because they're female. Women should have higher expectations of their friends, female or not.

What's completely unhelpful is imposing upon women an artificial sisterhood, a forced bonding based on weakness, not strength. In the wake of feminism, an anti-male "contract of female solidarity," as Kate Fillion puts it, seems to have developed among many women. This contract typically carries "an implicit pledge to remain equal and remain the same": sameness provides security. Many women, writes Fillion in *Lip Service*, "fear that if we achieve more or have more than other women, we will lose our connections with them."[6]

A fear of difference also arises out of the intense intimacy that characterizes female friendships. While men's bonding often depends on shared activities, women's typically depends on shared secrets. Women tell each other the most intimate details of their lives, from daily weight fluctuations to boyfriends' aptitude in bed. Astonished by the lack of intimacy in male friendships, women often say that they can invariably get more information out of a man in an hour than his best male friend would in a lifetime.

But intense intimacy can also be suffocating, stifling growth and achievement. In the film *Walking and Talking*, the central character becomes deeply despondent over the news of her best friend's engagement. "You used to need me," she tells her, betraying the unhealthy depth of her own dependency.

Out of fear of losing a connection, women often find themselves apologizing for their success. Instead of proudly talking about their triumphs, they emphasize their shortcomings and failures, practicing what Deborah Tannen and other sociolinguists call "downward competition." Women put themselves down not only to make other women feel better about themselves, but also to win the prize of "most downtrodden." A comment such as "I have gained so much weight" is typically followed by "Oh, you look great, but look at *my* thighs!" This is intimacy by complaint, and, amazingly, it works: women walk away feeling better about themselves and their relations with one another. But, as Fillion points out, this type of intimacy also prevents women from telling one another the truth, a truth that can often be of great use. " 'Judge not' is an unwritten commandment of female friendships," Fillion writes.[7]

Bonding based on weakness also promotes the habit of talking about problems instead of trying to solve them. "Women's expressive style," writes Carol Tavris in *The Mismeasure of Woman*, "leads many women to rehearse their problems and constantly brood about them, rather than learning to distract themselves or take action to solve them. Some women come to believe that talking *is* doing something about the problem, and that talking is enough." Perhaps the biggest waste of time are conversations devoted exclusively to psychoanalyzing men. By the time many women reach their mid-twenties, they have become experts at deconstructing a man's moods, behavior, and habits of speech (or, often, the lack thereof).[8]

Clearly, some of our friendships could use a few more "masculine" elements—sharing activities; talking about anything other than emotional traumas; learning to view disagreement as natural, not personal betrayal. Of course, if women (on average) continue to be more empathetic than men, their relationships with one another may always be based primarily on verbal connection. But overconnection can be just as harmful as underconnection. Bonding based on strength, however, would energize and challenge women to do their best. Female friends should be cheering each other on, supporting all goals and dreams, no matter how fanciful.

The contract of female solidarity, in other words, is not only no longer necessary, it has become quite harmful. Men (as a group) are not the enemy, and women are not always friends. Choice in friendship is as important as choice in everything else in a woman's life. And the fact is, a male friend can be a far better choice than a female friend who is resentful, overly dependent, or self-absorbed, let alone malicious and vindictive.

I I I

Sisterhood has been no more powerful in the political realm than it has been in the world of personal relationships. Women don't vote as a bloc, and have been only slightly more likely than men to vote for women candidates. While the vast majority of women (and men) believe that women deserve the same rights and opportunities as men, most feel alienated from the "women's movement," from the feminist theorists and activists who claim to speak for women and for feminism.[9]

Feminist theorists and activists, meanwhile, tend to blame this state of affairs on sexist socialization and the media, which, they claim, blatantly distorts everything about the movement. Well, it's no doubt true that most women get their ideas about feminism and the women's movement from the media and that the media tend to focus on the movement's most radical "leaders" and ideas (in part because that's what sells). But it's also true that in the past couple of decades the media haven't had to work very hard to find such extremism. Such theories as all sex is rape (Catharine MacKinnon and Andrea Dworkin), dieting is a political conspiracy (Naomi Wolf), women are forced to be heterosexual (Adrienne Rich), and fashion designers seek to disempower women (Susan Faludi) have been presented as mainstream feminism, and until recently no "insider" feminist tried to change this impression.

Of course, all political movements have their radical wings, and they can be quite useful in continually pushing for greater and greater reforms. A century and a half ago, the notion of giving women the vote was considered completely far-fetched, and just fifty years ago the idea of a female Supreme Court justice was in the realm of fantasy. The problem is not radical ideas but radical ideas presented as orthodoxy—you must accept these views or you are not a feminist—and the absence of more realistic alternatives. Indeed, at this point women are in far greater need of realistic and practical advice than of (ostensibly) utopian theories—*Working Woman*, not *Ms.*

Even now that the idea of feminism as a particular brand of politics has been deflated by Betty Friedan, Camille Paglia, and others, many feminists still refuse to accept the need for diverse views. A cover of *Ms.* magazine retorts, "No, Feminists *Don't* All Think Alike," and Gloria Steinem, bell hooks, Naomi Wolf, and Urvashi Vaid smile at us multiculturally. But inside they prove precisely the opposite. They all agree on what they assume are the basics of feminism: that an all-encompassing "patriarchy" continues to "oppress" women; that a "left, revolutionary movement" is needed to promote resistance and struggle; that men, capitalism, and Western culture are responsible for women's problems.[10]

In her book *Fire with Fire: The New Female Power and How It Will Change the Twenty-First Century*, Naomi Wolf makes another inconsistent attempt at disavowing the sisterhood model of feminism. Wolf writes, correctly, that "we are too diverse, our numbers too great and our relationships with one another, properly, too complex and impersonal now for this model of female connectedness to do its job." Yet the main theme of her book is that women must seize "power" with a "concerted, unified effort." The questions of which women should do this (all women? leftist women?), why "diverse" women would want to unify to "seize" power, and what should be done with this "power" once it is seized (institute quotas? ban cosmetic surgery?) are left largely unaddressed.[11]

What's interesting, however, is that while feminism turned into an orthodoxy sometime in the seventies, I don't think there have been many orthodox feminists—women who actually bought the entire package. Until recently, it certainly seemed as though they all did because a code of silence prevailed: an exaggerated desire for public solidarity impeded feminists from disagreeing with each other, at least outside of obscure feminist journals.

For instance, although a debate over pornography has roiled the feminist community since the sixties and although it was hard to find a feminist who actually took MacKinnon and Dworkin seriously in private, until fairly recently it was even harder to find evidence of the pornography debate or feminist criticism of either Dworkin or MacKinnon in mainstream public venues.

Unfortunately, dissent is still largely ignored or dismissed as part of the so-called backlash. In another article in *Ms.*, Susan Faludi calls women (including myself) who have lamented the fact that feminism has turned into an orthodoxy "Pod Feminists," a term that apparently means we were planted by the right. No doubt this book will also be dismissed by some in the feminist community as "conservative," maybe even "sexist," because, among other things, I refuse to say that women in this country are oppressed, because I argue against quotas, and because I believe that research on biological differences between the sexes can be helpful to women. The fact that I am quite liberal and fully committed to feminist principles will be purposefully overlooked.[12]

On one level you can understand the desire of feminist activists to "fight sexism instead of each other," as it is often put, to circle the wagons. There is still very real opposition to feminist matters large and (relatively) small, from reproductive rights to the idea that men are capable of ironing.

But by squelching all internal dissent, feminist writers have not only alienated most women (not to mention men), they have allowed hyperbolic rhetoric, false statistics, politicized scholarship, reverse sexism, and general silliness free rein. In *Who Stole Feminism?* Christina Hoff Sommers deflates many of the exaggerated statistics that feminist writers have used continuously regarding anorexia, date rape, and domestic violence. For instance, 150,000 women do not die of anorexia each year, as Gloria Steinem, Naomi Wolf, and countless others have asserted; the number is somewhere between 50 and 100.[13]

In this atmosphere, it was hardly surprising to find several prominent feminist writers having to explain why their personal lives—their relations with certain types of men, their desire to wear makeup, count calories, and be lushly photographed—seemed to contradict their theories. It's not that these writers were (necessarily) hypocrites. It's that they were concocting theories for a world in which no one—not even they—would want to live.

Of course, a good deal of the irrationality of contemporary feminism—the attempts to politicize every aspect of a woman's life and the bizarre insistence that there has been no progress—also has something to do with the felt need to keep activist fires burning. "It is hard, over the long run, to sustain feminism's moral presuppositions and activist style unless new issues can be found around which to crusade," write Daphne Patai and Noretta Koertge in *Professing Feminism: Cautionary Tales from inside the Strange World of Women's Studies.*[14]

Patai and Koertge teach women's studies courses, where the orthodoxy and ideological policing have been strongest. The feminism espoused in the vast majority of programs, they write, "bids to be a totalizing scheme resting on a grand theory, one that is as all-inclusive as Marxism, as assured of its ability to unmask hidden

meanings as Freudian psychology, and as fervent in its condemnation of apostates as evangelical fundamentalism. . . . It offers a
prescription for radical change that is as simple as it is drastic:
reject whatever is tainted with patriarchy and replace it with something embodying gynocentric values."[15]

In a field where dissidents not only are ostracized but can
actually lose their jobs (Elizabeth Fox-Genovese says she stepped
down as chair of Emory's women's studies program because of complaints from students and faculty that she wasn't radical enough),
Professing Feminism is a brave attempt by "insiders" to expose a good
deal of dirty laundry. It would be nice to think that the book is now
being used in women's studies classes, though given the level of
intolerance the authors describe that seems unlikely. Patai and
Koertge also recount a well-devised separatism (the exclusion of
male authors from course syllabi and scholarly papers) and a deliberate politicization: courses are judged in terms of relevance to the
political agenda, pedagogy is "thinly disguised indoctrination," and
faculty are appointed based on their commitment to community
organizing, not on their academic credentials.[16]

Most disconcerting, write Patai and Koertge, is that "scholarship itself becomes suspect as faculty members feel constant pressure not to betray the cause." Some professors feel obligated to
present the work of all women scholars who call themselves feminists, no matter how questionable their methodology or conclusions. "Feminist theory guarantees that researchers will discover
male bias and oppression in every civilization and time," says Mary
Lefkowitz, a classics professor at Wellesley and author of *Not out of
Africa*. No distinction is often made between "historical interpretation of the past and political reinterpretation."[17]

Women's studies is actually something of a misnomer. Most of
the courses are designed not merely to study women, but also to
improve their lives, both the individual students' (the vast majority
of whom are female) and women's in general. A few years ago I
took my own mini-tour of the world of women's studies for *Mother
Jones* magazine, visiting programs at the University of California

(Berkeley), the University of Iowa, Dartmouth, and Smith. Although most of the classes I attended stopped short of outright advocacy of specific political positions, virtually all carried strong political undercurrents in the choice of texts, lecture topics, and the lack of discussion of divergent points of view.

Many women's studies professors acknowledge their field's bias, but point out that all disciplines are biased. Still, there's a huge difference between, as Patai puts it, "recognizing and minimizing deep biases and proclaiming and endorsing them. Do they really want fundamentalist studies, in which teachers are not just studying fundamentalism but supporting it?"[18]

Despite the womb-like atmosphere of most of the classrooms I encountered, I didn't see many students question their professors or the texts. This is particularly ironic, given the fact that teaching students to "think critically" is considered one of the primary goals of women's studies. In a 1991 study by the American Association of Colleges, 30 percent of students taking women's studies courses at Wellesley said they felt uneasy expressing unpopular opinions; only 14 percent of non–women's studies students felt that way.[19]

In a response to my *Mother Jones* article, Susan Faludi wrote that the "capacity to analyze the world in political terms . . . should probably be a requirement for college graduation." Fair enough. But are the "political terms" of Jesse Helms acceptable as well?[20]

What women's studies does succeed at teaching many students is the ability to see the world through "gender-colored glasses." Indeed, the unremitting emphasis on women as oppressed victims can be quite effective. After just a few days of my research, I found myself noticing that the sign on the women's bathroom door in the University of Iowa's library was smaller than the one on the men's room door. It is not at all surprising to find the classes filled with angry and whiny young women. This too of course is ironic. At the schools I visited at least, the women were overwhelmingly white and upper middle class; not only have they not come into contact with much real oppression, but they are the first generation of women who have grown up with nearly every option open to them.

Of course, there is plenty to get angry about. Rape, domestic violence, and discrimination in this country; female infanticide in China; bride burning in India; genital mutilation in Africa. But a generalized, diffuse anger directed at *all* men, at some amorphous patriarchy or at capitalism or Western culture, seems to achieve little more than alienation—of both women and men.

The whininess is also turning up in much of the new writing by twentysomething feminists. In the anthology *Listen Up: Voices from the Next Feminist Generation*, being overweight, having to earn a living, having to put up with a man asking you out repeatedly through e-mail, getting pregnant in high school—all are classified as op-pression. In a *New York Times* essay, Wendy Kaminer labels this "therapeutic feminism": the writers equate feeling bad, having a bad day, with being oppressed. They take little or no responsibility for either contributing to their woes or solving them. Unlike self-help books, therapeutic feminism is all about accepting yourself the way you are—even if the way you are is miserable—in order to coyly undermine the patriarchy.[21]

Not coincidentally, the broader result of this adversarial polit-ical sisterhood is quite similar to the effect of an adversarial per-sonal sisterhood. The heightened desire for sameness produces a rigid conformity of politics, manners, and dress; an effort to hide one's abilities and accomplishments ("The feminist notion of 'em-powerment' seems to result above all in the equal disempowerment of each by all," write Patai and Koertge); a tendency to whine about problems instead of taking responsibility for solving them; and an atmosphere in which the only competition allowed is for the title of most oppressed.[22]

This, too, is bonding based on weakness, and the unsurprising result is, again, underhanded competition—backbiting, personal betrayal, sniping, accusations, and seething resentment. According to Patai and Koertge, the women's studies community calls this "horizontal hostility" and blames it on a patriarchy that "has taught women to distrust each other and to look only to men for leadership." What seems more apparent is that even women in a sisterhood based on love can't be forced to love one another. And whenever sisterly affection is contrived, it can turn quite ugly.[23]

I V

In recent years, critics have been writing feminism off as useless, irrelevant, dead. But that too is counterproductive. First of all, feminism—in the apolitical sense of the term—is not useless, irrelevant, or dead. It is critical to women's lives. Moreover, many of the illiberal ideas emanating from feminist scholars are directly changing laws and policies, and a "feminist"-influenced pedagogy is beginning to pervade much of the academy.

What we need to do instead is to retire—with confidence and resolution—the notion of a "women's movement" with a single voice and a single agenda. Even better, we should just abolish the term. This would mean that there would be no feminist leaders, no feminist spokespeople, no singular feminist agenda, no unified feminist political program, no totalizing feminist ideology.

This has already begun to happen. Multiculturalism has spawned a plethora of divisions and subsets among feminists—we now have Native American feminists, gay feminists, Jewish feminists, biracial feminists, and so on. An essay in *Listen Up* begins (with no tongue in cheek): "As an educated, married, monogamous, feminist, Christian, African-American mother, I suffer from an acute case of multiplicity." Unfortunately, the emphasis on difference still often stops at politics. Most self-described feminists still seem to believe that there is one primary source of women's troubles (men) and one surefire way to solve them (government intervention).[24]

Nevertheless, this splintering is a hopeful sign, and it has precedence. At the end of the last century, women also turned away from a self-consciously unified movement, which at that time was called the Woman Movement. The Woman Movement had increasingly developed a very narrow conception of "woman"—domestic, virtuous, religious, and subservient—and a rather puritanical attitude toward things like obscenity.

In its place, women began to form primitive consciousness-raising groups. One of the more prominent was called Heterodoxy, whose only requirement was that its members not hold orthodox views. It was during this period that the word *feminism* was coined. "Feminism means that . . . [a woman] wants to push on to the finest, fullest, freest expression of herself," wrote Rose Young, a novelist and charter member of Heterodoxy. "She wants to be an individual."[25]

The need to again move away from any sort of monolithic women's movement in no way undermines the work that has been done. Indeed, it is only because of this work that the contemporary women's movement was able to outlive its usefulness. "Justice sometimes comes," writes Leon Wieseltier in a *New Republic* essay on identity politics. "And when it comes, it is sometimes bewildering, because it proposes peace to selves that have been arranged for war. The identity that altered history yesterday is redundant today."[26]

And what would the new political identity of feminism look like? Heterodoxy. Women would fight for causes they believe in, join groups they believe worthwhile, support candidates and colleagues they respect, read books and magazines they enjoy. No presumptions would be made about a woman's—a feminist's—opinions, values, or goals.

If one of women's basic rights—most obviously, the right to abortion—is in jeopardy, women would band together: it's not a coincidence that women have turned out for abortion marches and rallies in droves in the past couple of decades. But men too would fight to keep abortion legal. Surveys consistently show that men believe in the right to abortion just as much as women do. In fact, they believe in all of the basic rights of feminism just as much as women do. And that, after all, was the goal.[27]

It is no longer even useful to characterize an issue as either "feminist" or "women's." Rape is a violent crime. Discrimination, sexual harassment, and child care are work and family issues. Breast cancer is a health issue. Calling these issues "women's issues" implies that only women care about them and that only women can solve them—neither of which is true or helpful.

Perhaps most important, in a post–women's movement world, there would be real debate. While the attacks by Paglia and others have been successful at chipping away at the orthodoxy of feminism, they were less successful at bringing about healthy debate among women. Indeed, the critique of feminism has at times become just as exaggerated and simplistic as what was under attack.

The worst offender has often been Paglia herself, who has written, among other things, that rape is natural so women may as well lie back and enjoy it; that there could never be a female Mozart; and that men are superior to women because, among other things, they can urinate standing up. Other critics have claimed that women are just as violent as men; that academic feminists promote anti-male, anti-sex theories because they are "homely"; and that date rape basically doesn't exist.[28]

Much of this is celebrity feminism, in which facts and ideas seem to matter less than self-promotion. No doubt the media encourage this; hyperbole is always marketable. No doubt the media have also encouraged the celebrity feminist catfights that have ensued between, for instance, Naomi Wolf and Camille Paglia; Gloria Steinem and Sally Quinn; Susan Faludi and anyone who has ever said anything critical about feminism. This happens not because editors are (necessarily) sexist, but because they crave controversy and often have no use for rational, sober analysis. I was once told by a magazine editor to make a critical review of a play written by a woman "bitchier." I refused, and the review never ran. Nevertheless, it's up to women themselves to say: I don't do catfights. At the very least, we need to limit attacks to ideas, not other women.

What we could also truly benefit from is a revival of consciousness-raising groups. Feminist activists who organize such dubious events as "Take Back the Night" rallies or sit-ins in Grand

Central Station to advertise domestic violence may want to consider redirecting their energies into work that can directly help women—both those who know the basics of feminism and those who don't.

In some ways, the success of feminism has caused more of a need for these groups now than thirty years ago. In addition to the stress of dealing with jobs and housework and childrearing, there's the phenomenon of what Shelby Steele has called "integration shock," the shock of being "suddenly accountable on strictly personal terms." As Barbara Findlen writes in the introduction to *Listen Up*, "If there is a troublesome legacy from the feminism that has come before, it's the burden of high expectations—of both ourselves and the world."[29]

Consciousness-raising groups can help not only women who wrongly believe that they have too few choices but also those women who feel paralyzed by too many. The fact is, most of the problems of women today (in this country at least) are not merely "structural": women have a great deal of power to change their lives. But women have to understand the complex origins of those problems—whether it be biology, parental neglect, or sexism—to know how to begin the process.

Most important, women need to understand that any type of artificial sisterhood is the antithesis of self-development, of individuality. Women can't find their identity in other women or in some conveniently preassembled collection of opinions labeled "feminism" any more than they can try to find an identity in men, a job, or motherhood. Feminism offers women only the opportunity to have a real identity; discovering its components is up to each woman.

◆

A LIBERATED
WOMAN

W H E N I S T A R T E D to write this book, my focus was on reviving the quickly deteriorating concept of women as autonomous individuals. I was annoyed at how the victim-based theories set forth in books such as *Backlash*, *The Beauty Myth*, and *The War against Women* and the group-think mentality of many activists were (inadvertently) working to deny women of precisely what feminism had offered them: their strength, their uniqueness, their independence. The contemporary women's movement, which had set out to dismantle socially mandated gender roles, government intrusion into women's private lives, and special privileges for women, was now trying to establish the Politically Correct Woman, providing her with a ready-made set of opinions, values, behaviors, even clothes. Worse, theorists and activists were trying to induce government to protect this paradoxically ultrasensitive woman not just from violence, harassment, and discrimination, but also from flirting, competition, the media, and Kate Moss.

Pointing out all of the ways that feminist theorists and activists have been undermining the individuality of women would have certainly filled a volume (or three). But I soon began to realize that this wasn't enough. Although most of the political work was done, feminism had to have more to say to women than "You are now free. Have a nice life."

Indeed, even with egalitarian marriages and half-female law schools and a nearly closed pay gap, many women today don't feel or act all that autonomously. Women no longer need men to live, but many are still staying in bad relationships as though they do. Nearly every opportunity is open to women now, but many aren't taking full advantage because of a lack of confidence. Despite tough discrimination and sexual harassment laws, many women allow themselves to be exploited or abused at work because they are too timid to confront their bosses.

Yet most of the prominent feminist writers, with the notable exception of Gloria Steinem, have been too busy focusing on the ills of pornography or fashion shows or mascara commercials to notice that women's emotional development may not have kept pace with their political or economic progress. In the past couple of decades, feminists have essentially relegated the interior lives of women to self-help books and talk shows.

What also seemed increasingly apparent is that many writers have intentionally ignored a crucial aspect of being a woman: our biology. Yes, women are individuals. But we also share a reproductive system that often seems to have a will of its own. Indeed, many of the personal problems that women contend with—from premenstrual depression to an unpleasant reaction to casual sex to our obsessions with men, food, even beauty—are, to a greater or lesser extent, rooted in our biology.

The more I read the new research on psychological differences between the sexes, the more I realized that we are living in a particularly interesting moment. The social restrictions on women's roles have been lifted enough so that we can now begin to see which traditional behaviors are more rooted in biology and which in culture. Clearly, the fact that within thirty years women went from being perceived as universally passive and unambitious to acting as assertive and competitive as many men shows the strong influence of culture on these traits. At the same time, women's conduct in the romantic realm has changed less dramatically; indeed, many women who tried more assertive behaviors in this arena are now reverting back to those allowing more discretion.

In another thirty years, these patterns could look quite different; we don't really know. Many girls are still socialized to submit, to be "good," to believe that marriage is a woman's greatest achievement in life. Contrary to much of what was thought until the sixties, the behavior of women does not completely stem from nature. Yet what seems equally clear at this point is that, contrary to most feminist theorizing throughout the past thirty years, all behavior doesn't stem from nurture either.

In the end, though, biology—like culture—can be used only to help explain situations and problems. Neither can be used as an excuse. No matter what the nature/nurture balance turns out to be, women have to see themselves primarily as individuals with free will, able to make rational choices and (to some degree) able to control their lives.

So I started this book focusing on women's individuality and ended up seeing that women's individuality is actually quite complicated. Women are different from one another—no assumptions can be made about a woman's opinions, values, or goals. But women also share a biology that may lead them to many similar thoughts, feelings, and experiences. Just, in other words, like men.

In the private sphere, this equal-but-different approach seems to be fairly straightforward. Women may end up reverting to—or choosing—some of the more traditional behaviors and customs. As long as those behaviors and customs aren't self-destructive, as long as they are chosen from positions of strength, then, it seems to me, there's nothing unfeminist about engaging in them. It's the lipstick proviso: if women want to spend a fair amount of time on their appearance, if women want men to court them and be chivalrous, if women want to stay home part time with their toddlers—no one can say in good faith that these choices ipso facto undermine their autonomy.

In the public sphere, though, the equal-but-different approach seems more problematic. The corporate world isn't yet sophisticated enough to respect women's legal and social equality while allowing differences room to thrive: stereotypes still reign. As increasing numbers of women break these stereotypes, the situation should improve. Yet it may always be more difficult for women to combine an uninterrupted high-powered career with raising a brood of children. Feminism, unfortunately, can't reset our biological clocks, help us fall in love at a career-convenient time, or increase the number of hours in a day. We can, though, prod our companies to install on-site day care centers, prod our husbands to do their share of the housework and childrearing, and prod ourselves to recognize our limits.

I grew up trying to run as far and as quickly as possible from the lifestyle of my mother, in search of some mythical idea of a liberated woman. I'm glad (and, I know, she's glad) that I had the opportunity to run, to develop in ways that would never have been possible had I followed my mother's path.

But in the process of writing this book I've come to accept two things. One, a woman can be president of the United States and not be liberated if she has no integrity or internal source of strength; a woman can raise five children at home and iron her husband's boxers and still be liberated if she knows her mind and follows her dreams. In her way, on her terms, my mother has always been a liberated woman.

The second thing I've realized is that it was my mother's constant, unconditional love that allowed me to run. Being a good mother doesn't have to mean complete self-denial and selflessness.

My mother pleased herself by cherishing me. Whether only mothers can provide that level of connection, no one yet knows. Nor do we know what, exactly, it takes to develop that connection. But feminism will in the end mean very little if we try to avoid finding out.

Clearly, finishing off the feminist revolution, as well as our own personal evolutions, is not going to get any easier. There are still more questions than answers, and the answers we do have are not always pretty.

Women have finally been freed to do what they want with their lives—without precise guidelines, a statement of purpose, even a good role model or two. Feminism brought women to this point, but it can offer only minimal information on where to go from here. That we must each decide for ourselves.

Ultimately, how each woman deals with this responsibility is a testament to her feminist fortitude. It is not a coincidence that one of the last speeches Elizabeth Cady Stanton gave was on the essential autonomy of each human being. "The strongest reason for giving woman a complete emancipation from all forms of bondage, of custom, dependence, superstition . . . is the solitude and personal responsibility of her own individual life."[1]

Feminism is not a set of commands, but a set of challenges. It represents an ideal to which not only society, but women themselves, must aspire. There are no correct feminist behaviors, opinions, values; there is no consolidated sisterhood; no one liberated woman. There is, in the end, only liberation.

NOTES

PREFACE: THE LIPSTICK PROVISO

1. Kim France, "Feminism Amplified," *New York*, 3 June 1996, 36.

ONE: LIBERATION

1. In the political world, see, for example, the National Organization for Women's proposed platform for its 21st Century Party: The party is pledged to "enacting laws, rules and programs to require and accomplish gender and racial balance in elected and appointed offices and in corporate decision-making bodies" (10). In the academic world, see sociologist Judith Lorber's *Paradoxes of Gender*, in which Lorber argues that not only should half of every workplace be made up of women but half the paintings in art museums, half the books published, and so on.

2. Fuller, *Woman in the Nineteenth Century*, 175.

3. Martha Burk and Heidi Hartmann, "Beyond the Gender Gap: What Must the Women's Movement Do to Recover?" *Nation*, 10 June 1996.

4. Cott, *Grounding of Modern Feminism*, 5. The more complicated reason why women don't constitute a political class is that the rights that feminism has obtained are held by individual women, not by women as a group. There are human rights, not men's rights and women's rights. That's why liberal feminism emphasizes the *liberty* of individual women, not the equality of women as a group.

5. April Lassiter, "A Women's Agenda for Real Women," *Washington Times*, 27 February 1996; Heidi Hartmann, "Feminism after the Fall," *Dissent*, Spring 1995, 159. Although MacKinnon and Dworkin deny ever saying that in a patriarchal society, all sex is basically rape, they have certainly written the following: "Compare victims' reports of rape with women's reports of sex. They look a lot alike . . . The major distinction between intercourse (normal) and rape (abnormal) is that the normal happens so often that one cannot get anyone to see anything wrong with it." (MacKinnon: *Toward a Feminist Theory of the State*, 146). "Perhaps the wrong of rape has proven so difficult to articulate because the unquestionable starting point has been that rape is definable as distinct from intercourse when for women it is difficult to distinguish them under conditions of male dominance. . . . It is difficult to avoid the conclusion that penetration itself is known to be a violation. Instead of asking, what is the violation of rape, what if we ask, what is the non-violation of intercourse?" (MacKinnon, "Feminism, Marxism, Method, and the State: Towards Feminist Jurisprudence," in *Feminism and Methodology*, 142). "Physically, the woman is a space inhabited, a literal territory occupied literally; occupied even if there has been no resistance, no force; even if the occupied person said, yes please, yes hurry, yes more" (Dworkin, *Intercourse*, 133).

6. "Improving Employment Opportunities for Women," testimony concerning H.R. 1 Civil Rights Act of 1991 before the U.S. House of Representatives Committee on Education and Labor, 27 February 1991.

7. See Michael Weiss and Cathy Young, "Feminist Jurisprudence: Equal Rights or Neo-Paternalism," *Cato Policy Analysis*, 19 June 1996.

8. "If no can be taken as yes, how free can yes be? . . . If sex is normally something men do to women, the issue is less whether there was force and more whether consent is a meaningful concept" (MacKinnon, *Feminism Unmodified*, 82). See Sanday, *Woman Scorned*, for a discussion of court action on this issue.

9. Georgia Warnke, "Surrogate Mothering and the Meaning of Family," *Dissent,* Fall 1994.

10. Also see "How Real Is PMS?" *Ms.,* January/February 1992.

11. Quoted on ABC News Special, "Boys and Girls Are Different: Men, Women, and the Sex Difference," 1 February 1995.

12. Richards, *Sceptical Feminist,* 5.

13. Study by Korn/Ferry International, quoted in Michael Lynch and Katherine Post, "What Glass Ceiling?" By *Public Interest,* Summer 1996; Costello and Krimgold, *American Woman.*

14. Quoted in Cott, *Grounding of Modern Feminism,* 281.

15. Hrdy, *Woman That Never Evolved.*

16. Gina Kolata, "Man's World, Woman's World? Brain Studies Point to Differences," *New York Times,* 28 February 1995. Also see Begley, Sharon, "Gray Matters," *Newsweek,* 27 March 1995.

17. Quoted on ABC News, "Boys and Girls Are Different."

18. *Woman That Never Evolved,* v.

TWO: FEMININITY

1. Dr. Laura Allen, who studies brain tissue at UCLA, quoted on ABC News Special, "Boys and Girls Are Different: Men, Women, and the Sex Difference," 1 February 1995: "I was told that [doing this research] just really wasn't a good idea, because it was politically provocative." According to an article in *Newsweek* (Sharon Begley, "Gray Matters," 27 March 1995), when neuroscientist Raquel Gur "gave a talk to M.D.-Ph.D. students in Illinois about sex differences in brains, a group of women asked her to stop publicizing the work: they were afraid women would lose twenty years of gains if word got out that the sexes aren't the same." See also Patai and Koertge, *Professing Feminism,* chap. 6, and "Vicious Cycle: The Politics of Periods," *Washington Post,* 8 July 1994. Dianne Schecter, a research biologist at Columbia University, and Jean Endicott, a professor of clinical psychology at Columbia University and director of the Premenstrual Evaluation Unit at Columbia-Presbyterian Medical Center, confirmed this as well.

2. Gilligan, *In a Different Voice.*

3. See, for example, Faludi, *Backlash;* Katha Pollitt, "Are Women Morally Superior?" *Nation,* 28 December 1992; Fillion, *Lip Service;* Sommers, *Who Stole Feminism?* Gilligan's methodology has been criticized as well as her conclusions. Critics such as Pollitt and Sommers have pointed out that in Gilligan's own interviews women frequently employ the supposedly male lan-

guage of rights while men fall into the idiom of care and compassion, showing that, at the least, there is a vast continuum.

4. See Tavris, *Mismeasure of Woman;* Fillion, *Lip Service;* Katherine Dunn, "Just as Fierce," *Mother Jones,* November/December 1994; Cathy Young, "Gender Poisoning: In the Bobbitt Era, Facing the Real Truth about Male Violence," *Washington Post,* 16 January 1994; Barbara Ehrenreich, "Sex and the Married Woman," *Mirabella,* June 1992; and Heyn, *Erotic Silence.*

5. For a review of the studies, see Konner, *Tangled Wing;* Wilson, *Moral Sense;* and Moir and Jessel, *Brain Sex.* Also, in studying children age two and a half to eight, Melissa Hines, a UCLA behavioral scientist, found that boys favored sports cars, fire trucks, and Lincoln Logs, while girls were more drawn to dolls and kitchen toys. The only group of girls to prefer the boy toys were those exposed to elevated levels of testosterone during their embryonic development.

6. Bem, *Lenses of Gender,* 196. Some feminists do concede that biology may have played some part in originating gender in prehistoric days, but they hold to the claim that centuries of socialization are primarily responsible for any and all gender differences in evidence today.

Regarding aggression, for example, Nancy Chodorow in *The Reproduction of Mothering* argues that the "contemporary reproduction of mothering occurs through social structurally induced psychological processes. It is neither a product of biology nor of intentional role playing." Then she continues: "there may be behavioral differences linked to biology, such as masculine aggressiveness" (7, 15).

7. Indeed, if anyone would have made this argument on the presumption that it would catch fire, it would have been Pat Buchanan during his campaign for president in 1996. Instead, he barely touched on women's issues—and didn't go anywhere without first checking in with his wife and sister. (See Laura Blumenfeld, "The Pat Paradox," *Washington Post,* 28 February 1996.)

8. It is also no doubt true, as Nancy Chodorow writes in *The Reproduction of Mothering,* that daughters learn a lot about how to be mothers from their mothers. Daughters define themselves by relating to their mothers; sons define themselves by separation from their mothers. But it doesn't seem, as Chodorow argues, that that's the *only* reason females are more empathetic and relationship-oriented.

As biological anthropologist Melvin Konner writes in *The Tangled Wing,* concentrations of all the sex hormones—testosterone, estrogen, progesterone—have been found to be highest in precisely the brain regions (the hypothalamus and the limbic systems) that play an important role in courtship, sex, maternal behavior, and violence—"just the behaviors in which the sexes most differ." Researchers at the Harvard Medical School have also recently found a gene in female mice that prompts them to care for their young. Female mice who lack this gene—called fosB—ignore their babies and allow them to die. Humans also have an fosB gene. But according to an article on the study in the *New York Times* ("Gene May Be Clue to Nature of Nurturing," 26 July 1996), the researchers would not speculate on whether this applies to human mothers as well. Also see Wilson, *Moral Sense,* and Moir and Jessel, *Brain Sex.*

9. See "Illuminating How Bodies Are Built for Sociability," *New York Times,* 30 April 1996.

10. See Moir and Jessel, *Brain Sex.*

11. And men, on average, are slightly better at spatial tasks, like visualizing figures rotated in three dimensions. This also explains why men are more often speech-impaired after a stroke to the left side of the brain. See Begley, "Gray Matters."

12. See Wright, *Moral Animal.* Evolutionary psychologists, by the way, may be either psychologists or anthropologists by formal training.

13 Symons, *Evolution of Human Sexuality,* 14.

14. Robert Wright, "Feminists Meet Mr. Darwin," *The New Republic,* 28 November 1994, 46.

15. See J. Richard Udry et al., "Androgen Effects on Women's Gendered Behavior," *Journal of Biosocial Science* 27, no. 3 (1995): 359–68. See also Moir and Jessel, *Brain Sex,* 31.

16. The rate of major depression (persistent for a minimum of two weeks) for women is 8 percent; for men, 3.5 percent. And the rate of dysthmia (chronic depressed mood more often than not) for women is 5.4 percent, 2.6 percent for men. Myrna Wiseman et al., "Sex Differences in Rates of Depression," *Journal of Affective Disorders* 29 (1993): 77–84.

Despite the fact that these higher rates for women have been found consistently in different social classes, ethnic groups, and cultures, this depression gap has been the cause of some controversy. Some researchers believe that women aren't really more depressed than men, that the gap is the result of the fact that women are better able to identify the problem and seek treatment. Men, according to this theory, get just as depressed as women but use alcohol or drugs to inhibit or mask depressive symptoms. While this may account for a small portion of the gap, specialists in the field—including Jean Endicott, a professor of clinical psychology at Columbia University, Mary Blehar, chief of mood, anxiety, and personality disorders at the National Institute for Mental Health, and the American Psychological Association's

Task Force on Women and Depression—believe that, given the consistency and the universality of the findings and the fact that the findings stem from community surveys (not clinical trials), this theory doesn't sufficiently account for the problem. Moreover, there has been no evidence of major gender differences in rates for bipolar disorder (manic-depression), and the rates for recurrence of major depression are similar for men and women.

17. According to McGrath et al., *Women and Depression*, and in conversation with Endicott.

18. Biologist Dianne Schecter of Columbia University has found that the more progesterone women produce in the second half of their menstrual cycles, the worse their symptoms of PMS. Conversely, the more estrogen in the first half, the more positive feelings. Schecter speculates that this may have some evolutionary basis. Since women are not fertile in the second half of their cycle, a less "receptive" mood would ward off other males so as not to jeopardize pregnancy.

Most researchers report that up to two-thirds of women suffer from mild to minimal mood or somatic changes (depressed mood, irritability, hostility, anxiety, changes in sleep, appetite, energy, and libido) premenstrually; an estimated 5 percent experience severe premenstrual symptoms. Curiously, despite the vast array of evidence, both empirical and scientific, of the existence of PMS, some feminist theorists as well as scientists still argue that PMS doesn't even exist. There was a huge fight over getting it listed in the *DSM-IV* (the American Psychiatric Association's Diagnostic and Statistic Manual). Schecter says that she's been ostracized by other female biologists for simply doing research on PMS.

The fear, of course, is that women will again be said to be driven by "raging hormones," which would prohibit them from, at the very least, being airline pilots or president. Given the often volatile and random nature of male aggression, this argument would seem a hard one to make at this time. Moreover, refusing to acknowledge the problem doesn't do women much good. It seems odd that feminists are implicitly telling women that their symptoms are all in their heads.

19. The "sad memory" study was conducted by psychiatrist Mark George at the National Institute of Mental Health. See Begley, "Gray Matters."

20. Men with low levels of "instrumentality" (a sense of agency or mastery) and increased levels of "expressiveness" (a sense of communion, or concern for others) tend to be just as depressed as women with those levels. Moreover, high-instrumentality women tend to be less depressed than those with low levels. And low instrumentality not only can make both women and

men more vulnerable to depression but can also set them up for failure. Optimistic people tend to recover more easily from rejection; worrying about failure increases the likelihood of failure.

21. Udry et al., "Androgen Effects." See Moir and Jessel, *Brain Sex*, for description of work at the Kinsey Institute.

22. Jack, *Silencing the Self.*

23. *Washington Post,* 4 August 1994.

24. Hrdy, *Woman That Never Evolved* (97). Hrdy also writes, "Experts writing about sex differences among primates have relied upon stereotypes of the female primate constructed in the early sixties. . . . There has been a prevailing bias among evolutionary theorists in favor of stressing sexual competition among males for access to females at the expense of careful scrutiny of what females in their own right were doing. Among their recurring themes are the male's struggle for preeminence and his quest for 'sexual variety' in order to inseminate as many females as possible. Visionaries of male-male competition stressed the imagery of primate females herded by tyrannical male consorts: sexually cautious females coyly safeguarding their fertility until the appropriate male partner arrives; women waiting at campsites for their men to return; and, particularly, females so preoccupied with motherhood that they have little respite to influence their species' social organization.

"As a result, until just recently descriptions of other primate species have told little about females except in their capacity as mothers. Natural histories of monkeys and apes have described the behavior of males with far greater detail and accuracy than they have described the lives of females" (2, 13, 14).

25. Brownmiller, *Femininity.*

26. "Feminist Fatale," *New Republic,* 16 March 1992; Tad Friend, "Yes," *Esquire,* February 1994.

27. Margaret Atwood, speech to the American Booksellers Association, 1993, quoted in Katherine Dunn, "Call of the Wild," *Vogue,* June 1995.

28. According to Darwin's theory of sexual selection, female preferences established competition among males and, to a lesser extent, male preferences established competition among females. (The sex contributing most to the production and rearing of offspring is the sex that gets competed for.) Females selected males for large body size, strength, and aggressiveness, for protection, resources, and good genes. The progeny of those who wisely chose a mate survived; those who didn't, perished.

THREE: BEAUTY

1. Researchers may have found a difference between how white and black girls view their bodies. The University of Arizona's Teen Lifestyle Project has found that while 70 percent of black teens said they were satisfied with their weight, 90 percent of the white respondents "expressed some degree of negative concern about their body weight." However, 30 percent of girls in both groups had tried to lose weight one or two times in the past year; in both groups, 1 percent said they always dieted. And in response to the question "Are you trying to lose weight now?" 54 percent of black girls said they were, while only 44 percent of white girls did. Sheila Parker et al., "Body Image and Weight Concerns among African American and White Adolescent Females: Differences That Make a Difference," *Human Organization* 54, no. 2 (1995): 105. Also see Thomas Cash, "Gender and Body Images: Stereotypes and Realities," *Sex Roles* 21, nos. 5/6 (1989); "Women's New Relationship with Fashion," *New York Times*, 5 August 1996.

2. David Kunzle in *Fashion and Fetishism* argues that while corsets were universal in Europe for six centuries, only a few women—those who wore them morbidly tight—were ever really harmed by them. Kunzle also notes that men wore tight clothes as well—very tight collars and tight shoes and boots; some even wore corsets.

3. See, among others, Bartky, *Femininity and Domination*; Chapkis, *Beauty Secrets*; Wolf, *Beauty Myth*; Faludi, *Backlash*.

4. Wolf, *Beauty Myth*, 187; Faludi, *Backlash*, 173.

5. Wolf, *Beauty Myth*, 12.

6. See, for example, Buss, *Evolution of Desire*.

7. In 1972, according to Cash, 23 percent of U.S. women said they were dissatisfied with their appearance; today, that figure has more than doubled, to 48 percent. Also, the younger a woman is, the more dissatisfied she is with her appearance.

8. Victor Johnston and Melissa Franklin, "Is Beauty in the Eye of the Beholder?" *Ethology and Sociobiology* 14 (1993): 183–99; Langlois, Judith, et al., "Infant preferences for attractive faces: Rudiments of a stereotype," *Developmental Psychology* 23 (1987): 363–69.

9. See Buss, *Evolution of Desire*.

10. Cowley, Geoffrey, "Biology of Beauty," *Newsweek*, 3 June 1996, 63.

11. Buss's study was of thirty-seven cultures in thirty-three countries. In a different five-decade study, sociologists Elaine Hatfield and Susan Sprecher came up with similar results. See *Mirror, Mirror . . . The Importance of Looks in Everyday Life*.

12. Buss, *Evolution of Desire.*

13. "The Economic Reality of *The Beauty Myth,*" Working Paper Series, National Bureau of Economic Research, 1993.

14. See Ehrenreich, *Fear of Falling.* Also see Buss, *Evolution of Desire.*

15. Alan Farnham, "You're So Vain," *Fortune,* 9 September 1996, 66.

16. Wolf, *Beauty Myth,* 19, 66.

17. "Economic Reality of *The Beauty Myth.*"

18. Timothy Schellhardt, "Attractiveness Aids Men More Than Women," *Wall Street Journal,* 18 October 1991.

19. Wolf, *Beauty Myth,* 28; Richards, *Sceptical Feminist,* 194.

20. According to a 1992 *Glamour* magazine survey, 84 percent of respondents say they enjoy the time, effort, and money they put into their appearance. Leslie George, "Your Love/Hate Relationship with Looking Good," *Glamour,* April 1992, 222.

21. *Glamour* survey.

22. Meryl Gordon, "Hillary Strikes Back," *Elle,* May 1994.

23. Kathy Davis, "Remaking the She-Devil: A Critical Look at Feminist Approaches to History," *Hypatia* 6, no. 2 (Summer 1991): 23. Davis subsequently published *Reshaping the Female Body.*

24. "Female Image of the Male Ideal, in a Faulty Mirror," *New York Times,* 22 July 1992. Researchers have also discovered that men assume that women long for a larger male chest size than women actually favor.

25. *Glamour-Hanes* 1995 survey. American Cancer Society, *Cancer Facts and Figures: 1996* (Atlanta: American Cancer Society, 1996), 12.

26. American Cancer Society, *Cancer Facts,* 11. Lung cancer now surpasses breast cancer as the chief cause of cancer death among women. According to a June 1996 study by the National Center on Addiction and Substance Abuse ("Substance Abuse and the American Woman"), one in five pregnant women smokes, drinks, and/or uses drugs.

27. American Medical Association, *1993 Final Conference Report on Tobacco Use.*

28. Wolf, *Beauty Myth,* 187. See also Bordo, *Unbearable Weight.*

29. The restaurant is a woman-run co-op called Bloodroot in New Haven, Connecticut.

30. Morton Shaevitz of the University of California, San Diego School of Medicine, found this through clinical observations. Cash, "Gender and Body Images."

31. "Obese" is defined as exceeding acceptable weight by 20 percent or more. According to a 1994 study by the National Center for Health Statis-

tics, reported in "Despite Awareness of Risks, More in U.S. Are Getting Fat," *New York Times*, 17 July 1994.

32. "Even Moderate Weight Gain Can Be Risky," *New York Times*, 14 September 1995.

33. In a 1995 study, Walter C. Willet and other researchers from the Harvard School of Public Health and Harvard Medical School found that the weight gain allowed in the 1990 charts was not healthy. Walter C. Willet, "Weight, Weight Change, and Coronary Heart Disease in Women," *Journal of the American Medical Association* 273, no. 6 (8 February 1995): 461–65.

34. According to psychiatrist Albert Stunkard at the University of Pennsylvania Medical School, based on his research, specifically of twins. It has also been found, though, that the human body is programmed to defend a particular weight range or a certain amount of stored fat—"a set point"—making it harder to both lose and gain weight.

35. "Nutrition and Your Health: Dietary Guidelines for Americans," 1995, U.S. Department of Agriculture and U.S. Department of Health and Human Services.

36. Aimee Lee Ball, "How the Elite Eat," *Harper's Bazaar*, September 1996, 446.

37. Geoffrey Cowley, "The Biology of Beauty," *Newsweek*, 3 June 1996, 65, and Ridley, *Red Queen*. Men apparently do not have an evolved preference for a particular amount of body fat per se. Rather, they have an evolved preference for whatever features are linked with status.

38. Study by Devandra Singh of the University of Texas at Austin, cited in Cowley, "Biology of Beauty."

39. However, Miss America contestants and *Playboy* centerfolds became increasingly thinner between 1960 and 1979. David M. Garner et al., "Cultural Explanations of Thinness in Women," *Psychological Reports* 47 (1980): 485.

40. See Anderson, J.L., and Crawford, C.B., "Modeling costs and benefits of adolescent weight control as a mechanism for reproductive suppression," *Human Nature* 3 (1992): 229–334.

41. Brett Silverstein et al., "Possible Causes of the Thin Standard of Bodily Attractiveness for Women," *International Journal of Eating Disorders* 5, no. 5 (1986): 907.

42. Quoted in text of "Are American Standards of Beauty Obsolete?" symposium sponsored by Women, Men, and the Media at Columbia University Graduate School of Journalism, 8 December 1994.

43. Dr. Michael Strober, quoted in "How Thin Is Too Thin?" *People*, 20 September 1993.

44. See Gordon, Richard, *Anorexia and Bulimia: Anatomy of a Social Epidemic.*

45. According to Jean Rubel of Anorexia Nervosa and Related Eating Disorders, Inc. (ANRED), some studies show a rise and some do not. According to the American Psychiatric Association, between 0.5 and 1.0 percent of females age twelve to twenty-five suffer from anorexia nervosa, and between 1.0 and 3.0 percent suffer from bulimia. Jowel Yager, M.D., et al., *Practice Guidelines for Eating Disorders*, American Psychiatric Association, February 1993.

46. Steinem, *Moving Beyond Words*, 97.

47. Faludi, *Backlash*, 189.

48. Anne Hollander, personal note to author.

49. Hollander note.

50. Wollstonecraft, *Vindication of the Rights of Woman,* 132.

FOUR: SEX

1. According to a 1995 *Glamour* survey, only 14 percent of female respondents said they asked their dates out.

2. "Sex and America's Teenagers," 1994 survey by the Alan Guttmacher Institute.

3. Wright, *Moral Animal*, 30.

4. See page 204, note 5.

5. Buss, *Evolution of Desire.*

6. Hrdy, *Woman That Never Evolved.*

7. Buss, *Evolution of Desire*, 20. Buss also writes: "No biological law of the animal world dictates that women invest more than men. Indeed, among some species, such as the Mormon cricket, pipefish seahorse, and Panamanian poison arrow frog, males invest more. . . . Among these so-called sex-role reversed species, it is the males who are more discriminating about mating. Among all four thousand species of mammals, including the more than two hundred species of primates, however, females bear the burden of internal fertilization, gestation, and lactation" (20).

8. Symons, *Evolution of Human Sexuality*, 274.

9. Hrdy, *Woman That Never Evolved*, 134.

10. Buss, *Evolution of Desire.*

11. Hrdy, *Woman That Never Evolved*, 176.

12. Fisher, *Anatomy of Love.*

13. Fisher, *Anatomy of Love.*

14. Fisher, *Anatomy of Love.*

15. Ackerman, *A Natural History of Love.* Hrdy, *Woman That Never Evolved,*

139: "In 1978, a team of psychologists—David Adams, Anne Burt, and Alice Ross Gold—studying married women in a college community in Connecticut reported a statistically significant peak in sexual behavior around time of ovulation." This finding was replicated by Martha McClintock, a psychology professor at the University of Chicago: "We found a clear increase in initiation of sex by women before and during ovulation" (quoted in *Ms.*, July/August 1994, 59).

16. Helen Fisher, conversation with author.

17. Buss, *Evolution of Desire*. Confirmed by another study by psychologists Michael Wiederman and Elizabeth Allgeier. According to Buss, both women and men are choosy about long-term mates. Yet women retain high standards when selecting for just a sexual relationship, whereas men's standards for a sexual partner drop substantially.

18. Sanday, *Woman Scorned*. Fairstein, *Sexual Violence*.

19. Fillion, *Lip Service*.

20. Susan Sprecher, "Token Resistance to Sexual Intercourse," *The Journal of Sex Research* 31, no. 2 (1994).

21. Quoted in "When Is It Rape?" *Time*, 3 June 1991, 53.

22. Michael Weiss and Cathy Young, "Feminist Jurisprudence: Equal Rights or Neo-Paternalism?" *Cato Policy Analysis*, 19 June 1996; Roiphe, *Morning After*, 51.

23. Sex in America survey of nearly 3,500 men and women, age eighteen to fifty-nine conducted in 1992 by the National Opinion Research Center at the University of Chicago.

24. Buss, *Evolution of Desire*. Men also report desiring an average of eight partners to women's one over the next two years. And men are more likely than women to be currently seeking a short-term relationship. Also see Sex in America survey.

25. Natalie Angier, "Science Is Finding Out What Women Really Want," *New York Times*, 13 August 1995. Research by Ellen T. M. Laan, a psychologist at the University of Amsterdam, found that women were equally turned on by male-friendly porn films and female-friendly porn films, but *reported* that they were aroused only by the latter. "The results suggest that [women and men] have more or less equal potential for sexual arousal," Laan was quoted in the *New York Times* story. "But there's an evolutionary rationale for why women might be more discriminating, and why they might screen the situation before taking action. Women are, after all, the ones who get pregnant." Laan also suggested that this may explain why women get physiologically aroused during rape: "getting wet is automatic."

26. Buss, *Evolution of Desire*.

27. Wright, *Moral Animal*, 73. According to Buss's cross-cultural survey, American men view promiscuity as especially undesirable in a potential spouse—and they view lack of sexual experience as desirable. Women known as promiscuous suffer reputational damage even in relatively promiscuous cultures such as Sweden (Buss, *Evolution of Desire*).

28. Buss, *Evolution of Desire*.

29. See, for example, Cynthia Grant Bowman, "Street Harassment and the Informal Ghettoization of Women," *Harvard Law Review* 106, no. 3 (January 1993).

FIVE: LOVE

1. Firestone, *Dialectic of Sex;* French, *Women's Room*, 460; Ti-Grace Atkinson, quoted in Kay Hymowitz, "The L Word: Love as Taboo," *City Journal* (Spring 1995): 32.

2. Wollstonecraft, *Vindication of the Rights of Woman. Women and Economics.* Charlotte Perkins Gilman.

3. Suzanne Fields, "What Do Feminists Want?" *Washington Times*, 7 August 1995. Mary Frances Berry's *Politics of Parenthood* is one of many books that argue that fathers are just as suited to child care as mothers. In a review of these and other books in the *New Republic* ("Home Repairs," 16 August 1993), Ann Hulbert writes, "in the all-important battle between the sexes about rights, the priority is not so much care that's suitable for kids as care that suits parents."

4. Fisher, *Anatomy of Love*. Fisher reports that in a 1992 survey of 168 cultures, anthropologists William Jankoviak and Ed Fischer found direct evidence of romantic love in nearly 90 percent of them. The people in many of these cultures not only reported experiencing romantic love but had coined specific names for it.

5. Faludi, *Backlash*.

6. Faludi, *Backlash*.

7. Faludi, *Backlash*.

8. Faludi, *Backlash*.

9. "Women's Work on Television," *Washington Post*, 27 August 1995.

10. Fisher, *Anatomy of Love*. Small, *What's Love Got to Do With It?*

11. Steinem, *Revolution from Within*.

12. Fisher, *Anatomy of Love*.

13. Fisher, *Anatomy of Love*. Michael Liebowitz and Donald Klein of the New York State Psychiatric Institute gave romance junkies antidepressant drugs that block the action of monoamine oxidase (MAO), a class of sub-

stances that break down PEA. The patients were then able to sustain relationships and not crave a PEA high. This research was confirmed by psychiatrist Hector Sabelli, who found that partners in good relationships had high levels of PEA.

14. McGrath, *Women and Depression.*

15. Gina Kolata, "Man's World, Woman's World? Brain Studies Point to Differences," *New York Times,* 28 February 1995.

16. Buss, *Evolution of Desire.*

17. Steinem, *Revolution from Within,* 283.

18. Buss, *Evolution of Desire.*

19. Moreover, as social scientist Pepper Schwartz reports in *Peer Marriages,* many egalitarian couples who get too close lose the sense of mystery that fuels passion.

20. Fisher, *Anatomy of Love.*

21. "Women: The New Providers," Whirlpool Foundation Study by the Families and Work Institute, May 1995. Thirty-three percent would prefer to work part time, 31 percent would rather care for their families, and 20 percent would like to do volunteer work. Among eighteen-to-twenty-four-year-olds, 29 percent would work part time, 32 percent would care for their families, 17 percent would do volunteer work. Other polls show that 60 to 70 percent of mothers with jobs outside the home want to continue working.

22. Gilman, *Women and Economics,* 98. Gilman also wrote: "The labor of women in the house, certainly, enables men to produce more wealth than they otherwise could; and in this way women are economic factors in society. But so are horses" (47).

23. "In the typical hunter-gather village, mothers can reconcile a home life with a work life fairly gracefully, and in a richly social context," writes Robert Wright. "When they gather food, their children stay either with them or with aunts, uncles, grandparents, cousins or life-long friends. When they're back at the village, child care is a mostly public task—extensively social, even communal." According to Wright, in one society studied it was common for a woman to breastfeed her neighbor's child while the neighbor gathered food. "The Evolution of Despair," *Time,* 28 August 1995.

One of the largest studies was done by Dr. Ethel Roskies and Silvie Carrier, psychologists at the University of Montreal. Reported in "For the Professional Mother, Rewards May Outweigh Stress," *New York Times,* 9 December 1992.

24. According to Linda Thompson and Alexis J. Walker, "Gender in Families: Women and Men in Marriage, Work, and Parenthood," *Journal of Marriage and the Family* 51 (November 1989). Also, in a 1995 study of income

and housework, University of Washington sociologist Julie Brines found that wives do the overwhelming amount of chores no matter what percentage of the family's income they bring home. Women's work is greatest in traditional families, and it decreases as family income increases. Interestingly, though, when women's earnings skyrocket past their mates' earnings, the mates do much less.

25. Hochschild, *Second Shift.*

26. Conversations with sociologists; McGrath, *Women and Depression.*

27. Gina Maranto, "Delayed Childbearing," *Atlantic Monthly,* June 1995.

28. National Center for Health Statistics. At the moment, nearly five out of six women become mothers.

29. Natalie Angier, "Illuminating How Bodies Are Built for Sociability," *New York Times,* 30 April 1996. Also, author interview with Dr. C. Sue Carter of the University of Maryland, College Park, who is renowned in the field of oxytocin research.

30. In, for instance, *Mother-Infant Bonding,* Diane E. Eyer proposes that the term be abolished. See Jay Belsky and Jude Cassidy, "Attachment: Theory and Evidence," in Rutter and Hay, *Development through Life.* During the seventies, a theory that came to be known as "mother-infant bonding" suggested that mothers and infants who spend time together right after birth form a crucial psychological attachment that will prove instrumental in later stages of childrearing. While the theory finally rid hospital obstetrics of some very outdated practices (mothers can now spend time with their newborns), it has now largely been discredited. Fuller, *Woman in the Nineteenth Century,* 175.

31. Mahony, *Kidding Ourselves.* Mahony also writes that more women should consider "marrying down," to musicians, artists, and the like, who often earn less money, work flexible hours, and might be able to take on more child care.

32. One of the most authoritative reviews of the research can be found in McLanahan and Sandefur, *Growing Up with a Single Parent.* Reviewing five large-scale social surveys and other evidence (and after adjusting for many income-related factors), the sociologists concluded: "Children who grow up in a household with only one biological parent (nearly always the mother) . . . are twice as likely to drop out of high school, twice as likely to have a child before age twenty, and one and a half times as likely to be 'idle'—out of school and out of work—in their late teens and early twenties" (1–2).

Children living with divorced mothers, though, fare far better than those living with never married mothers. The income of families headed by divorced mothers is more than double that of families headed by never married mothers. Two-thirds of the children living with never married mothers live below the poverty line, compared with just over a third of children of divorce. Children in single-parent families headed by fathers do better than those headed by mothers, but not as well as those in two-parent families.

33. "For Women, Varied Reasons for Single Motherhood," *New York Times,* 26 May 1992.

34. Maggie Gallagher, "An Unwed Mother for Quayle," *New York Times,* 24 September 1992. Ackerman, *Natural History of Love,* 16.

35. Ross, *What Men Want.* Interestingly, Nancy Chodorow also makes this point in *Reproduction of Mothering.* See also David Popenoe, "The Vanishing Father," *Wilson Quarterly,* Spring 1996.

36. Marcelle Clements, "Battered Women: Why Do They Go Back for More?," *Elle,* January 1995, 45.

SIX: POWER

1. Karen Lehrman, "The Ploy of Sex," *Washington Post,* 20 December 1992.

2. Supreme Court of the United States Syllabus: *United States v. Virginia et al.* Certiorari to the United States Court of Appeals for the Fourth Circuit, no. 94, 33 (1941). Argued 17 January 1996; decided 26 June 1996.

3. See Michael Weiss and Cathy Young, "Feminist Jurisprudence: Equal Rights or Neo-Paternalism?" *Cato Policy Analysis,* 19 June 1996, and Elizabeth Kiss, "Alchemy or Fool's Gold? Assessing Feminist Doubts about Rights," *Dissent,* Summer 1995.

See NOW's 21st Century Party pledge, note 1, p. 203.

4. According to Costello and Krimgold, *American Woman,* only 41 percent of employed mothers are covered by FMLA, because they either work at companies with fewer than fifty employees or have not worked the required 1,250 hours a year.

5. See, for example, Gilligan, *Meeting at the Crossroads;* Gordon, *Prisoners of Men's Dreams;* and Noddings, *Ethics of Care.*

6. Costello and Krimgold, *American Woman.* Nearly six in ten working women in 1994 were concentrated in service, sales, and clerical jobs. According to the Bureau of Labor Statistics, three-quarters of women work in traditionally female occupations.

7. "Work and Family Benefits Provided by Major U.S. Employers in 1994," Catalyst 1996 Fact Sheet on Working Women, Hewitt Associates, New York, 1994. Michael Lynch and Katherine Post, "What Glass Ceiling?" *Public Interest,* Summer 1996.

8. Lynch and Post, "What Glass Ceiling?"

9. See, for instance, Heidi Hartmann testimony concerning H.R. 1 Civil Rights Act of 1991 before the U.S. House of Representatives Committee on Education and Labor, 27 February 1991.

10. For example, see *How Schools Shortchange Girls*. a report commissioned by the American Association of University Women and researched by the Wellesley College Center for Research on Women, 1992. Criticism by, among others, Sommers, *Who Stole Feminism?*

11. According to a 1995 Catalyst study, female executive respondents cite the following top three factors holding women back: male stereotyping and preconceptions of women; exclusion from informal networks of communication; and lack of significant general management/line experience.

12. Lynch and Post, "What Glass Ceiling?" See also Stephanie N. Mehta, "Number of Women-Owned Businesses Surged 43% in 5 Years through 1992," *Wall Street Journal*, 29 January 1996.

13. Lynch and Post, "What Glass Ceiling?"; *Working Woman*, February 1996.

14. Costello and Krimgold, *American Woman*.

15. "Mr. Mom Goes Mainstream," *American Demographics*, March 1994.

16. U.S. Bureau of Labor Statistics.

17. Costello and Krimgold, *American Woman*.

18. Felice Schwartz, "Management Women and the New Facts of Life," *Harvard Business Review*, January/February 1989.

19. Gilligan, *In a Different Voice*; Wolf, *Fire with Fire*.

20. Polly Toynbee, "Is Margaret Thatcher a Woman?" *Washington Monthly*, May 1988, 34; Mark Potok, "Texas' Hutchinson a Battler and Survivor," *USA Today*, 11 June 1993; Naomi Wolf, "Are Opinions Male?" *New Republic*, 29 November 1993, 22.

21. Fillion, *Lip Service*, 73.

22. Lani Guinier et al., "Becoming Gentlemen: Women's Experiences at One Ivy League Law School," *University of Pennsylvania Law Review*, November 1994.

23. Jeff Rosen, "The Book of Ruth," *New Republic*, 2 August 1993.

24. "When 'La Difference' Means Votes," *Washington Post*, 27 November 1995.

25. "The Public Perspective," Roper Center Review of Public Opinion and Polling, August/September 1996. Also see "Do Women Vote for Women?" December 1995 National Women's Political Caucus. Thomas Edsall, "Clinton Benefited from Huge Gender Gap," *Washington Post*, 6 November 1996.

26. Personal interview with author.

27. Alison Mitchell, "Holtzman Draws Criticism from Feminists Over AIDS," *New York Times*, 27 August 1992, 36.

28. Sonia Nazario, "Views of Women Are as Varied as the Women," *Wall Street Journal*, 18 October 1991.

29. John M. Broder, "Hillary Clinton Defends Past Investments," *Los Angeles Times*, 23 April 1994; Katha Pollitt, "First-Lady Bashing: The Male Media's Hillary Problem," *Nation*, 17 May 1993; and again in *Nation*, February 1996: The reason for the attention on Hillary Clinton is that "a lot of people still expect the wives of politicians to concentrate on the Kinder-Kirche-Kuche side of life."

30. "Sexual Harassment: A History of Federal Law," Congressional Research Service report, 7 May 1993.

31. Weiss and Young, "Feminist Jurisprudence." Also see, for example, the New York Bar Association's model policy for law firms: "A partner or an employee who enters into a sexual relationship with another employee, where there exists a difference in seniority or power between the individuals involved, should be aware that, if a complaint of sexual harassment is subsequently made, it could be exceedingly difficult to prove immunity on grounds of mutual consent." In other words, even completely consensual relationships can be considered sexual harassment—if a woman (or a man) at any point decides to call them that.

32. "Feminist Jurisprudence." *Ellison v. Brady*, 924F2d 872, 879 (9th Cir 1991).

33. "If no can be taken as yes, how free can yes be? . . . If sex is normally something men do to women, the issue is less whether there was force and more whether consent is a meaningful concept." MacKinnon, *Toward a Feminist Theory*.

34. Amy Rosenberg, "Glanton's Accuser Tells of Seduction," *Philadelphia Inquirer*, 13 July 1993; "Plaintiff Vague on Sexual Encounters," *Philadelphia Inquirer*, 14 July 1993.

35. Joseph Slobodzian, "Lawyers Dark on Firing in a Deposition," *Philadelphia Inquirer*, 24 July 1993. It also came out in the trial that Frederick gave Christmas gifts to Glanton and his children a month after she allegedly broke off the affair and that she had sought "romantic relationships" with several of the firm's married lawyers and "pursued" one partner unsuccessfully for two years.

36. Dale Russakoff, "Lawyer Found to Have Harassed Associate," *Washington Post*, 7 August 1993.

37. Molly Haskell, "Managing Your Sexuality," *Working Woman*, August 1994, 33.

SEVEN: SISTERHOOD

1. *Marie Clare*/Gallup poll, September 1994. The poll also found that only 34 percent of women believe that feminist leaders reflect the views of women and that 51 percent believe that the contemporary movement is hurting relations between the sexes. Also, a February 1996 poll by Wirthlin Worldwide found that 29 percent of women call themselves feminist.

2. Personal interview with author.

3. Hrdy, *Woman That Never Evolved.*

4. Hrdy, *Woman That Never Evolved,* 100.

5. Elizabeth Kaye, "What Women Think of Other Women," *Esquire,* August 1992.

6. Fillion, *Lip Service,* 75.

7. Fillion, *Lip Service,* 54.

8. Tavris, *Mismeasure of Woman,* 268.

9. *Marie Clare*/Gallup poll; "Do Women Vote for Women?" National Women's Political Caucus, December 1995.

10. *Ms.,* September/October 1993.

11. Wolf, *Fire with Fire,* 294.

12. Faludi, "I'm Not a Feminist, but I Play One on TV," *Ms.,* March/April 1995, 32.

13. Sommers, *Who Stole Feminism?;* National Center for Health Statistics.

14. Patai and Koertge, *Professing Feminism,* 2.

15. Patai and Koertge, *Professing Feminism,* 183–84.

16. Patai and Koertge, *Professing Feminism,* xvi.

17. Patai and Koertge, *Professing Feminism,* 9. Lefkowitz is quoted in Karen Lehrman, "Off Course," *Mother Jones,* November/December 1993.

18. Lehrman, "Off Course."

19. "Courage to Question: Women's Studies and Student Learning," American Association of Colleges 1991 survey, 109.

20. Susan Faludi, "Backtalk," *Mother Jones,* November/December 1993.

21. Findlen, *Listen Up.* Also see Wendy Kaminer, "Feminism's Third Wave: What Do Young Women Want?" *New York Times Book Review,* 4 June 1995.

22. Patai and Koertge, *Professing Feminism,* 35.

23. Patai and Koertge, *Professing Feminism,* 46.

24. Findlen, *Listen Up,* 221.

25. *Radical Feminists of Heterodoxy,* 25.

26. Leon Wieseltier, "Against Identity," *The New Republic.* 28 November 1994.

27. For example, according to a survey by NBC News/*Wall Street Journal*, 10–14 May 1996, 57 percent of women and 53 percent of men believe the choices should be left to women and their doctors.

28. "If you get raped, if you get beat up in a dark alley in a street, it's okay. That was part of the risk of freedom. . . . The uncontrollable aspect of male sexuality is part of what makes sex interesting. And yes, it can lead to rape in some situations. . . . If [rape] is a totally devastating psychological experience for a woman, then she doesn't have a proper attitude about sex" (Interviews with Camille Paglia, "Antihero," *Spin*, September 1991, October 1991).

"Male urination really *is* a kind of accomplishment, an arc of transcendance" (Paglia, *Sexual Personae*, 21). "If civilization had been left in female hands, we would still be living in grass huts" (38). Also see Katherine Dunn, "Just as Fierce," *Mother Jones*, November/December 1994; Tad Friend, "Yes," *Esquire*, February 1994, 55, quotes Christina Hoff Sommers: "There are a lot of homely women in women's studies. Preaching these anti-male, anti-sex sermons is a way for them to compensate for various heartaches—they're just mad at the beautiful girls." Roiphe, *Morning After*.

29. Steele, *Content of Our Character*, 23; *Listen Up*, xv.

EPILOGUE: A LIBERATED WOMAN

1. Elizabeth Cady Stanton, "Solitude of Self," speech given on 20 February 1892, before the U.S. Senate Committee on Woman Suffrage.

Bibliography

◆

Ackerman, Diane. *A Natural History of Love.* New York: Random House, 1994.

Bartky, Sandra. *Femininity and Domination: Studies in the Phenomenology of Oppression.* New York: Routledge, 1990.

Bem, Sandra Lepsitz. *The Lenses of Gender: Transforming the Debate on Sexual Inequality.* New Haven: Yale University Press, 1993.

Berry, Mary Frances. *The Politics of Parenthood.* New York· Penguin Books, 1993.

Bordo, Susan. *Unbearable Weight: Feminism, Western Culture, and the Body.* Berkeley: University of California Press, 1993.

Brown, Lyn Mikel, and Gilligan, Carol. *Meeting at the Crossroads: Women's Psychology and Girls' Development.* Cambridge: Harvard University Press, 1992.

Brownmiller, Susan. *Femininity.* New York: Fawcett Columbine, 1984.

Buss, David M. *The Evolution of Desire: Strategies of Human Mating.* New York: Basic Books, 1994.

Chapkis, Wendy. *Beauty Secrets: Women and the Politics of Appearance.* Boston: South End Press, 1986.

Chodorow, Nancy. *The Reproduction of Mothering: Psychoanalysis and the Sociology of Gender.* Berkeley: University of California Press, 1978.

Costello, Cynthia, and Barbara Kivimae Krimgold, eds. *The American Woman: 1996–97.* New York: W. W. Norton & Co. and the Women's Research and Education Institute, 1996.

Cott, Nancy. *The Grounding of Modern Feminism.* New Haven: Yale University Press, 1987.

Davis, Kathy. *Reshaping the Female Body: The Dilemma of Cosmetic Surgery.* New York: Routledge, 1995.

Dworkin, Andrea. *Intercourse.* New York: The Free Press, 1987.

Ehrenreich, Barbara. *Fear of Falling: The Inner Life of the Middle Class.* New York: HarperCollins, 1990.

Eyer, Diane E. *Mother-Infant Bonding: A Scientific Fiction.* New Haven: Yale University Press, 1992.

Fairstein, Linda. *Sexual Violence.* New York: Morrow, 1993.

Faludi, Susan. *Backlash: The Undeclared War against American Women.* New York: Crown, 1991.

Fillion, Kate. *Lip Service: The Truth about Women's Darker Side in Love, Sex, and Friendship.* New York: HarperCollins, 1996.

Findlen, Barbara. *Listen Up: Voices from the Next Feminist Generation.* Seattle: Seal Press, 1995.

Firestone, Shulamith. *The Dialectic of Sex: The Case for Feminist Revolution.* New York: Morrow, 1970.

Fisher, Helen. *The Anatomy of Love: The Natural History of Monogamy, Adultery, and Divorce.* New York: Norton, 1992.

Fox-Genovese, Elizabeth. *Feminism without Illusions: A Critique of Individualism.* Chapel Hill: University of North Carolina Press, 1991.

French, Marilyn. *The Women's Room.* New York: Ballantine Books, 1977.

Fuller, Margaret. *Woman in the Nineteenth Century.* 1845. Reprint, New York: Norton Library, 1971.

Gilligan, Carol. *In a Different Voice: Psychological Theory and Women's Development.* Cambridge: Harvard University Press, 1982.

Gilman, Charlotte Perkins. *Women and Economics.* New York: Prometheus Books, 1994 (original date: 1898).

Gordon, Richard. *Anorexia and Bulimia: Anatomy of a Social Epidemic.* London: Blackwell, 1990.

Gordon, Suzanne. *Prisoners of Men's Dreams: Striking Out for a New Feminine Future.* Boston: Little, Brown, 1991.

Harding, Sandra, ed. *Feminism and Methodology.* Bloomington: Indiana University Press, 1987.

Hatfield, Elaine, and Sprecher, Susan. *Mirror, Mirror . . . The Importance of Looks in Everyday Life.* New York: State University of New York Press, 1985.

Heyn, Dalma. *The Erotic Silence of the American Wife.* New York: Turtle Bay Books, 1992.

Hochschild, Arlie. *The Second Shift.* New York: Avon, 1989.

Hrdy, Sarah Blaffer. *The Woman That Never Evolved.* Cambridge: Harvard University Press, 1981.

Konner, Melvin. *The Tangled Wing: Biological Constraints on the Human Spirit.* New York: Harper Colophon, 1982.

Jack, Dana Crowley. *Silencing the Self: Women and Depression.* Cambridge: Harvard University Press, 1994.

Jaggar, Alison. *Feminist Politics and Human Nature.* Lanham, Md.: Rowman and Littlefield, 1983.

Kaminer, Wendy. *A Fearful Freedom: Women's Flight from Equality.* New York: Addison-Wesley, 1990.

Kunzle, David. *Fashion and Fetishism: A Social History of the Corset, Tight Lacing, and Other Forms of Body-Sculpture in the West.* Totowa, NJ: Rowman & Littlefield, 1982.

Lorber, Judith. *Paradoxes of Gender.* New Haven: Yale University Press, 1994.

MacKinnon, Catharine. *Feminism Unmodified: Discourses on Life and Law.* Cambridge: Harvard University Press, 1987.

————. *Only Words.* Cambridge: Harvard University Press, 1993.

————. *Toward a Feminist Theory of the State.* Cambridge: Harvard University Press, 1989.

McGrath, Ellen, et al., eds. *Women and Depression: Risk Factors and Treatment Issues.* Washington, D.C.: American Psychological Association, 1990.

McLanahan, Sara, and Sandefur, Gary. *Growing Up with a Single Parent.* Cambridge: Harvard University Press, 1994.

Mahony, Rhonda. *Kidding Ourselves: Why Women Won't Achieve Equality Until Men Really Share Parenting and How to Make It Happen.* New York: Basic, 1995.

Moir, Anne, and Jessel, David. *Brain Sex: The Real Difference Between Men & Women.* New York: Lyle Stuart, 1991.

Noddings, Nell. *Caring: A Feminine Approach to Ethics and Moral Education.* Berkeley: University of California Press, 1984.

Orbach, Susie. *Fat Is a Feminist Issue.* New York: Berkley, 1978.

Paglia, Camille. *Sexual Personae: Art and Decadence from Nefertiti to Emily Dickenson.* New Haven: Yale University Press, 1990.

Patai, Daphne, and Koertge, Noretta. *Professing Feminism: Cautionary Tales from the Strange World of Women's Studies.* New York: Basic Books, 1994.

Pollitt, Katha. *Reasonable Creatures: Essays on Women and Feminism.* New York: Knopf, 1994.

Richards, Janet Radcliffe. *The Sceptical Feminist: A Philosophical Inquiry.* London: Routledge and Kegan Paul, 1980.

Ridley, Matt. *The Red Queen: Sex and the Evolution of Human Nature.* New York: Macmillan, 1993.

Roiphe, Katie. *The Morning After: Sex, Fear, and Feminism on Campus.* Boston: Little, Brown, 1993.

Ross, John Munder. *What Men Want: Mothers, Fathers, & Manhood.* Cambridge: Harvard University Press, 1994.

Rossi, Alice, ed. *Sexuality Across the Life Course.* Chicago: University of Chicago Press, 1994.

Ruddick, Sara. *Maternal Thinking: Toward a Politics of Peace.* New York: Ballantine Books, 1989.

Rutter, Michael, and Hay, D., eds. *Development Through Life: A Handbook for Clinicians.* London: Blackwell, 1994.

Sanday, Peggy Reeves. *A Woman Scorned: Acquaintance Rape on Trial.* New York: Doubleday, 1996.

Schwartz, Judith. *Radical Feminists of Heterodoxy: Greenwich Village 1912–1940.* Norwich, Vt.: New Victoria Publishers, 1986.

Schwartz, Pepper. *Peer Marriages: How Love Between Equals Really Works.* New York: Free Press, 1994.

Small, Meredith F. *What's Love Got to Do With It?: The Evolution of Human Mating.* New York: Anchor, 1995.

Sommers, Christina Hoff. *Who Stole Feminism?: How Women Have Betrayed Women.* New York: Simon & Schuster, 1994.

Steele, Shelby. *The Content of Our Character: A New Vision of Race in America.* New York: St. Martin's Press, 1990.

Steinem, Gloria. *Moving Beyond Words.* New York: Simon & Schuster, 1994.

———. *Revolution from Within: A Book of Self-Esteem.* Boston: Little, Brown, 1992.

Symons, Donald. *The Evolution of Human Sexuality.* New York: Oxford University Press, 1979.

Tavris, Carol. *The Mismeasure of Woman: Why Women Are Not the Better Sex, the Inferior Sex, or the Opposite Sex.* New York: Simon & Schuster, 1992.

Taylor, Joan Kennedy. *Reclaiming the Mainstream: Individualist Feminism Rediscovered.* New York: Prometheus, 1992.

Tong, Rosemarie. *Feminist Thought: A Comprehensive Introduction.* San Francisco: Westview Press, 1989.

Willis, Ellen. *No More Nice Girls: Countercultural Essays.* Hanover: Wesleyan University Press, 1992.

Wilson, James Q. *The Moral Sense.* New York: The Free Press, 1993.

Wolf, Naomi. *The Beauty Myth: How Images of Beauty Are Used against Women.* New York: Doubleday, 1992.

———. *Fire with Fire: The New Female Power and How It Will Change the Twenty-First Century.* New York: Random House, 1993.

Wollstonecraft, Mary. *A Vindication of the Rights of Woman.* 1792. Reprint, New York: Penguin, 1992.

Wright, Robert. *The Moral Animal: The New Science of Evolutionary Psychology.* New York: Pantheon, 1994.

Acknowledgments

◆

T H I S   B O O K   W O U L D   not have happened without the constant (and tireless) support of about a dozen people. Leon Wieseltier and Ann Hulbert provided the initial encouragement that started the process. Kate Boo and Jay Tolson suffered through endless rough drafts, endless discussions, and endless complaints, providing masterful editing all the while. Ellen Ladowsky, Nancy Jacobson, Pamela Erens, Susie Linfield, Susan Chumsky, Louise Palmer—all offered crucial emotional support. Bruce Feiler was a constant source of not only ideas and editorial direction, but of optimism, especially when it was in rather short supply. And a special thanks to Alex Boyar for offering an endless supply of humor and perspective, and more than anything, for simply being there.

This book would also not have happened without the support of three institutions—the Brookings Institution, the Woodrow Wilson Center for Scholars, and the Cato Institute—whose guest scholarships allowed me refuge from my apartment and, thus, sanity. And a special thanks to Jim Morris at the Wilson Center for support much above and beyond the call of duty.

I would also like to thank all of my readers at various stages of the process: Amy Schwartz, Mickey Kaus, Robert Wright, Sarah Blaffer Hrdy, Alice Rossi, Anne Hollander, Jeff Rosen, Nicole Tapay, Tom Palmer, David Boaz, Elizabeth Kaplan, Pamela Erens, Debbie Springhorn, and Leda Cosmides. And without the grunt work of a handful of interns—Sarah Carlson, Bennah Sirfaty, Derek Warner, Jeremy Hildreth, Maren Boedeker, and Matthew Sargent—the footnotes would never have gotten done. And a special thanks to the Institute for Humane Studies for funding Sarah's work.

I would also like to thank my editor, Arabella Meyer, and agent, Gail Ross, both of whom have remained enthusiastic throughout what often seemed like a process that had no end. And a special thanks to Howard Yoon, for bringing calm and order when both were nowhere to be found.

Finally, and most especially, I would like to thank my family for putting up with all of this. My brother, sister-in-law, cousins, and grandfather probably now feel as though they can write a book themselves. Most especially, I would like to thank my mother and father. Without their constant and unconditional love and support, this book truly would never have made it beyond an amorphous idea. All writers should be blessed with parents willing to not only endure, but encourage one through all of the turmoil of writing a book, and I dedicate this one to mine.

ABOUT THE AUTHOR

Karen Lehrman, a former editor at the *New Republic* and the *Wilson Quarterly,* is a journalist and social critic whose articles have appeared in the *New York Times,* the *Washington Post,* the *Wall Street Journal,* the *New Republic, Vogue,* and other periodicals. Her critique of women's studies programs in *Mother Jones* has been reprinted in several anthologies. Lehrman lives in New York City.